SEXUALITY IN ORGANIZATIONS:

SEXUALITY IN ORGANIZATIONS:
romantic and coercive behaviors at work

•

Edited by
DAIL ANN NEUGARTEN
and
JAY M. SHAFRITZ,
University of Colorado at Denver

MOORE PUBLISHING COMPANY, INC.

OAK PARK, ILLINOIS

362.83
S518

Library of Congress Cataloging in Publication Data

Main entry under title:

CC.

Sexuality in organizations.

    Bibliography: p.
    Includes index.
    1. Sexual harassment of women—United States. 2. Sex in business. I. Neugarten, Dail Ann. III. Shafritz, Jay M.
HD6060.5.U5S49   362.8'3   80-20737
ISBN 0-935610-14-6

Copyright © 1980 by Moore Publishing Company, Inc. All rights reserved. Printed in the United States of America. No part of this publication may be reproduced, stored in a retrieval system, or transmitted, in any form or by any means, electronic, mechanical, photocopying, recording, or otherwise, without the prior written permission of the publisher, except by a reviewer who may quote brief passages in a review.

Moore Publishing Company, Inc.
701 South Gunderson Avenue, Oak Park, Illinois 60304

Contents

UNIVERSITY LIBRARIES
CARNEGIE-MELLON UNIVERSITY
PITTSBURGH. PENNSYLVANIA 15213

Foreword

Eighty years ago, 20 percent of the U.S. population was self employed. In 1980, more than 90 percent work in organizations and more than 50 percent work in organizations with more than 100 members. At the turn of the century, it was not unusual for a person to be born at home, to be educated at home, to spend his or her life working on the family farm, and then die at home and be buried by his or her family. Today, it is likely that a person will be born and educated in an organization and that he or she will work, die, and be buried in or by an organization.

Because of the important role that organizations play in our world, they have been the subject of much study. As a consequence, we are coming to a better understanding of the advantages and difficulties of living in hierarchical systems. One of the most surprising things about our learning in this area is that it has only been in the last six or seven years that we have become aware of one of the most potent and seemingly obvious difficulties of modern life—the management of human attraction within hierarchical structures.

Few problems could be more volatile. Values associated with objective decisionmaking clash with the norms of intimacy and human bonding. The problems that result are significant and complex, but we are gradually learning about some important aspects of the process.

The first thing we have discovered is that organizations are environments that facilitate the dynamics of attraction. The organization provides a setting where instrumental goals spawn common interest, where proximity sustains lasting interaction patterns, and where transactional structures facilitate the exchange of social and physical rewards.

We have also learned that physiological drives are not left in the parking lot or the train station. People bring their sexuality to work and many have difficulty managing that sexuality. This has proven to be a considerable difficulty, especially for those who are victimized in some manner.

Finally, we have begun to explore the responses to the problems of sexuality in the working place. From both an administrative and a legal point of view, the problem presents a puzzle of considerable complexity.

The organization of this book reflects the four areas of which we have become most aware. In the first section, we learn of the sexual dynamics that are inherent in the work setting. We come to understand the interplay of sexual attraction and hierarchical processes. In the second section, we learn about the nature and scope of sexual harassment. In the third, we find a focus on organizational responses to the problem. In the fourth, legal issues are covered.

In bringing together this volume of reading, Neugarten and Shafritz sensitize us to the fact that we must better understand and manage the dynamics of sexuality in organizational settings. They also provide a valuable reference book, for this collection is a relatively comprehensive representation of the literature that will facilitate the flurry of research efforts that are now underway. Clearly, from both a practical and research perspective, *Sexuality in Organizations: Romantic and Coercive Behaviors at Work* is a book of considerable importance.

ROBERT E. QUINN
State University of
New York at Albany

Acknowledgments

We are grateful to a number of individuals who aided us in producing this book. Valuable substantive insights were provided by Robert E. Quinn, State University of New York at Albany, and David H. Rosenbloom of Syracuse University. More general advice and support were generously offered by Robert F. Wilcox. Fritz and Jerrold Neugarten and Richard A. Wehmhoefer granted a special kind of encouragement, and James R. Favor offered a particularly important perspective. Bernice Neugarten deserves special mention for her keen insights and editorial polish.

Research assistance was provided by Todd Jonathan, Noah Justin, Louise Alexander, and Sheri Dawn. The staff of the Graduate School of Public Affairs, University of Colorado at Denver—Margaret Benjamin, Berna LoSasso, Patricia McClure and Bonnie Ramer—deserves particular thanks for their care in typing the manuscript and for their general professionalism in assisting in the multitude of tasks that allowed for the completion of this book.

Overview

This book is an exploration of the romantic and coercive relations between men and women as they develop in work organizations. Romantic relationships are usually pleasurable and rewarding for the individuals involved and can have a positive effect on motivation and productivity. Coercive relationships are another story; they are painful for at least one of the persons, they inhibit organizational harmony and effectiveness, and they may pose legal problems.

Our intent is to provide the managers of organizations in both the public and private sectors the perspective they need to understand the problem of sexuality in organizations and to provide concrete information for dealing with the issue.

We began the planning of this book with several questions in mind. To what extent is the issue of sexuality in the workplace a concern of management? To what extent is it a management responsibility? Are there existing organizational policies to deal with the issue?

In reviewing the literature, we found that sexual harassment at work was a topic of growing concern. Several new questions then arose. What is sexual harassment in the workplace? How widespread is it, and what empirical research exists to document its nature? Do organizations have policies prohibiting sexual harassment and grievance procedures for adjudication? Is sexual harassment as aspect of sex discrimination as defined in Title VII of the Civil Rights Act of 1964? To what extent is an employer responsible for the actions of employees? What legal precedents exist in this field?

RELATIONS BETWEEN THE SEXES: THE CONTEXT

Work organizations are contexts in which the relationships between men and women are cultivated. Sometimes these relationships are based solely on role requirements, such as those of boss and secretary. In these cases, behaviors are based on the requirements of the job and are geared toward the accomplishment of specific tasks. At other times, relationships are more personal and interactions are broader than those demanded by the job. The issue of sexuality in organizations is gaining the attention of researchers and managers as more and more women enter the labor force and as more women rise to managerial ranks.

Many of the social and economic factors that have contributed to the increase in women workers have indirect, but important, implications for the changing relations between women and men in the work setting. With more than half of all women now in the labor force, an increasing proportion are heads-of-households and are either self-supporting or the sole support for their families. But in addition to single women, it is now married women and women with children who are at work, and the greatest increases have recently been among well-educated wives in middle-class families. It is, in fact, the case that the more education a woman has, the more likely she is to be in the labor force. And whereas the major reasons that women work are economic, just as is true for men, there are other reasons. Especially at higher educational levels, women work for intellec-

1

tual and social stimulation, for self-development and because they find the work intrinsically interesting and rewarding.

These factors, among others, have led to changing expectations and changing behaviors on the part of both men and women. Increasing numbers of women aspire to economic independence and increased professionalism; men's career goals and patterns of professional mobility change in response to this trend. Unfortunately, the realities of the workplace often collide with women's desired goals; for instance, clerical workers—secretaries, typists, bank tellers, and telephone operators—the largest job category for women, still includes six of every ten women in the labor force. Although women are more likely than men to be in white collar jobs, those jobs are usually less skilled and lower paid, as shown in the big earnings gap between men and women, a gap that is present even within the same job categories, but which is narrower at higher occupational levels.

While proportionately more women are moving into management jobs, these tend to be mid-level rather than top level positions. The stereotypes which influence the interactions between men and women in the labor force, and organizational policies which have become institutionalized over the years, have tended thus far to leave women in subordinate positions.

Yet that picture, too, is changing. For instance, of young women workers (those under 30) one-fourth are already working in professional and technical jobs, a proportion that will probably continue to rise as successive groups of young women finish their education and enter the labor force. The overall pattern, however, does not yet reflect the impact of the dramatic educational gains that have been occurring for women in recent years.

Another important factor influencing the relations between men and women at work is that the Congress has mandated equal opportunity, equal protection and equal treatment of women in the labor force. As the weight of protective legislation increases, the relationships between men and women at work will change. As women move into positions of management and as they become more vehement about their rights and responsibilities, sexual relationships at work will no longer be viewed as one of those issues that lies outside the realm of organizational policy. Instead, they will become a predominant concern, not only of researchers who are interested in the broader issues of organizational behavior, but also of managers who are anxious to achieve organizational harmony and to avoid lawsuits.

SEXUAL HARASSMENT: THE CONDITION

Information on the frequency of sexual harassment is primarily impressionistic and anecdotal and based mainly on women's observations about themselves and others. The phenomenon, nevertheless, is real. It arises, at least in part, from a social context in which men have traditionally exerted power over women both at home and at work and in which women have been viewed as subordinates. Men have been the sexual initiators, and women, the sexual objects.

This pattern has grown from the tradition of women's dependence on men for their material survival, and it has led to the condition in which women, in large part, have been socialized to assess their personal worth in terms of their desirability to men. Although these historical patterns are changing, men and women alike have long accepted the validity of the more powerful man and the less powerful woman, and in accepting this pattern, both sexes have legitimized male sexual dominance in the workplace as well as in the society at large. From this perspective, sexual harassment of women in the workplace may be viewed as a social mechanism which preserves the status quo, one which reflects, more than sexuality itself, the issue of power.

There are, of course, instances in which women exhibit a form of sexual harassment of men, usually by unwelcomed seductive behaviors. And there are instances of sexual harassment which result from a particular personal pathology—as when, for example, a man makes unwanted sexual overtures toward a woman, or a woman to a man, that are prompted by maliciousness or by an intent to do psychological harm. Whether any or all such behaviors are due to culturally ingrained habits, power politics, or occasional character flaws, women are usually the objects of sexual harassment, and the impacts on women are usually negative.

SEXUAL HARASSMENT AT WORK: DEFINITIONS AND EFFECTS

The term *sexual harassment* has come to describe a variety of undesirable sexual behaviors, some of them overt, some subtle; some physical, some verbal. Some are conscious acts intended to gain power or to force compliance, others are unconscious acts that grow out of long-ingrained sex roles. Sometimes sexual harassment is a single encounter; sometimes, a recurrent pattern. At times, it is a condition of employment as, for example, when being hired, retained or promoted rests on the granting of sexual favors. At other times it is a pervasive and condoned condition of the work environment and a part of the organizational climate. It is viewed by some as a management problem, and by others as a problem that falls outside the realm of management responsibility.

Sexual harassment has been defined by the Working Women's Institute as any repeated or unwanted verbal or physical sexual advances; sexually explicit derogatory statements; or sexually discriminatory remarks made by someone in the workplace which are offensive or objectionable to the recipient,

or cause the recipient discomfort or humiliation, or interfere with the recipient's job performance.[1] While this definition seems on the surface to be straightforward, it is nevertheless the case that what one person defines as offensive another person defines as flattery. A physical touch or a suggestion of intimacy to one person might be objectionable; to another, humorous.

Although, as has been said, sexual harassment is occasionally directed at men, it is women who are more often harassed, and for whom the problem arises for management. It is apparent that sexual harassment has the potential to affect a woman's economic status, her self-esteem and self-concept, her ability to perform on the job and her career opportunities, even her mental and physical health. A woman's negative response to sexual overtures may have a wide range of outcomes, from no action by her superiors, to an unfavorable report in her personnel file, to a reduction in responsibilities, to a demotion, a salary cut, or a disciplinary dismissal.

Sexual harassment too may be a significant factor in analyzing women's higher rate of unemployment or job turnover. Lin Farley, for example, is one investigator who contends that many women are forced from their jobs or choose voluntarily to leave a place of employment because of sexual harassment.[2] If they are forced from their jobs, they suffer the stigma of being "fired," and this influences their future employment opportunities. If they choose to leave their jobs voluntarily, they are technically ineligible for unemployment compensation. The National Commission on Unemployment Compensation established a subcommittee in 1979 to examine this latter issue. Members of the committee concluded that women who suffer from sexual harassment are often in these "Catch 22" situations. The committee argued strongly that a federal standard be adopted to prohibit any state from imposing a disqualification from unemployment compensation to a claimant who has quit or been terminated because of sexual harassment on the job.

The psychological effects of sexual harassment have often been described for women, with only fleeting acknowledgment that they may also arise for men. Many women fear being blamed, ostracized or fired, so they react in ways which are less than direct and forceful. Feelings of intimidation, frustration, guilt, embarrassment, degradation, anger and fear are the most common psychological reactions to sexual harassment. A woman may internalize her emotional reactions and become physically ill or depressed.

And what about the effects of sexual harassment on men? Although the research findings are almost non-existent, the effects can be expected to vary, depending upon whether a man is the perpetrator or the observer; if perpetrator, depending on his motives; if observer, depending on whether he becomes directly involved. A man who often harasses women may be unaware of the effects of that behavior, whether on the women involved, on other men, or on himself. Or if aware, he may be unconcerned.

The effects on men who are observers of sexual harassment vary also. For a husband whose wife is being harassed, feelings of anger toward the perpetrator and possibly toward the wife, and feelings of helplessness or revulsion may arise. In a different context the observer may have his own feelings of power reaffirmed and his sense of male-bonding reinforced. The man who comes to the defense of a woman may feel embarrassed in the eyes of other men, or he may feel self-righteous. Many men, because of their own socialization, find sexual harassment of women to be comic or a matter of indifference.[3]

Regardless of the motivation, the most extreme outcome for the man who harasses women may be a disciplinary action taken by his supervisor—a reprimand, a demotion, or a dismissal due to a formal complaint. To judge from the literature on the topic, however, these are uncommon occurrences; it has been women who have usually been the recipients of whatever organizational action is taken.

THE SCOPE OF THE PROBLEM

Although the sexual harassment of women may not be a major national problem, Representative James M. Hanley, chairman of the Subcommittee on Investigations of the House Committee on Post Office and Civil Service, in recent Hearings on Sexual Harassment in the Federal Government, observed that "several surveys done by private groups and individuals have indicated that sexual harassment is widespread. Unfortunately, our preliminary investigation has shown that the problem is not only epidemic, it is pandemic, an everyday, everywhere occurrence."[4]

In an effort to gather information on the extent and handling of sexual harassment, several surveys have been undertaken recently in the United States. Although the methodological approaches leave much to be desired, the studies are nevertheless valuable for illustrating the dimensions, if not the exact measure of the problem. Among such studies have been the following:

1) In May 1975 the Working Women's Institute of New York, a research and advocacy center devoted to furthering the goals of equal employment opportunity for women, surveyed 155 women on the subject. Seventy percent reported that they had experienced sexual harassment at least once; of these, the majority ignored it, only to find that the behavior continued or worsened. Of those who ignored it, some were penalized by unwarranted reprimands, sabotage of their work, transfers or dismissals. Only a minority of those harassed complained through established channels; and of these complaints, no action was taken in over half the cases. The women who did not complain said it was

because nothing would be done, or their complaints would be ridiculed, or they themselves would be blamed. For the women who experienced it, sexual harassment had negative emotional effects, with the large majority feeling angry or upset, and some feeling frightened or guilty. Some felt powerless, diminished in their ambition, and impaired in their job performance.[5]

2) In 1976 *Redbook* magazine solicited its readers' views about sexual harassment. Some 9000 women returned the questionnaire, an overwhelming response according to the *Redbook*'s editors. The majority of respondents were married, in their 20s and 30s, working at white collar jobs and earning between $5,000 and $10,000 per year. Nearly 90 percent reported that they had experienced some form of sexual harassment on their jobs and over 90 percent considered the problem to be a serious one. The majority indicated, further, that they found the behaviors embarrassing, demeaning or intimidating, while only a small minority said they had felt flattered.[6] (These findings may not be representative, for it is likely that those women who had experienced sexual harassment were more likely than other women to respond to *Redbook*'s questionnaire.)

3) Also in 1976 the United Nations Ad Hoc Group on Equal Rights for Women polled all 875 women employed by the U. N. in professional and clerical positions and found that half said that sexual pressure currently existed on their jobs. Slightly less than one-third had complained. The reason most frequently cited for not complaining was the perceived absence of proper channels for lodging a complaint.[7]

4) In 1977 sociologist Sandra Harley Carey interviewed 401 working women on the topic of sexual politics in business. All these women, interestingly enough, reported experiencing sexual harassment, but only a minority felt embarrassed or intimidated or thought the behavior demeaning. Over 20 percent indicated that they would not report an incident of sexual harassment because their superiors would take no action. Over one-third of the companies for which these women work were reported to have no policy on sexual harassment. Over one-third of the women did not know if their company had a policy at all.[8]

5) In 1978-79 a small sample of 198 federal employees in the Departments of Health, Education and Welfare, Justice and General Services Administration were interviewed by New Responses, Inc., a non-profit organization of women's policy consultants based in Washington, D.C. Of the 79 women in the sample who reported experiencing sexual harassment, one-fourth had had promotions withheld, some were transferred, and a few were fired or were looking for another job. The majority of the respondents indicated that they were experiencing sexual harassment on a continual basis and reported feelings of anger, helplessness and physical illness which interfered with their performance. A few indicated that sexual harassment took the form of rape or attempted rape.[9]

6) In 1979 Peggy Crull surveyed 325 women who had written unsolicited letters to the Working Women's Institute indicating that they had personally experienced sexual harassment. One-fourth indicated that they had been fired from their jobs, and over 40 percent said they had been pressured into resigning. Although this is a self-selected sample whose reports may be far from generalizable, almost all these women indicated they had emotional stress symptoms such as nervousness, fear, anger and sleeplessness; most of them said that the incidents interfered with job performance; most of them reported physical stress symptoms; and one-fourth said they had sought psychological therapy.[10]

7) In contrast to the figures cited in the preceding studies, are those from a study in 1979 of barriers to upward mobility undertaken by the Women's Advisory Council to the Salt Lake County Merit Council. Of 1,051 women employed by the Salt Lake County Government, over half responded to a questionnaire in which some of the questions related to sexuality and sexual harassment. Only a few of the respondents, less than 10 percent, said women in their office had been upgraded or promoted because they encouraged sexual advances, or that they themselves tolerated intimacies from superiors or co-workers in order to be upgraded. Of those who responded to the question of how they dealt with advances made by male co-workers, most said they ignored it, only a few told their boss, and most told the offender that he was out of bounds. It is of interest that in the recommendations sec-

tion of this study no mention is made of the need to prohibit sexual harassment as a condition of employment.[11]

In addition to the surveys eliciting data from women about their experiences with sexual harassment, several studies have been undertaken to determine organizational policies and practices:

1) In 1977 the Working Women's Institute mailed a questionnaire to 540 state and local civil rights enforcement agencies inquiring about their practices regarding sexual harassment complaints. Only 74 of the 540 agencies returned the questionnaires, and of those that did, most were unable to document the numbers or types of sexual harassment complaints they had received. Only two agencies had kept track of the sexual harassment complaints. More often than not, agencies included such complaints in the general category of sex discrimination. Apparently one of the major difficulties of documenting sexual harassment cases is that sexual harassment had not been the primary cause of action, but had been included in a broader complaint. The most complete documentation of cases and their dispositions came from the New York State Division of Human Rights which, in 1976, counted 65 complaints. This study's conclusion was that, despite what seemed to be a genuine concern as expressed by many fair employment practices agencies, most of these agencies had not established policies or mechanisms to deal with the special requirements of sexual harassment cases.[12]

2) In 1979 the Rocky Mountain Regional Office of Personnel Management conducted an informal study of state personnel agencies on the topic of sexual harassment. The study concluded that none of the states in the region have laws or regulations specifically prohibiting sexual harassment; that all the state personnel agencies, felt that state civil rights statutes covered sexual harassment under prohibitions against sex discrimination; that no state had a good workable written definition of sexual harassment; that no state had established a specific system to handle complaints of sexual harassment; and that, with regard to negotiated contracts, none of the jurisdictions in the region had contracts under which sexual harassment (as an item separate from sex discrimination) could be referred to binding arbitration.[13]

3) In 1979 the Office of Intergovernmental Personnel Programs, Office of Personnel Management, surveyed the states for information about sexual harassment. Most states indicated that they had no special provisions for dealing with the issue, but felt that such cases could be prosecuted adequately under laws that prohibit sex discrimination. Two proposed bills and one statute were uncovered that specifically deal with the issue. In California a bill is pending to amend the labor code (covering organizations in the private sector) to make discrimination an unlawful employment practice when it is based on the refusal of a person to engage in sexual behavior with an employer, supervisor, client, customer, or fellow employee. In New York a bill is pending that allows a victim of sexual harassment who resigns from employment to obtain unemployment insurance, and in Maryland a new criminal code makes coercive sexual demands a fourth-degree sexual offense.

According to the survey findings, successful prosecutions of sexual harassment cases are rare. For instance, in Colorado a case will not be heard in court unless the harassment is directly involved in an adverse personnel action.

No states had systems for receiving or resolving complaints of sexual harassment, and no states reported union contracts in which sexual harassment is an issue that can go to arbitration. In the state of Connecticut, however, two labor agreements have an Employee's Bill of Rights clause stating that an employee must be able to work "in an environment free of significant abuse or arbitrary conduct by a supervisor."[14]

It can be argued that the findings from the various studies cited here may not be generalizable to the population of working women in the United States, nor to organizational practices, and that the studies are, therefore, of limited value in describing the dimensions of the problem. These studies are useful, however, in giving a general overview of the topic of sexual harassment, even if they do not produce a definitive analysis. It is likely that other studies will accumulate. For example, the U.S.

Merit System Protection Board now has a mandate by the House Subcommittee on Investigations to conduct a systematic survey of sexual harassment in the federal government.[15]

The surveys cited above, with their limitations, represent the state-of-the-art or the extent of our knowledge about sexual harassment in the workplace. Three conclusions are probably warranted:

1) Sexual harassment is widespread and it occurs regardless of a woman's age, marital status, ethnicity, occupation, or salary level.

2) If sexual harassment is as pervasive as the studies indicate, the inequitable treatment of women, the discriminatory effects and the potential for abuse are enormous.

3) Public sector agencies, which are presumably sensitive to issues of human rights—to say nothing about private sector organizations—have not yet acknowledged the magnitude of the problem, undertaken systematic investigations of its effects, nor instituted preventive or corrective measures.

ORGANIZATIONAL RESPONSES TO SEXUAL HARASSMENT

A recent article in *Fortune* magazine asserts that concerns about sexual harassment are coming into vogue primarily because the Equal Employment Opportunity Commission (EEOC) has gone "maybe six weeks without finding a new form of discrimination to outlaw."[16] Yet it is becoming clear that sexual harassment is a significant management concern. Congress has held hearings on the topic, the Working Women's Institute is undertaking research, as is also the Alliance Against Sexual Coercion, and a National Sexual Harassment Legal Backup Center has recently opened in New York. In 1979 the Office of Personnel Management was mandated by Congress to proffer a definition of sexual harassment and to issue a directive stating that it is a prohibited personnel practice in the federal government. In the same year, as already mentioned, the Merit Systems Protection Board was requested by Congress to do a major survey on sexual harassment in the federal government, to ascertain the extent of the problem and the channels for recourse. The Secretary of the Department of Health, Education and Welfare (now Health and Human Services) has issued a statement prohibiting sexual harassment in her agency, as has the mayor of the District of Columbia. Perhaps most importantly, the EEOC has in this same year drafted provisional guidelines regarding the practice.

Management's role is to assure that the work environment is safe, conducive to high performance and non-discriminatory. Generally speaking, sexuality has been considered "personal" and, therefore, not a behavior that management can change.[17] Until very recently, management's response to complaints of sexual harassment has been to do nothing. Three reasons stand out:

1) *Management has failed to take the problem seriously or to identify sexual harassment as a problem at all.* This reflects the general social context, but also the reluctance to let the problem surface for fear of maligning the reputation of the organization.

2) *Organizations have lacked adequate policies or guidelines.* Until recently, there have been no governmental policies prohibiting sexual harassment as an unfair or discriminatory labor practice, and most organizations have dealt with the few complaints that do surface as if they were complaints of sex discrimination. The guidelines and grievance procedures that insure adequate administrative hearings have not incorporated the special requirements of sexual harassment cases. More significantly, it has not been clear whether sexual harassment is a form of sex discrimination under Title VII of the Civil Rights Act, or whether Title VII guidelines and procedures even apply to these cases.

8 OVERVIEW

3) *There is confusion regarding who it is in the organization who has responsibility.* Indeed, one of the major legal questions surrounding the issue of sexual harassment is whether or not it is employment related. Does management bear any responsibility? Does responsibility lie with the Federal Women's Program Director or the EEO Director or the Affirmative Action Officers? This confusion is aptly represented in the U.S. Department of Housing and Urban Development's March 1980 issue of *Huddle*, (HUD's in-house newsletter) which states:

Employees who are subjected to sexual harassment by other HUD employees on the job may consider taking the following actions where appropriate:
- File a grievance under the Department's grievance system or a union contract grievance procedure
- Notify the Office of Inspector General by calling the HUD Employee Hotline
- File a formal complaint of discrimination; and
- Contact any of HUD's Federal Women's Program or EEO Coordinators[18]

Beginning in 1978, however, there have been some important positive steps taken to prohibit sexual harassment. At the federal level, agencies must now conform to a policy statement indicating that sexual harassment is a prohibited personnel practice. The U.S. Office of Personnel Management, on December 12, 1979, issued an umbrella policy, applicable to all federal agencies and departments that indicates each agency and department head should:

1. Issue a very strong management statement clearly defining the policy of the federal government as an employer with regard to sexual harassment;
2. Emphasize this policy as part of new employee orientation covering the merit principles and the code of conduct; and
3. Make employees aware of the avenues for seeking redress, and the actions that will be taken against employees violating the policy.[19]

In addition, several "Memoranda of Understanding" between the Investiga-

tions Subcommittee of the Post Office and Civil Service Committee, U.S. House of Representatives and various federal agencies have appeared as outcomes of the congressional hearings on sexual harassment. These memoranda outline the responsibilities and tasks of each of these agencies as mandated by the Congress of the United States. For example, the memo between the subcommittee and the EEOC states the following: the EEOC will require each agency, as a part of its affirmative action plan, to inform federal employees that coercive sexual advances are prohibited by Title VII and to distinguish it from behavior which does not violate Title VII; the EEOC will require agencies to take specific steps to make the work environment free of sexual intimidation; the EEOC will design a training module on sexual harassment for equal employment opportunity personnel; and the EEOC will issue directives to federal agency EEO counselors to be circulated also to Federal Women's Program Coordinators, etc.[20]

It is not only within federal agencies themselves that positive steps have been taken. The Office of Personnel Management has recently completed a training package on sexual harassment which is available to all federal, state and local government agencies,[21] and the Equal Employment Opportunity Commission has just drafted proposed guidelines that cover both the private and public sectors.[22] The mayor of the District of Columbia, on May 24, 1979, issued an Executive Order that not only prohibits sexual harassment, but establishes a procedure by which allegations of sexual harassment may be filed, investigated and adjudicated. It further requires all agencies in the District to develop programs and monitoring systems to prevent sexual harassment.[23] To clarify these organizational responses, the State of Wisconsin is the first state to pass a law banning sexual harassment as an unfair labor practice. The law also qualifies for unemployment insurance anyone who quits a job because of sexual harassment.[24] Such a law is pending in the State of New York. The Minnesota Supreme Court ruled, in June 1980, that a company can be held liable for the sexual harassment of a woman by her co-workers.[25] This decision is the first to hold that an employer is responsible for sexual harassment conducted by non-supervisory personnel.

More broadly, in private as well as public organizations, women and men, too,[26] are now initiating complaints of sexual harassment. These complaints are being made to higher management, to personnel departments, to Federal Women's Coordinators, and to union officials. It is still the case, however, that whereas most agencies, both public and private, have grievance procedures that purportedly serve to adjudicate complaints of discrimination or unfair labor practices, there is reason to question the timeliness and effectiveness of these procedures in dealing with sexual harassment cases.

If these organizational sources of redress are not satisfactory, a victim of sexual harassment may file a charge with the EEOC. All complaints must be filed within 180 days of the alleged violation; the complainant must identify the parties and clearly describe the discriminatory acts. If there is a state or local fair employment practices agency or human rights commission, the EEOC must first turn the complaint over to this unit. The EEOC or state agency involvement is primarily investigative. If evidence is found during an investigation, the EEOC or state representative will then decide whether there is reasonable cause to believe there has been a violation of the law. If there is such a finding, the EEOC will try to negotiate a settlement informally. If a successful conciliation cannot be reached, the complainant may file a civil court suit. But to file a complaint with the EEOC, in effect, takes the matter out of the hands of management.

Within the past two years, especially in the public sector, management has begun to take the issue of sexual harassment seriously and has undertaken to establish organizational procedures to insure a safe and non-discriminatory workplace. These efforts represent a major step forward, but they are still initial and relatively untested efforts. Because most organizations have thus far been unable to cope with allegations of sexual harassment, some complainants have felt they had no choice but to go to court.

LEGAL ASPECTS OF SEXUAL HARASSMENT

Victims or alleged victims of sexual harassment have in the past, and will in the future, turn to the courts in order to seek redress. Sexual harassment is becoming a "cause of action." However, contradictory legal findings have raised the question: Cause of action under what legislative mandate? Under what constitutional provision?

Several of the major sexual harassment cases deserve mention, because they illustrate the complexity of the legal issues and the absence of an explicit legal doctrine in this field.

In a 1974 case, **Barnes v. Train**,[27] a woman hired as the administrative assistant to the male director of the Environmental Protection Agency's Equal Opportunities Division, filed a suit in district court alleging that her job was abolished because she refused to engage in sexual relations with the director. The District Court dismissed the case, arguing that although Barnes was discriminated against, the discrimination was not because she was a woman, but because she refused to engage in sexual behavior with her supervisor. Thus, the District Court decided that sexual harassment was not treatment "based on sex within its legal meaning."

Barnes appealed the ruling and in **Barnes v. Castle**[28] the appellate court reversed the decision, stating that: "We think that the discrimination as portrayed was plainly based on the appellant's gender. Retention of her job was conditioned upon submission to sexual relations—an exaction which the superior would not have sought from any male." The appellate court thus argued that sexual harassment did constitute sex discrimination. The Environmental Protection Agency was held accountable, and Barnes received $18,000 in back pay as damages for lost promotions.

In *Monge* v. *Beebe Rubber*[29] a case was filed on the basis of wrongful dismissal. The plaintiff, a married woman with three children, worked in a factory where her foreman told her that if she wanted a promotion she would have to "be nice." She refused and was purportedly so ridiculed and verbally abused that she became ill and was hospitalized. Beebe Rubber decided that her absence constituted a "voluntary resignation," and Monge sued for wrongful dismissal. The court held that her discharge, based on her rejection of sexual advances, was a breach of an employment contract. The court stated: "The foreman's overtures and the capricious firing, the seeming manipulation of job assignments, and the apparent connivance of the personnel manager in this course of events all support the jury's conclusion that the dismissal was maliciously motivated." Monge won a jury verdict and $2,500.

In re. Carmita Wood. In a case brought to the attention of the New York State Department of Labor Unemployment Insurance Appeals Board, Carmita Wood claimed that she was forced to resign because of the physical and emotional repercussions resulting from her superior's sexual advances. Wood claimed that because of the conditions prompting her resignation, she was eligible to collect unemployment compensation. Her request was denied, and she appealed to the New York State Department of Labor, Unemployment

Division Appeal Board. Her appeal, too, was denied.[30]

In a similar case in Wisconsin, *Hamilton* v. *Appleton Electric Company*,[31] a contrary finding emerged. Hamilton, like Wood, claimed that she was forced to resign because she was being sexually harassed. Her unemployment compensation appeal was the first case to hold that sexual harassment, as a pervasive condition of work, was employment discrimination and, therefore, an unfair labor practice. The Commission of the Department of Industry, Labor and Human Relations found that under Wisconsin's Fair Employment Law, Hamilton was discriminated against and that, therefore, upon her termination, she was eligible for unemployment compensation.

In *Corne* v. *Bausch & Lomb, Inc.*[32] two women sued for a violation of their civil rights under Title VII, stating that their male supervisor had taken unsolicited and unwelcome sexual liberties with them both. The District Court in Arizona dismissed the case on several grounds: first, that Title VII outlawed sex discrimination where such discrimination arose out of a company policy, whereas the supervisor in this case was merely satisfying a "personal urge"; second, that Title VII did not prohibit "verbal and physical sexual advances where the behavior was a nonemployment related encounter"; third, that Title VII was inapplicable because the conduct could be directed equally toward men. The court went on to say, "An outgrowth of holding such activity to be actionable under Title VII would be a potential federal lawsuit every time an employee made amorous or sexually oriented advances toward another. The only sure way an employer could avoid such charges would be to have employees who were asexual." This case was appealed, and the decision was reversed.

In *Miller* v. *Bank of America*[33] the District Court determined that sexual harassment was an isolated misconduct not attributable to employer policy. In this case, a black woman charged that her white male supervisor promised her a better job if she would be "sexually cooperative." She refused and was fired. Miller sued for reinstatement, back pay, and attorney's fees. The District Court dismissed the complaint, stating that Miller should have filed a complaint with the Employee Relations Department of the bank which would have conducted an "appropriate investigation." The court, in making this determination, stated:

> The attraction of males to females is a natural sex phenomenon and it is probable that this attraction plays at least a subtle part in most personnel decisions. Such being the case, it would seem wise for the court to refrain from delving into these matters short of specific factual allegations describing an employer policy which in its application poses or permits a consistent, as distinguished from isolated, sex-based discrimination on a definable employee group.

(Miller's appeal is pending as this book goes to press.)

Williams v. *Saxbe*[34] was the first case in which sexual harassment was clearly said to be "treatment based on sex" under Title VII. Williams, an employee in the United States Department of Justice, asserted that her supervisor "engaged in a continuing pattern and practice of harassment and humiliation. . . ." When she refused his sexual advances, he fired her on a Friday afternoon and told her not to return on the following Monday. The District Court to which Williams appealed sent the case back to the Department of Justice finding that the burden of proof during the administrative hearing had been incorrectly placed upon the plaintiff. The adjudication officer in the Department of Justice, found that the facts of the case did not warrant a claim under Title VII, whereupon the case was returned to the court. In a precedent-setting opinion, Judge Richey then ruled that the retaliatory actions of the male supervisor *did* constitute sex discrimination under Title VII. The case, however, remains unsettled.

In 1977, three female undergraduates and one male professor brought a class action suit against Yale University, charging that the university condoned the sexual harassment of its students. Yale asked the case be dismissed on the grounds that the complainants were without a legal basis for the suit. A court ruled that the trial could go forward on its merits and said that a case of sexual harassment at an education institution receiving federal funds was a form of sex discrimination. No decision has been handed down in this case to date.

In *Tomkins* v. *Public Service Electric and Gas Company*,[35] Tomkins, an office worker, complained to the company that her supervisor made physical sexual advances, had told her that a sexual relationship was essential to an effective working relationship, had threatened her with work-related reprisals when she refused, and had physically restrained her. Fifteen months after her complaint was filed, she was fired. The New Jersey District Court dismissed her case stating that Title VII "was not intended to provide a federal tort remedy for what amounts to a physical attack motivated by sexual desire on the part of a supervisor, and which happened to occur in a corporate corridor rather than in a back alley." The court further stated that "sexual harassment is neither employment related nor sex-based, but a personal injury properly pursued in state court as a tort." Tomkins appealed this finding and the decision was reversed. Tomkins received $20,000 and attorney's fees, and her employer was told to notify all employees that sexual harassment is against the law.

Finally, in *Heelan* v. *Johns Mansville Corp.*,[36] Heelan claimed that because she refused to have sexual relations with her supervisor, she was fired. She made a formal complaint, but the company's response was deemed insufficient. The court held that "an employer is liable under Title VII when refusal of a super-

visor's unsolicited sexual advances is
the basis of an employee's termination."
Heelan won $100,000 in an out-of-
court settlement.

These cases, and there are many
others, illustrate the complexity of the
legal arguments and focus attention on
four major legal questions which are as
yet unresolved: Is sexual harassment sex
discrimination as defined by Title VII of
the Civil Rights Act? What, if any, are
the available avenues for legal recourse
other than Title VII? In cases of sexual
harassment, are employers (organizations) liable for the acts of their employees (supervisors), and if so, under what
conditions? If a woman or a man resigns
from employment because of sexual
harassment, is he/she entitled to unemployment compensation?

With respect to the first question, the
legal trend, despite the fact that some of
the findings cited in the cases above are
contradictory, seems to indicate that
sexual harassment is sex discrimination
under Title VII.

Title VII states:

a) It shall be an unlawful employment
practice for an employer to discriminate
against any individual with respect to his
compensation, terms conditions, or
privileges of employment because of such
individual's . . . sex . . . ; or
b) to limit, segregate, or classify his employees or applicants for employment in
any way which would deprive or tend to
deprive any individual of employment opportunities or otherwise adversely affect
his status as an employee, because of such
individual's . . . sex.[37]

Generally, a plaintiff filing a sexual
harassment case under Title VII must
show that sexual advances were a condition of employment and were not personal, non-employment-related encounters. The body of law developed to date
seems to indicate that in order to show
a violation of Title VII, the plaintiff must
establish that (1) submission to sexual
advances of a supervisor was a term or
condition of employment, (2) rejection
of sexual advances substantially affected

the plaintiff's employment (e.g., resulted
in a demotion or discharge), and (3) the
behavior was gender-related—i.e., that
employees of the opposite sex were not
affected in the same way.

With respect to the question, what
avenues for legal recourse are available
other than Title VII, it appears from the
legal cases to date that the only other
legitimate grounds for court actions are
wrongful dismissal (Monge v. Beebe
Rubber) and unfair labor practices
(Hamilton v. Appleton Electric Co.). In
cases of wrongful dismissal, the courts
generally cannot provide for reinstatement, but can provide a financial compensation.

Outside of such civil actions, the
criminal courts are the only other potential avenue for legal recourse in cases of
sexual harassment. In order, however,
for a plaintiff to sue in criminal court,
charges of assault or battery must be
proved beyond a reasonable doubt; and
only the perpetrator, not the employer,
can be brought to trial. In the United
States to date, there have been no criminal cases in the area of sexual harassment.

The legal precedent is even more
nebulous with regard to the question of
employers' (organizations') liability for
the acts of their employees. The evolving precedent in federal law seems to be
that the plaintiff may include the employer (the organization) in sexual
harassment suits. Yet Miller v. Bank of
America is the only case in which this
precedent has been established.

Finally, in the only two cases dealing
with the question of eligibility for unemployment compensation, the court
findings have been contradictory, with
the first legal precedent having been
overturned.

In summary, this overview indicates
that (1) literature on sexual harassment
is sparse, (2) organizational policies are
new and not yet institutionalized, and
(3) the law is unclear and evolving. Yet
the concerns are widespread. The chap-
ters to follow have been selected to in-

form managers of the complexities of the problem and of its organizational, legal and human consequences.

NOTES

1. "Sexual Harassment on the Job: Questions and Answers" (New York: Working Women's Institute, 1978).

2. Lin Farley, *Sexual Shakedown: The Sexual Harassment of Women on the Job* (New York: McGraw Hill, 1978), pp. 45-51.

3. *Ibid.*, p. 176.

4. "Sexual Harassment in the Federal Government," Hearings before the Subcommittee on Investigations of the Committee on Post Office and Civil Service, U.S. House of Representatives, Ninety-Sixth Congress, First Session, October 23, 1979, serial no. 96-57. (Washington, D.C.: U.S. Government Printing Office, 1980), p. 1.

5. "Sexual Harassment on the Job: Results of Preliminary Survey" (New York: Working Women's Institute, 1975).

6. Claire Safran, "What Men Do To Women on the Job: A Shocking Look at Sexual Harassment," *Redbook* (November 1976): 149, 217-24.

7. United Nations Ad Hoc Group on Equal Rights for Women, "Report on the Questionnaire XXXVI," Report on file at the New York University Law Review reported in Note 51, *New York University Law Review* (1976): 148, 149 n.6.

8. Sandra Harley Carey, "Sexual Politics in Business" (unpublished, University of Texas at San Antonio, 1976).

9. Statement of Mary Ann Largen, Director, New Responses, Inc. in "Sexual Harassment in the Federal Government," *op. cit.*, p. 39.

10. Peggy Crull, "The Impact of Sexual Harassment on the Job: A Profile of the Experiences of 92 Women," Research Series, Report No. 3 (New York: Working Women's Institute, Fall 1979).

11. The Women's Advisory Council to the Salt Lake County Merit Council, "Study on Barriers to Upward Mobility," Personnel Division and Merit Systems Council, Salt Lake County, Utah, July, 1979.

12. "Responses of Fair Employment Practices Agencies to Sexual Harassment Complaints: A Report and Recommendations," Research Series, Report No. 2 (New York: Working Women's Institute, Fall 1978).

13. Office of Personnel Management letter to D. Neugarten (March 14, 1980).

14. Elizabeth Sulliven, "Survey Shows Few States Have Systems to Resolve Sexual Harassment Complaints," *Intergovernmental Personnel Notes*, U.S. Office of Personnel Management, November-December 1979, p. 3.

15. Statement of Mrs. Ruth T. Prokop, Chairwoman, Merit Systems Protection Board, in "Sexual Harassment in the Federal Government," *op. cit.*, pp. 162-65.

16. "Sex at the Office," *Fortune* (April 7, 1980): 42.

17. Catharine A. MacKinnon, *Sexual Harassment of Working Women* (New Haven, Conn.: Yale University Press, 1979), p. 83.

18. Department of Housing and Urban Development, *HUDDLE*, vol. 10, no. 3 (March 1980).

19. U.S. Office of Personnel Management, "Memorandum to Heads of Departments and Independent Agencies, Subject: Policy Statement and Definition of Sexual Harassment," Washington, D.C., December 12, 1979.

20. "Memorandum of Understanding between the Investigations Subcommittee of the Post Office and Civil Service Committee and the Equal Employment Opportunity Commission concerning the Problem of Sexual Harassment of Federal Employees," unpublished, undated.

21. "Workshop on Sexual Harassment, Participants Manual and Trainers Manual," Washington, D.C.: Supervisory and Communications Training Center, U.S. Office of Personnel Management, undated.

22. Equal Employment Opportunity Commission, "Title 29–Labor, Chapter XIV— Part 1604—Guidelines on Discrimination Because of Sex under Title VII of the Civil Rights Act of 1964, as Amended—Adoption of Interim Interpretative Guidelines," Washington, D.C., April 1980.

23. Government of the District of Columbia, "Mayor's Order 79-89, Subject: Sexual Harassment," May 24, 1979.

24. *Wisconsin Statutes*, Bill #450, May 1978.

25. *Continental Can Co., et al.* v. *State by William Wilson, Commissioner, et al.* June 6, 1980. Minnesota Supreme Court.

26. In a precedent-setting case in Bonn,

West Germany, a female private in the U.S.
Army has been convicted for indecently as-
saulting a male soldier. A 1980 Court Martial
convicted the woman of assault and battery
and of sexually molesting a male soldier. She
was sentenced to thirty days at hard labor
and fined $298. *Rocky Mountain News*, 9
April 1980.

27. *Barnes* v. *Train* 13 FEP Cases 123, 124
(D.D.C. 1974).

28. *Barnes* v. *Costle* 561 F.2d. 983 (D.C.
Cir 1977).

29. *Monge* v. *Beebe Rubber* 316 A.2d. 549
(N.H. 1974).

30. *In re. Carmita Wood*, Case No. 75-
92437. New York State Department of Labor
Unemployment Insurance Appeals Board,
Decision and Notice of Decision, March 7,
1975 (unreported), Appeal No. 207,958,
New York State Department of Labor, Un-
employment Insurance Division Appeal
Board (October 6, 1975).

31. *Hamilton* v. *Appleton Electric Co.*,
E.R.D. Case #7301025, State of Wisconsin,
Department of Industry, Labor and Human
Relations, October 1, 1976.

32. *Corne* v. *Bausch and Lomb, Inc.* 390 F.
Supp. 161 (D. Ariz. 1975), reversed 562 R.
2d. 55 (9th Cir 1977).

33. *Miller* v. *Bank of America*, 418 F.
Supp. 233 (N.D. Cal. 1976).

34. *Williams* v. *Saxbe*, 413 F. Supp. 654
(D.D.C. 1976).

35. *Tomkins* v. *Public Service Electric and
Gas Co.*, 422 F. Supp. 533 (D.N.J. 1977), reversed on appeal 568 F. 2d. 1044 (3rd. Cir.
1977).

36. *Heelan* v. *Johns Mansville Corp.*, 451
F. Supp. 1382 (D. Colo. 1978).

37. Title VII of the Civil Rights Act of 1964,
as amended by the Equal Employment Opportunity Act of 1972, section 703 (a) (1) and
(2), codified at 42 U.S.C. Section 2000e (2)
(a) (1) and (2).

I

Sexuality in Organizations: The Context

Introduction. Organizations are natural environments for the emergence of romantic relationships. These relationships can be short- or long-term, pleasurable or painful for the parties directly involved, and they can be an asset or a liability for colleagues and for management.

In their article "The Executive Man and Woman: The Issue of Sexuality," Bradford, Sargent and Sprague introduce the topic of sexuality in the work-place and describe it as a behavior that causes many of the difficulties men and women experience in their working lives. The authors share insights about ritualized sex role behaviors—the "macho and the seductress," the "chivalrous knight and the helpless maiden," the "protective father and the pet," and the "tough warrior and nurturant mother,"—and about how these traditional behaviors are changing. The reality of sexuality at work, they argue, must be openly acknowledged so that men and women alike can better deal with themselves and others in the pursuit of professional excellence.

Jennie Farley's "Worklife Problems for Both Men and Women," ad-dresses the set of problems which exist in a work setting between the sexes and suggests that personnel directors and personnel staff need to take re-sponsibility for enlightening themselves, as well as line administrators, about ways of resolving them. The problems, which are not new, but which are becoming exaggerated because of women's increased labor force participation, anti-discrimination laws, the women's movement and litigations, include (1) the "Sex Plus" problems, defined as those factors which are unique to women—the responsibility for child care, for instance—and which, therefore, make women's occupational tenure and performance patterns significantly different from men's; (2) sexual harass-ment, which is a complex issue because of the question of whether or not or under what conditions it constitutes sex discrimination under Title VII of the Civil Rights Act of 1964; and (3) The office romance, a phenomenon which is clearly on the rise as more women enter and rise-in-rank in the labor force. All these problems are interrelated and expand the thrust of personnel policies and procedures.

Robert E. Quinn's "Coping with Cupid: The Formation, Impact and Management of Romantic Relationships in Organizations," is the original and, in fact, the only systematically conducted research in the field of sexuality at work. Quinn was interested in identifying the variables related to the formation of romantic relationships in organizations. He found that proximity, motivation and certain work group characteristics were factors associated with the development of romantic involvements. Quinn identifies the effects of such involvements on the parties immediately involved, on other organizational members and on the system as a whole, and he discusses the potential range of actions available to management as it responds to the outcomes of romantic liaisons.

Margaret Mead, in closing this section of the book, advances "A Proposal: We Need Taboos on Sex at Work." Mead describes the modern social context as an environment in which traditional role relationships—husband and wife, parent and child, male and female—are breaking down. Men and women need to and are confronting the necessity of working out new forms of acceptable behavior. In so doing, Mead argues, there needs to be a "new climate of opinion," and strict taboos on sexual behavior in work organizations. Mead's code dictates that in order to "protect and nurture the most meaningful human relations . . . you don't make passes at or sleep with the people you work with."

1. The Executive Man and Woman: The Issue of Sexuality*

DAVID L. BRADFORD
ALICE G. SARGENT
MELINDA S. SPRAGUE

When the issue of hiring women in management arises, a frequent response from male executives is joking about the sexual implications: "Won't that make field trips more interesting!" "No woman would be safe in this office with Bill here." Such comments enrage advocates of affirmative action, who see the issue as one of fairness and the opportunity for options other than housewife or secretary. We believe the problem of women in management is complex, encompassing far more than sexual interplay, but this joking reveals more than simple prejudice. Many of the difficulties men and women experience in their relationships at work revolve around sexuality.

Sexuality covers a wide area, and so initially we need to distinguish several ways sex influences managerial behavior. The first refers to the effect of *differential socialization* of males and females. This socialization covers a wide area of which only a part relates to sexual behavior per se. A substantial body of research demonstrates that from birth boys and girls are consistently treated differently. The types of games, toys, and books given to boys, as well as the kind of behavior for which boys are rewarded and punished, teach boys different values, aspirations, and behavioral skills than girls. Boys are sup-

ported for being aggressive, assertive, analytical, and competitive, while girls are praised for being helpful, passive, deferential, and concerned with interpersonal relationships.

Teachers as well as parents support these differences. One example is the research by Serbin (1973), who found that elementary school teachers, both male and female, responded more often to questions raised by boys than girls, and gave the boys longer answers that were richer in content. Girls received more perfunctory answers often accompanied by a pat on the head or arm around the shoulder—as if support and not cognitive content were the important response. Little wonder that this differential training is excellent preparation for men to succeed in management while handicapping women who want to travel the same route.

By college the differences are learned well. Aries (in press) found in a mixed sex group of college students that men typically talked two-thirds of the time. When women did communicate, they directed their comments to men rather than to other women and were more concerned about acceptance and relationships while men were more attuned to authority and impressing each other.

A second way sex influences managerial behavior is through *stereotypes* of

*Source: "The Executive Man and Woman: The Issue of Sexuality," chapter 3, from *Bringing Women into Management*, Francine E. Gordon and Myra H. Strober, eds. Copyright © 1975 by McGraw-Hill Book Company. Reprinted by permission.

the other sex. Definite expectations exist regarding the values, interests, aptitudes, and abilities of a person just because the other happens to be male or female. Women, as well as men, often expect other women to be interested in fashion design, not finance, and in personnel, not line management. Managers assume that a married woman will not want out-of-town job assignments while such consideration is not given to a married man.

Many times, expectations about competence levels differ solely on the basis of sex, so that the *same* output is often judged of lower quality when observers believe it to have been done by a woman rather than a man. Goldberg (1968) and Pheterson *et al.* (1971) found that females also have lower expectations of a woman's competence. In these studies women evaluated paintings and written reports as of lesser quality when they bore a female signature than when a male's. Clearly, these perceptions and expectations influence the type of job assignments male supervisors allocate, the performance level they expect, the way they assess tasks performed, and the candidates they consider when opportunities for advancement arise. Fear of failure may be a major concern for most men, but Horner's (1970) research on college students found that because women are punished for success by being ostracized by other women and rejected by men, they are ambivalent about success. In fact, in Horner's research college women and black men demonstrated a comparable conflict.

The third area deals with how *sexuality* per se influences how men and women work together. Sexuality here refers not just to sexual attraction and office affairs but to the various ways in which a male manager sees himself as a sexual male and responds to the sexuality of a female coworker—and the ways a female manager experiences her own sexuality in responding to males.

This article will focus on this third area of sexuality and discuss the following four aspects:

1) the way that men define and measure their masculinity and females their femininity, and the relation of these self-images to work success;

2) the sexual messages behind many male-female interactions;

3) the likelihood that introducing females to all levels of management will be disruptive to the way men commonly relate to other men; and

4) the matter of mutual attraction leading to sexual intercourse.

Obviously these four aspects do not apply to all males or females in management, nor is each necessarily of the same intensity as one moves from first-level supervision to the executive suite. What we are suggesting is that sexuality in one form or other helps to explain why managers feel ambivalent about affirmative action for women, why many men and women have difficulty relating to each other in the office, and why women executives are handicapped in their search for success.

A. HOW SEXUALITY IS DEFINED

1. MASCULINITY AND WORK SUCCESS: THE COMPATIBLE EQUATION

An important aspect of the sense of self-identity for both males and females is their masculinity and femininity. The charge of not being masculine is as devastating an attack for a man as questioning a woman's femininity is for a woman. How do males assert their sexuality? Teen-agers resort to fistfighting, playing "chicken" with cars, playing football, and competing against one another to see who can consume more beer or have more dates. While this may do for youth, an educated adult must find more discreet and indirect proofs.

For many men, work serves as the major vehicle defining their identify, including sexual identity. A job indicates not only a person's competence and worth but even who he is. When people meet socially, one of the first questions asked is, "What do you do?", for the answer is seen as telling a great deal about the individual. Being a plumber or a physicist, an executive or an engineer, is perceived as saying a lot about the individual's values, abilities, personality, and worth. Conversely, as Bakke's (1934) work of the Depression showed, being unemployed has a detrimental effect on a person's self-image and worth.

Status and pay of the job also bear an element of sexuality. The lumberjack and construction worker exemplify the rough masculinity of physical labor, but there is an aura of sexuality around success itself, as most clearly seen with famous individuals whose power and male sexuality are highly correlated. Not only does sexuality frequently contain elements of competition, dominance, and power, but power often takes on sexual implications. Even some of the terms used for the former are borrowed from the latter. A person's program is said to have been "emasculated" by a certain decision, and the manager who fails is described as "impotent."

This equation of power with affirmation of masculine sexuality relates not only to the type of occupation, but also to specific task accomplishments on the job. Not infrequently a task dispute in a staff meeting takes on an overtone of interpersonal rivalry, often with a *macho* flavor. Logical arguments, the pros and cons of various positions, can mean more than just arriving at the best solution. Certainly there are other motives at work so that the "winner" feels more competent and valued by the organization, but we suggest he might also feel more masculine and reaffirmed as a man. Men once dueled physically, but now verbal wit and repartee have replaced the sword. In academic circles this has been perfected to an art, where

logical arguments between colleagues are the forum for dominance.[1]

For men and for the women who admire them and help them stage these roles, there is congruence between sexuality and work performance. This refers not only to the compatibility between how boys are socialized (*i.e.*, raised to be verbally aggressive, competitive, concerned with the task more than the relationship) and requirements of the workplace, but also to a similar congruence between work success and affirmation of masculinity. Thus men strive to advance, build up their programs, and compete in meetings partially to obtain status and financial records that connote masculine success, but also to affirm their masculinity more directly. Even those who do not use success for sexual reassurance may feel threatened as males if they experience work failure.

This perception of the overlap between sexuality and professional success may help to explain some of the opposition to the advancement of women. To lose to a woman is inevitably more shattering to a male's self-image than to be bested by another male. Men often apply the term "castrating" to an aggressive or competent female, implying that her intentions are to lessen the masculinity of the male. But the same action or behavior may vary in its apparent impact depending on whether it comes from a male or female colleague. Behavior that is acceptable in a man is denigrated in a woman. A man may be assertive, but a woman is overly aggressive. A man may attack, but a woman castrates! Are there that many women who really try to de-

---

1. Another sign that verbal arguments can have a sexually competitive component is the behavior that not infrequently arises when an attractive female is in an otherwise all-male group. While she is not directly addressed, the men compete among themselves to see who is wittiest and sharpest.

stroy the masculinity of male coworkers? Or is the real issue that because so many men make the connection, often unconsciously, between their masculinity and job performance, any assertiveness or task success by women is experienced by the male as a threat at that level?

2. THE PERCEIVED INCOMPATIBILITY OF FEMININITY AND WORK SUCCESS

Task competence and sexuality interact for women as well, but for women an incompatibility exists between behaviors intrinsic to task success. Such traits include being passive, acting emotionally, being supportive, and relating well to others. Since high school, many women have felt a conflict between "being competent" and "being popular." These women must find validation of their sexuality elsewhere, since the charge of nonfemininity is a common response to any show of competence by a woman.

The options are not very satisfying for women who feel this dilemma. One alternative is to hold back from expressing competence or to express it through others. The latter ploy may mean saying things through a male, preferably the boss, so that he and others think it is his idea. When a woman does present an idea or suggestion, it is often in a deferential manner without the assurance or bluster that enables men to get their ideas accepted. Furthermore, when her idea is attacked, she is more likely to concede than to rebut: even when a woman can have ideas, she is not expected to defend them very staunchly. These evasions help some women to preserve their femininity, as traditionally defined, but at the cost of inhibiting competence.

The other extreme is forfeiting acceptance as a female to facilitate the more direct expression of ability. This is the stereotype of the "iron maiden" who is so determined to battle it out in

the man's world that any warmth or softness is suppressed.[2]

These are extreme positions, whereas in actuality most females in the managerial world work out a solution somewhere in between. Clearly this dilemma exists for women but not for men. The male executive, finding work and sexuality synergistic, does not have to spend time and energy working out a compromise. Furthermore, the very term "compromise" implies some concession whereby competence and/or sexual self-identity is lessened in the resolution.

B. MALE-FEMALE RELATIONSHIPS

The way males and females relate to one another at work has a sexual component in that the behavior of each is constantly influenced by the sex of the other. Most obviously this occurs when that person is viewed in terms of sexual attractiveness. One manager put it this way:

> I don't know whether it's right for me to act this way, or whether it makes me a Male Chauvinist Pig, but the first time I meet a woman, I respond to her as a sexual object and only later as a person.

We are not suggesting that all males or females have this same initial orientation, but even with those who don't, their interactions with the opposite sex have a sexual component even when sexual attraction is not involved.

In our culture certain ritualized ways of relating to the opposite sex have developed that have their roots in courtship behavior. For men, this may take the form of respectful deference to the "fair sex." Or it could include a protectiveness and solicitousness. To illustrate

---

2. Henning (1974) reports that a not infrequent occurrence for the woman who has gone this route is, around age forty, to realize the personal cost and begin to express the warmth and softness so long suppressed.

this point, imagine the following incident at a cocktail party. Three men have been discussing the state of the economy when a woman joins their group. They pull in their stomachs, stand a little straighter, and shift the subject to some mild flirtatious bantering, compliments on her attire, or some solicitous query about the family. If the conversation moves back to business, it would not be unusual to see some competitive jostling among the men to determine who sounds more astute and attempts to one-up the other. Approving comments from the female are welcomed, inane comments tolerated, but highly perceptive comments from her would certainly produce astonishment. It would be even more unsettling if she were to disagree with one of the males on a business issue, particularly if she were to correct him. If the male thus corrected replied defensively, the others would rush to her defense.

Yet this is a cocktail party. So what if the men are showing off a bit to the female present? What harm is there in some mild flirting? What is wrong with chivalry? And what does this scenario say about sexuality and women in management?

This interaction reinforces, in the minds of all of those involved, the woman's inferior position. She is expected to be naive and submissive, ignorant about business matters, unable to take care of herself and therefore in need of a man for protection. But if she is to be successful in the work world, she must learn how to operate in that more hostile environment. Passivity and deference will not get her far. One woman described it thusly: "None of the behaviors I learned from watching my mother talk to my father are helpful at work. In fact, they are dysfunctional."

The type of relating described at the cocktail party reflects the typical courtship behavior that is part of the dating-relating game males and females have engaged in since puberty. The problem

is that such interaction has permeated society. Being influenced and responding either consciously or unconsciously to the sexuality of the other is the primary way men and women have learned to relate to each other.[3]

1. ROLES AND THEIR USES

The problem is that this set of attitudes and behavior cannot be confined to the date or cocktail party but carries over to the office. It is most clearly seen between the manager and *his* secretary. The mild flirtation, compliments on her new hair style, perfume, or dress, is part and parcel of the daily interaction.[4] As long as it is verbal, this interaction probably causes few problems and is the kind of friendly banter that makes interaction between the sexes enjoyable. But this mode of relating may not be limited to occasional kidding. It may underly much of the relationship between males and females on the management level.

---

3. If this seems a bit farfetched to the reader, we would like to suggest the following exercise. The next time you observe a male and female interacting, change the sex of the woman so that "he" is using the same words, tone, gesture, and way of relating. It works just as well to change the man's sex instead. In either case, having the two be of the same sex produces a jarring effect. In both cases the sexuality will become apparent, for with the sex the "same," the interaction takes on a homosexual flavor.

4. Note that a similar relationship between a female manager and her *male* secretary would not be deemed quite appropriate, because that contradicts rather than complements the organizational hierarchy for a male is usually dominant sexually. The quasi-sexual aspect of the boss-secretary relationship not infrequently develops between a person with a great deal of power and his personal assistant. A major politician, top executive, or company president may never think of having sexual intercourse with his personal secretary, but part of her devotion and loyalty is based on more than her job responsibilities.

This kind of relationship is not attributable solely to the male; the tendency exists in both directions. The female is aware that she is relating to males and acts accordingly. Thus men and women get locked into reciprocal roles that have a semisexual basis. While not the only ways that they interact, the following four role relationships are illustrative of the assertion that ways of relating developed on the outside carry over to the office in a manner that limits the potential of both parties by isolating the person and limiting the range of behavior rather than encouraging the full scope of self-expression.[5]

a. *The* Macho *and the* Seductress. The primary mode of relating for these two roles is sexual. Actual seduction may not occur, but the nature of their interaction usually has a sexual flavor with elements of flirting and game playing. The man is concerned that women see and value him as a potent male and makes constant verbal efforts to emphasize this. He frequently attempts to assert his dominance over the woman by kidding with her about her attractiveness and then by putting her down for her incompetence in some other area. The cost to the woman is that she is seen more as a sexual object than as a person who has business-related knowledge and competence. The satisfaction for both is that it reaffirms their sexuality.

The Seductress role is similar for the woman. In some cases she is actively seeking affirmation that she is sexually desirable and wants to have men respond to her as highly attractive. At times men place her in that role and respond to her as potentially available. Being Seductress, either through her own efforts or the expectations of men, gives her great power, for she confers

potency on those men to whom she gives approval. This role has the advantage for the woman of affirming her femininity, but it inhibits direct expression of competence.

The presence of such a woman, particularly if there are only one or two females in the group, can be an energizer as the men compete for her approval, but such a situation rapidly becomes dysfunctional if there is a highly interdependent task which requires collaboration. In addition, the competence of the woman is not fully available, since her concern is to be valued as an attractive woman, not as a skilled colleague.

b. *Chivalrous Knight and Helpless Maiden.* This is perhaps the most common set of roles, for they are highly engrained in our culture. Here the male sees himself as stronger and more competent than women and responsible for them. While politely tolerant of women, and respectful of them as women, he would not perceive a woman as having many task-related skills. Consequently he would be less likely to challenge her or make the same demands on her that he would on males.

With this relationship the female, playing the role of Helpless Maiden, can use these stereotypes to manipulate the male for her own ends. Korda (1972) quotes just such a person.

> . . . When it's a question of using my sex, I use it. I don't mean to sleep around—I don't. But if you have any kind of looks and you're not scared yourself you can get what you want. You listen to them, flirt a little, cry when things go wrong, and say, "Gee, I wish you could show me how to do this, you know so much more about this than I do." It's a snap. [p. 29]

Rather than truly being helpless and withdrawing from the competition, the Helpless Maiden in this case feigns ineptness and derives a sense of power because men serve her. Many men become furious at having become ensnared into this protective stance, for the woman is taking his stereotype, usu-

5. This analysis owes much to the thinking of Rosabeth Kanter (1974), who developed the concept of stereotypic roles women play in male-dominated settings. "Seductress," "Pet," and "Mother" are her terms.

ally used to legitimize female subservience, and turning it against him for her own advantage. To add insult to injury, the very beliefs the men hold—that give Helpless Maiden her power—prevent men from directly confronting her and calling her on this game. To do so would be to treat her like a strong, competent person, i.e., another male. The damage to the Helpless Maiden is great, too. She may "overlearn" these behaviors and never get free of them, losing the opportunity to learn to take care of herself. This reinforces her dependency on a man, which limits her mobility as she fails to develop the direct assertiveness necessary for self-expression and success in the work world.

c. *Protective Father and the Pet.* A combination that crops up, particularly between an older man and younger woman, is a protective father-daughter relationship. This differs from the Knight-Maiden in that the Father tends to be more active in assuming a protective role and the woman's dependence is less likely to be a means of manipulation. The Pet functions almost as a cheerleader for the men she works with. If the Pet, or mascot, goes to lunch with a group of men, she laughs at their jokes, encourages them to talk about themselves and their ideas, but rarely contributes to the content herself.

Not infrequently the Pet and the Seductress get linked with high-status males, which increases the power of both. As in the case of the Seductress, this can validate the Pet's femininity, but at the cost of not being able to show competence directly. The two roles differ in that the Pet, like the overdeveloped but underaged teen-ager, is not perceived as sexually available.

d. *Tough Warrior and Nurturant Mother.* For many men, masculinity is defined in the "John Wayne" tradition of being tough and independent and suppressing all emotions. While functional at times for occupational success, this role definition is costly. This artificial self-sufficiency not only has personal costs, but can interfere with task success as well. Work requires collaboration as well as competition, interdependence as well as independence, and giving and receiving of support and help as well as giving and receiving of ideas.

The reciprocal of this role is that of the Nurturant Mother who serves as the confidant to whom others can bring their problems and seek support. While they are not relating to her as a sexual object, they do not respond to her as a total person; rather they respond to one aspect of the female stereotype. At least, this role removes her from sexual competition, but as Kanter points out, it has three major costs:

1) she is valued because of the support and service she can provide to the males and not because of her individual abilities or actions—thus it tends to cut down on her tendency to take independent initiative around task areas;

2) she often is placed in the role of the "good, accepting mother," which inhibits the extent to which she can use her critical abilities; and

3) she becomes the specialist in emotional issues and shields men from accepting responsibility in their areas; this division of labor serves to further the stereotype that men are rational and logical while women are overly emotional.

We have given these four descriptions of male-female roles as examples of how each can be trapped when relating to the other. While they have been paired, each can exist without the counterpart. A man can play Chivalrous Knight even when none of the women are acting helpless. These roles are overlearned from a multitude of past situations, and so the mere fact of being the only woman present might encourage a woman's tendency to nurture others without any of the men turning to her for support. But it is also likely that a dominant style from one sex evokes the the reciprocal in the other. It is difficult to be *Macho* to the Nurturant Mother but easy if the woman is playing Seductress.

Clearly not all interactions are of this type, for people of the opposite sex can relate to each other as individuals with a minimum of such role playing.[6] Furthermore, these ritualized ways of relating are less prevalent in the higher echelons of the organization. These four role types all limit expressions of competence in women and thus are dysfunctional for success. Males do not experience the reciprocal roles as much of a hindrance. Their roles are evoked only by the presence of women, but women executives almost always work with men and so their roles are more likely to emerge.

More and more women, and to some extent men, are attempting to break these role constraints, but change is slow. For example, it is hard for a woman to keep from being the protected child when her boss treats her as one. She may not be aware of the extent to which he shields her from assignments that are challenging and risky, but which are necessary if she is to develop and advance. Even if she is aware, how can she confront someone who is "only trying to help"?[7]

In the same way, men often feel confused about how to deal with women. While some females are attempting to change the norms governing interaction between the sexes, there is far from universal agreement by women about how they want to be treated. Males often feel confused about such simple issues as "Should I open the door, help her on

with her coat, pick up the tab, or call her Ms.?" Or issues of more substance: "Will she feel I'm patronizing her if I give her some advice about her career?" Relationships have become much more complex, with greater ambiguity about what is expected and what is correct. Like the white liberal who feels helpless when called a racist by a black, so many males feel constrained for fear of being labeled "sexist."

Ironically, the reason men often feel so uncertain about how to relate to women is that they are trapped in traditional sex roles themselves. They are shackled by the social mores of how gentlemen should relate to ladies: protecting them, taking care of them, being responsible for them. Men and women need the freedom to respond to each other as one individual to another.

C. MALE-MALE BONDING: THE INTERFERENCE OF WOMEN

When men are together, a bonding process develops that does not occur when women are present (Tiger, 1969). The mechanisms are many and varied. For some it can be a discussion of last weekend's football game, cars, or an offhand comment about the physical dimensions of a passing secretary. For others it can be comparing golf scores, or discussing politics and the stock market, or working together on a task. But whatever the subject, the style and tone are such that the message is clear: this is a "man's world." The rapport is perpetuated only so long as the membership is totally male.

Why the change when a female appears? One reason is that these topics serve as one way to assert a traditional definition of masculinity. This form of bonding is based on the exclusion of women. What is shared are interests supposedly not held by women rather than what the members have in common as a result of working on the same project or being employed by the same company. What would happen if a

---

6. The term "role playing" does not imply that the male or female is necessarily consciously "playing a role." As we have mentioned, roles can be so ingrained from countless encounters as to have become an integrated part of that individual's personality and behavioral style.

7. One of our female colleagues made the point that she has been held back more by "friends" than by enemies. "With the latter you know where you stand, but with friends they are forever trying to protect you from situations where you might fail."

woman in the group were equally knowledgeable and vocal about sports, cars, and politics? If the basis for bonding were solely common interests, then her contributions should be welcome. But isn't it likely that men would feel uncomfortable if a woman corrected them on Monday night's game, knew more about the racing specs of the Porsche, or had a lower handicap? The conversation would soon die out and men would lose the camaraderie that had existed before.

The points raised in the previous section give a clue to another reason why women interfere with the bonding that occurs in an all-male group. The introduction of a woman could activate male-female relationships so that men would feel great consternation not only about how they should act, but also about what subjects and language are appropriate and inappropriate. The bantering among men often has a veiled competitive tone that attempts to score points without hurting feelings or causing retaliation. Many men feel uncomfortable treating women in a similar fashion or even demonstrating such behavior in front of them. It would be even more threatening if a woman were attractive and fit the Seductress role. This could provoke a different kind of rivalry among the men that would undermine any sense of trust and solidarity among them.

Even when the female is not responded to as the Seductress, concerns about sexuality can interfere with other activities used by men for bonding. Frequently work goes on during lunch and over a drink after five. Not only is work conducted, but people become better acquainted, both crucial in facilitating later business interactions as well as the individual's career development. But men may be hesitant to involve women in such activities. Will luncheon meetings be seen by the woman and co-workers in the same light as if one were to go out with a male peer? Similarly, going out on the town while at conven-

tions or on business trips may not be the same when women are present.

D. THE FEAR OF SEXUAL ENTANGLEMENTS

Sexual liaisons within the same organization, while not unknown, still tend to be negatively sanctioned. Data from the Sex Research Center at the University of Indiana suggest that at least three-fourths of the males in this country commit adultery, but it is not clear how this is spread throughout the management hierarchy. A recent study (Johnson, 1974) reported that only 20 percent of top executives acknowledge having sex outside of marriage. Of these, only one in four indicates involvement on a regular basis; and only 8.8 percent of those, or less than 2 percent of the total sample, reported an affair with a woman in the office. Most of these men go outside of their marriage between the tenth and twentieth years of marriage and are between the ages of thirty-five and forty-five. Regrettably, there are no comparable data on women.

Questions can be raised about whether this sample is representative and whether information were gathered under conditions where the executives would be completely candid. But whatever the actual incidence of office affairs, the fear of their occurrence is very high. Hence the need exists for greater understanding of some of the issues and feelings involved.

Many people with whom we have talked say that when women and men work together in a noncompetitive relationship, it is only a matter of time before sexual attraction starts to develop. It is doubtful that this occurs in all, or nearly all cases, but one of the most consistent findings in social psychological research is that contact leads to liking, which in turn leads to more interaction. Two people who work together for some time learn to trust, rely on, and respect each other with a corresponding increase in liking.

Obviously this does not occur in all cases. Knowing another more fully may lead to discovering something we don't like, and working on a project can also be a source of strain and conflict. Also, knowing a man or woman as an equal may remove the mystique and could lead to a rich friendship without sexual involvement.

There are two reasons why it is likely that the incidence of sexual attraction will increase, in addition to the obvious fact that the presence of more women in management raises the number of potential pairs. One is the changing internal structure of contemporary organizations, and the other is the changing cultural norms. As organizations grow more complex with a wide distribution of offices, plants, and clients, travel will increase. The companies that send only males to the field, thus hindering the career opportunities of female executives, may become targets for affirmative action litigation. No longer are women working just eight to five; trips, evening meetings, and conferences set up conditions that make affairs easier to occur.

Societal norms about premarital and extramarital sexuality are changing. While such behavior is not sanctioned by organizations or society, there is greater tolerance for what was once considered highly deviant behavior. Although an affair may still bring great personal pain and can incur costs to job success and reputation, particularly for the female, it is not likely to be as shattering as in the past. Behavior at work cannot be isolated from societal trends, and changes in the culture are likely to be reflected in the office.

Sexual attraction and affairs obviously have their cost, but often overlooked are costs incurred when managers are overly concerned about preventing intimacy from developing. Such vigilance can prevent the emergence of normal relationships. The fear of getting emo-

tionally involved can lead male and female executives to bend over backwards to avoid situations that might appear compromising, like having dinner together or working after hours, but that might increase their task performance. The female can be so worried about appearing seductive that she becomes totally asexual and inhibits all expressions of warmth and caring. The wife at home may be jealous of the female coworker who is able to display skills that the wife has had to submerge. In order to avoid such conflict, the husband may avoid contacts with the female office mate for fear this will cause difficulties at home.

E. WHERE DO WE GO FROM HERE?

The problems we have discussed are complex and deeply rooted in our culture. No easy solutions exist, but as men and women begin to work together to build adult relationships, a first step seems to be to acknowledge the various ways sexuality may be expressed in the office. With this awareness, executives can become sensitive to the possibilities of responses based on sexual stereotypes. They can be more attuned to how men respond to women differentially so that such personally limiting ways of relating can be avoided.

Until recently, consciousness raising has been seen as the domain of women and then of only a few. In several urban areas—Berkeley, Boston, and New York—parallel groups of men have developed to look at the constraints of the male sex role. Such activity has rarely been seen as the concern of organizations. Executives have taken the stance that, at best, participation in such groups is an aspect of personal growth that can be undertaken after hours but it is nothing that business should initiate.

If our analysis is correct, the constraints men and women feel in relating to each other have direct application to work effectiveness. The manager, to be effective, needs to explore to what extent he has been enslaved by sex-role stereotypes, how he feels constrained from arguing with and directly confronting women, how confined he is by traditional definitions of masculinity as seen in films and advertising. The ultimate goal is not one of women's liberation or men's liberation but of human liberation that permits personal development according to individual interests rather than societal sex-role constraints.

For the long run this requires a major shift in cultural mores, but one does not have to wait for societal norms to change before changing the climate in the office. The superior can be very influential in determining what behavior is valued and what is not. Clear signals that competence in women is desired can provide the needed reassurance to the female who is afraid that assertiveness will be seen as unfeminine or castrating. Discouraging the games that men and women play can prevent their continuation.

For such changes to be permanent there must be support throughout the organization. Management development seeks to train executives to better handle technical and administrative aspects of their jobs. Training on the issues we have discussed would be equally useful to increase their awareness of sexism and to develop their ability to more effectively relate to and work with members of the opposite sex.

It is neither possible nor even desirable for people to ignore the sex of one another. At this point in our cultural development it is more desirable to increase awareness so that one can understand how the sex of another is affecting one's behavior. The statement "I want to treat her like I would any other person" is often a veiled form of sexism, for it usually means "like I would any other male." Growing up male or female has had a major impact on the person and how he or she relates to others.

What we are suggesting is that in order for the male executive to understand a woman as an individual, he needs to be aware of how being male has influenced his perceptions and responses to women. Likewise, the woman needs to be aware of how her stereotypes influence her behavior and limit her options in responding to the male executive. What is crucial is that the reality of sexuality as an issue can be acknowledged so that men and women in organizations can begin to recognize and explore these issues.

F. SEXUAL ATTRACTION

Increased awareness of the roles that sexuality and sexism play in male-female interaction may help with many of the issues we have discussed but may be less useful in resolving the problem of sexual attraction. If history is any predictor of the future, there may be no simple answer. Troy was not the first, nor last, empire to be lost over sexuality. Each person has to work out his or her own resolution. Some resolve it by working hard to make sure feelings never develop. However, although such a solution prevents the problem from arising, it may have a hidden cost, for to be so concerned and guarded against ever developing attractions can produce a greater than necessary distance and formality. After all, friendship and interpersonal liking are important facilitators in work, be they between the sexes or with the same sex.

Another resolution distinguishes between feelings and behavior. The former need not dictate the latter. People have much more control over their actions than over their emotions. When verbally attacked, it is difficult not to feel anger but easy to refrain from slugging back. So it is with sex. A person can have strong feelings of attraction, and these can continue to exist without leading either to an affair or to disruption of the work relationship.

When feelings of attraction do develop, should they be communicated? In our discussions with managers, no clear outcome emerges. In some situations, sharing of feelings appears to reduce some of the intensity and ambiguity so that individuals can continue to work together and even go out for lunch without fear that intentions will be misinterpreted. Open discussion also allows both people to decide how to deal with their attraction. The attraction then becomes a fact of life and people are free to turn to the task at hand.

For others, such a discussion is uncomfortable; they would much prefer not to acknowledge the attraction. There are no simple answers. What is important is that the issue of sexuality be recognized as a fact of organizational life.

Women in management have been described as a "problem" and an "issue" that must be faced. But equal employment may be the source of greater enrichment for the individual and for the total society as well as for the enlightened organization, and thus any problems encountered may be well worth the price.

NOTES

Elizabeth Aries, "Male-Female Communication in Small Groups," in Alice G. Sargent (ed.), *Beyond Sex Roles* (St. Paul, Minn.: West, in press).

E. W. Bakke, *The Unemployed Man* (New York: Dutton, 1934).

P. A. Goldberg, "Are Women Prejudiced against Women?" *Trans-Action* (April 1968).

Margaret Hennig, "Family Dynamics and the Successful Woman Executive," in Ruth B. Knudsin (ed.), *Women and Success: The Anatomy of Achievement* (New York: Morrow, 1974).

Matina Horner, "Femininity and Successful Achievement: A Basic Inconsistency," in Judith Bardwick, Elizabeth Douvan, Matina Horner, and David Guttmann (eds.), *Feminine Personality and Conflict* (Belmont, Calif.: Brooks/Cole, 1970).

Harry J. Johnson, *Executive Life Styles: A Life Extension Institute Report on Alcohol, Sex and Health* (New York: Crowell, 1974).

Rosabeth Moss Kanter, "Women in Organizations: Change Agent Skills," paper presented at the NTL Conference on New Technology in Organization Development, 1974, published in the conference proceedings.

Michael Korda, *Male Chauvinism!* (New York: Random House, 1972).

G. I. Pheterson, S. B. Kiesler, and P. A. Goldberg, "Evaluation of the Performance of Women as a Function of Their Sex, Achievement, and Personal History," *Journal of Personality and Social Psychology*, vol. 19, no. 1 (1971).

Lisa Serbin, unpublished doctoral dissertation, Department of Psychology, State University of New York at Stony Brook, 1973; presented at the American Psychological Association, Philadelphia, Spring 1973.

Lionel Tiger, *Men in Groups* (New York: Random House, 1969).

2. Worklife Problems for Both Women and Men*

JENNIE FARLEY

The personnel practitioner can get heat from both the feminist who seeks instant change in management policy and the line manager who wants immediate waivers of legally mandated responsibilities. People in personnel can, of course, grant neither. Enthusiasts on both sides periodically discover "new issues"—the very ones personnel has been struggling with for years—and label them (depending on their perspective) as gross inequities hitherto unnoticed by anyone or as fresh examples of absurd demands that no rational person outside of government would expect a manager to meet.

This chapter will consider five problems that personnel is both thought to be ignorant of and expected to resolve the moment they are mentioned. The problems are not new, but they may well be exacerbated by the rising expectations of government with respect to the power of law to eliminate discrimination and of feminists with regard to the willingness of profitmaking companies to deal with the social problems faced by women. These issues, which are troublesome both for women workers and for personnel managers, include the three "sex plus" problems—sex discrimination based on age, sexual preference, and status as parent—the prevention of sexual harassment on the job, and the "office romance."

THE "SEX PLUS" PROBLEMS

Some women workers face problems over and above their sex but related to it: they are parents, they are old, or they are homosexual. Each brings a set of complications that can make employers reluctant to have young mothers or old women or lesbians in their companies. One can understand managers' reluctance, but one cannot agree that any of these conditions alone is sufficient to deny an individual either employment in the first place or a fair chance to work in peace once on the job.

The great increase in the female workforce in the last decade has come about because, as noted earlier, mothers of small children are much more likely to work for pay than was the case in the past. Economist Juanita Kreps has demonstrated that women's pattern of labor force participation is very different from that of men. When age is charted against proportion working, the male pattern resembles an arc: by and large, men enter the workforce and continue in employment until they retire. Women's participation shows a sharp dip in the middle years—the childbearing lapse—then rises again as great numbers of women return to work when their children grow up. Students call this the M curve—M for mother.

This intermittent labor force participa-

*Source: Reprinted, by permission of the publisher, from *Affirmative Action and the Woman Worker: Guidelines for Personnel Management,* by Jennie Farley. Copyright © 1979 by AMACOM, a division of American Management Associations, pp. 167-182. All rights reserved.

tion is a uniquely American pattern. In
no other country do so many women
stay home when their children are little.
But the pattern here is changing rapidly.
The curve is approaching men's with
every passing year, as fewer and fewer
women either want to or can stay home
with children. Grossman notes that
nearly half the children in the United
States now have mothers who work for
pay.[1] There is every indication that that
proportion will rise. One reason for the
rise in the future may be that the daughter of a working mother is more likely to
plan to work for pay than the daughter
of a housewife.[2]

If mothers work, who—as Phyllis
Schlafly asks over and over—who will
take care of the children?[3] Perhaps the
more pertinent question to ask is: Who
is taking care of the children? About half
the preschool children of working
mothers are cared for in their own
homes either by a relative or (much less
frequently) by a hired caregiver. A third
of the preschool children are taken to
someone else's home, to be supervised
by a relative or by a hired caregiver.
Only 5 percent of preschool children
are in group day care centers or nurser-
ies. The others are taken to work by
their mothers. As the children grow, the
likelihood of their being cared for by a
neighbor increases.

During World War II, when women's
contribution to the workforce was
sought, there were child care facilities
in abundance. After the war, when the
women workers were let go to provide
room for the returning veterans, the centers were closed. In the early 1970s
there was a flurry of interest in com-
pany-sponsored child care centers; but
today these centers, like the govern-
ment-sponsored programs, are by and
large gone or serving a limited population.

In the United States (unlike other
modern countries), the care of small
children is seen as a personal, not social, responsibility. Mothers who have
to work are expected to make their own
arrangements, and they do. Feminists
have demanded that government and/or
private industry take cognizance of the
problem, but little has been done. One
reason cited for the lack of federal and
corporate response is that such social
support for a working mother would encourage otherwise responsible mothers
to leave their children. This attitude
does not, unfortunately, take into ac-
count the harsh reality that many
mothers of small children must work to
eat.

George Milkovich's research suggests
that it is to the company's advantage to
provide onsite care, since this reduces
both turnover and days lost by working
mothers.[4] Other studies suggest that the
provision of onsite care will serve the
needs of some working mothers but by
no means all. What appears needed is a
network of facilities in the community
to serve the diverse needs of residents.
Parents who travel some distance to
work prefer community facilities near
their homes. Those with school-age
children cannot take advantage of a
company-provided center after school
hours. A community center as envisioned by Harlow—one controlled by
the parents, open at the hours when the
parents work, willing to accept both in-
fants and children of school age in the
afternoons, providing for care of sick
children, staffed in part by senior citizens, and available to all who need
it—seems ideal.[5]

Until such centers come into being,
companies can still help attack the
problems faced by the working mother
of small children. There are measures
short of financing an entire child care
center attached to the factory that may
in fact be more effective, at least until
(and if) the national conscience is
aroused to the severity of the problem.
A study undertaken in Tompkins County, New York, suggested that such stop-
gap measures may help very much indeed. Among the solutions proposed:

• *The recognition that a woman's
work performance may not reflect lack*

of commitment to the job. If a hitherto responsible and reliable employee is absent more than usual over one winter, a casual look at her record may suggest that she just isn't as good as she used to be. The fact may be, however, that her child's illness is keeping her home. Once her child's ailment is cured, she is herself again. One personnel manager has devised a recordkeeping system for distinguishing between absences due to children's illness and those due to other causes. In this way he feels that his first-line supervisors will have more information about the individual worker's performance. One additional benefit, cited by the women workers who proposed the system, is that they no longer have to lie (masking their children's illnesses as their own) when they call in.

● *The presence in personnel of a staff member who is knowledgeable about community child care resources and benefits.* Women report that, especially when they are new to a community, information about the availability of child care centers, drop-in centers, and people trained to take over when children are sick is difficult to come by. Such information is especially valuable to women who are already working and cannot seek help through service agencies during working hours. A small company could assign the responsibility to a person already on staff. Bigger organizations could hire or train a specialist to serve as liaison between the service agencies and the women who need them. The representative in turn could be part of a network of child care referral specialists in all companies in the community with working mothers.

● *A system of granting parents a certain number of leave days each year, to be taken when children are sick.* These leave days could be taken by either father or mother. Indeed, planners of all child care programs should recognize that the number of single parents is increasing and that the increase is made up of working fathers as well as working mothers.

A second type of "sex plus" discrimination is that encountered by the older woman returning to the workforce. As outlined earlier, she may suffer a collapse of confidence as a result of her time out of the workforce. This helps her not one whit in getting the equal consideration for a responsible job that she deserves. The experience of Catalyst, Higher Education Resource Services (HERS), Washington Opportunities for Women (WOW), and other groups seeking solutions to these problems has shown that the older woman worker is a bargain for the company with imagination enough to hire her and promote her as warranted.

The presentation of credentials in the form of a businesslike résumé—seemingly a small matter—looms large in the concerns of older women. A study of application forms shows that even the most skilled and experienced returnees tend to do themselves a disservice when they present their credentials in writing.[6] A busy personnel officer turns away from the amateurishly completed application because he or she cannot imagine it represents an employable person. The woman who answers the question "Type of job sought?" with a phrase such as "Anything," "Any small way I can help," or "My deepest interest has always been in creativity" surely diminishes her chances of getting an interview, never mind a job.

Sociologist Helena Lopata has noted that there are ambiguities in the social definition of a housewife's role. She outlines four stages through which the housewife passes:

1. Becoming—the new bride learns homemaking and learns to be a shopper and consumer of household goods.
2. Maintaining the expanding circle as she bears and rears small children.
3. Reaching the "full-house plateau."
4. Managing the shrinking circle as the children leave home.[7]

If we analyze this role progression as a career ladder, it can be seen that the ladder is in the form of a horseshoe. No matter how well the housewife does her job, it decreases relentlessly in importance as the children grow up. Indeed, some would say that the more effective she is in assisting her children to be independent, the sooner she will do herself out of a job.

As Lopata points out, the social role of housewife is a low-prestige job. It can gain in prestige, she notes, if the family members for whom the housewife provides staff support gain in prestige or increase in number. So it is that the wife of a famous man or mother of a famous child is honored. So it is that the housewife who has a great many children and perhaps aged parents depending on her may also be lauded.

In any case, she is, as a rule, retired in her prime. The wife of a corporate executive, as Kanter notes, is in unusual circumstances in that she is expected to provide helping services for her husband when he is starting out but has limited duties during his middle years. When and if he reaches top management, she is once again on call.[8] Women married to corporate presidents, college presidents, politicians, ministers, and high-level military men are among those whose jobs as wives are demanding at least intermittently in the so-called golden years. But other wives are out of work at age 35, and it is they who need and deserve equal opportunity in the workplace. A representative of personnel can spot older women who need help by the fact that they often (and understandably) define themselves in terms of their husbands, using the "Mrs. John Jones" name style and including irrelevant information about their husbands' jobs or their children's activities in their applications for work.

It should be recognized that the older wife has every right to take credit for the success of members of her family. She may well have had a great deal to do with it. But this information is not pertinent to her job application. The casual discrimination against older women who have 25 years' potential working life ahead of them when they seek to reenter the workforce has not begun to be recognized. Banks are among the few institutions that truly welcome older women; their customs may spread to other organizations as more and more actions are instituted against violations of the law that protects both women and men from discrimination on the basis of age.

One sad footnote is that companies subject to consent degrees sometimes agree to favor some women over others. At least they are perceived to be acting that way. AT&T agreed to set up a management assessment program for women hired between 1965 and 1971 (to match one it had had for men hired during that period). Of those assessed, 43 percent were put on a "fast track" as "recommended women" but not without arousing resentment from women middle managers who had made it on their own. "Why shouldn't I be included?" complains a woman in middle management at New York Telephone Co. She started as a business office representative in 1951 and now says, "All I have is a law protecting old people."[9]

These two types of discrimination—on the basis of status as parent and of age—are intimately tied to sex discrimination. The link is apparent when we contrast the situation of women with that of men. There is clear legal precedent stating that a woman cannot be denied employment or promotion solely because she has small children unless a man with young children has the same restrictions placed on him.[10] Similarly, flight attendants have won the case based on the fact that stewardesses were considered "too old" to do the work when there were men of the same age in similar jobs. It is clear that women age socially before men do. President John F. Kennedy was 46 at the time of his assassination. His death was seen as especially poignant because he was cut down in his prime. A woman of 46 is not seen as so young. This assertion is difficult to prove—but it is clear, for example, that actors can be cast as romantic leads long after actresses their age are playing grandmothers.

A third type of "sex plus" discrimination has to do with homosexuality. The extent of employment discrimination based on sexual preference is little documented, but it seems clear that homosexuals who choose to identify themselves as such suffer problems in access to housing, opportunity to practice religion, freedom of speech, and freedom of assembly. One defense of current practices is that homosexuals are sick and, as is said, "queer." But the roots of homosexuality are nowhere clear, despite the assertion of some psychiatrists that the condition is pathological. Proponents of gay rights, as well as a substantial number of professional psychologists and psychiatrists, hold the condition to be normal though less common in the population than heterosexuality.

Early proponents of the idea that homosexuality was "within the normal range psychologically" were dismissed as biased or criticized for their methodology, since the majority of studies showed homosexuals to be less well adjusted than their opposite numbers who were heterosexual.[11] We can speculate that this maladjustment may be of social origin, a reaction to being discriminated against. However, if we accept the assumption that homosexuality is an illness, it may well be seen as a handicap entitling those who "suffer" from it to equal opportunities under the Rehabilitation Act.

Regardless of cause, homosexuality is a reality in American life and still carries with it a considerable social stigma, despite efforts of gay alliances. One personnel manager spoke for many when he said,

We have to think of the good of the whole community. If I were a banker and two men approached me for a loan to build a house, I'd certainly give it to the family man before I gave it to some gay.

After reflection, he went on to say,

Why do they have to flaunt it? I guess I don't care what they do at home, but when they are so open about it I can't stomach it.

And there, in a nutshell, is the best defense of gay rights. So long as homosexuals are denied credit, employment, advancement, loans, and housing, that long will they be fierce and furious about their sexual orientation. Should the day come when homosexuals are truly given equal treatment, when the old taboos are no more, they will no longer need to organize so militantly—a behavior that some find offensive whether it is undertaken by minority men or women of all races or homosexuals.

Lesbians carry an extra burden not borne by homosexual men. As females, they face limitations on their access to education, employment, and participation in political life. As lesbians, however, they know that they will have to support themselves; there will be no question of their working merely to "supplement their husbands' earnings."

This home truth was apparent to the lesbians at the National Women's Conference held in Houston, Texas, in November 1977. They worked hard to make certain that protection of their rights was among the resolutions included in the final roster. Indeed, it was. The resolution on sexual preference had three parts: first, that laws should be enacted to protect the civil rights of homosexuals; second, that state legislatures should repeal laws that restrict private sexual behavior between consenting adults; and third, that child custody cases should be determined on the basis of "which party is the better parent without regard to that person's sexual and affectional orientation."

In November 1977 the Supreme Court refused to review the case of James Gaylord, a homosexual high school teacher in Tacoma, Washington, who was fired for "immorality."[12] The issue was not his homosexual conduct,

but his status. The school board members asked Gaylord if he was homosexual; he responded that he was. They
dismissed him. Now he says to fellow
gays: "Lie if you are asked about your
sexual preference." Personnel managers
may find that any expression of views
on the employment rights of homosexuals will be scorned, because this is a
class not yet protected. But practitioners
may find that their consciences bother
them if they do not stand up for gays.

SEXUAL HARASSMENT AT WORK

The extent to which Title VII (or any
other federal law) protects women
against harassment because they are
women is unclear. As Ginsburg and
Koreski note, some judicial decisions
suggest that sexual harassment is illegal;
other decisions are quite specific in
considering that behavior beyond the
purview of current law. In theory, they
note, a bisexual supervisor who harassed both male and female staff members would not be making any distinction on the basis of sex and so would be
"clean" with respect to Title VII. Here,
as elsewhere, practitioners need to be
certain that they can distinguish between behavior that is clearly unjust
and behavior that is illegal.

One judge cited by Ginsburg and
Koreski went to great pains to make it
clear that Title VII cannot be interpreted
to include grievances involving sexual
harassment. The implication? There
would be too many cases for the courts
to handle. Indeed, he said, every time a
manager asked his secretary to lunch,
there'd be potential for a federal case.[13]

Feminists have expressed growing
discontent on the issue of harassment.
One difficulty is semantic. Exactly how
is harassment to be defined? It is clear
that a manager who makes sexual favors
a requirement for advancement or
promotion is harassing employees. But
what about the dirty remark? The pinch
on the rear end? The half-serious invitation to bed? A community group in
Ithaca, New York, conducted a
"speak-out" on the subject that drew
more than 100 women. These activists
went into local factories and shops and
interviewed 155 women (of whom
some were self-selected in that they
chose to come forward). No less than
two-thirds reported that they had suffered sexual harassment in the workplace. Of those, 10 percent said that
they had been flattered by the advances; the others felt quite the opposite. But, significantly, only a small proportion had reported the problem.

Personnel practitioners have traditionally handled the issue on a case-
by-case basis, perhaps telling the man
privately to cut it out and advising the
woman to not let it bother her—that's
just the way some men are. This may be
the reason for the low reporting rate,
since satisfaction is seldom granted to
the grievant.

A review of the experiences of managers in handling these issues suggests
only two guidelines. The first is that the
presence of a staff member in personnel
who is known to be sensitive to wom-
en's problems may well increase the incidence of reporting. At the same time,
it may solve more of the problems in
the long run, especially if they can be
caught before they mushroom. The second counsel to personnel managers is
that protecting the rights of grievants
also protects the company. It appears
that an organization can be held liable
if it can be demonstrated that the organization either condoned or profited from
acts of sexual harassment. It is, therefore, to the advantage of the personnel
department not only to protect those
who are being sexually harassed but to
make public the company's posture toward such behavior and to keep careful
records of the actions taken.

THE OFFICE ROMANCE

A separate issue is the organizational
romance. Using third-party reports,
Quinn has analyzed 130 cases of men

and women co-workers who became romantically involved. In 10 percent of the cases, the romance was felt to have a positive impact on the work or the workers in the department. In a third of the cases, the impact was felt to be negative but not severely so. In another third, the organizational romance was reported to have lowered morale and production and resulted in job loss.

Quinn charted management's responses to the romances, which ranged from taking no action to offering friendly counsel to taking punitive action. Out of 130 reported intrigues, 12 women lost their jobs as opposed to 5 men.

> The female is twice as likely to be terminated as is the male. Because the male is usually in a higher position, he apparently is seen as less dispensable as the female. The female is also thought to be much less likely to benefit from an open discussion or from counseling by superiors. The latter two conditions, however, are mediated by the fact that the female's superior is often the other participant in the relationship.[14]

Although it is difficult to assess the effectiveness of intervention, it is clear that women, because of their subordinate status, are more likely to lose their jobs if they sleep where they work than men are.

The personnel practitioner is well advised to intervene only if the relationship appears to be impeding the work or causing other workers to feel their rights to be infringed upon. If personnel is in the delicate position of having to "censure up"—that is, to talk with a vice president about his behavior with his secretary and to ask why she is earning three times as much as other vice presidents' secretaries—the difficulties are trebled. If it is a top management issue, personnel may well make the sound decision to let even topper management resolve it as it sees fit. But managers must, in all fairness, be certain that equal participants in any romance are punished equally. If she is transferred, he should be too. And let both of them explain that at home.

Perhaps the most ominous aspect of the office romance is that it is so often seen as inevitable. Schein has noted that fear that such relationships may develop can affect the reception accorded to women in management.[15] Sometimes managers claim that women are not placed in certain jobs because the company would get heat from men's wives if it permitted mixed-sex teams. This defense would be more credible if companies refrained from sending husbands on business trips, providing them with women secretaries, or moving executives from one part of the country to another on short notice—all because they feared the reaction of the wives. Company wives have precious little influence on company policy; it is difficult to believe that in this one area corporate gallantry prevails. It is particularly galling when the ones who suffer from such courtly decisions are women.

Increased proximity of women may cause misunderstandings to arise. Ginger-Lei Collins, driver of a semi-end dump truck on the Alaska pipeline, reports that her foreman often transferred a male driver if she had lunch with him too many times. "I went to a bar with one of the drivers one night and [the foreman] didn't speak to me for four days."[16] There is such unease about possible romantic complications among personnel at the Youngstown General Electric lamp plant that, according to a woman manager there:

> even developing simple friendships can present a challenge. Of course, there's no rule that says we have to be "good buddies" with our co-workers, but some men seem to have a more difficult time building a relationship, other than at a strictly business level, for fear that a wrong assumption might be made. It's unfortunate that mixed company at lunch, for example, is still suspect.[17]

One such suspicion resulted in personnel actions that proved to be quite expensive for management. Schoolteacher Joyce Rucker of Bowling Green, Ohio, filed a complaint under Title IX when she was demoted because of rumors that she was having an affair with a male teacher—something she denies. The male involved was promoted to an administrative job. HEW ruled it unfair to discipline only one of the teachers and has started action to cut off the more than $100,000 in federal funds going annually to the district.[18]

It is true that increased proximity of women may cause romantic relationships to develop. But having men and women as equals in a romantic intrigue may ease personnel problems substantially. The possibility of exploitation is much diminished when both participants are geologists or advertising salespeople or whatever. At least it is not automatic that one partner pays more dearly than the other.

It appears, then, that personnel can take a laissez-faire attitude. When men and women are more evenly distributed at all levels in all job sites, perhaps we can all come to experience the attraction between the sexes as something other than a terrible danger signal. No less an authority on these matters than Helen Gurley Brown, editor of *Cosmopolitan*, has written:

> There are no friendships between virile men and womanly women anywhere, in my opinion, completely devoid of sexual overtones. And that's good. A man always wonders what a woman is like in bed, not necessarily with him but with anybody. She wonders the same thing about him. All this speculating about men and women in offices, even if nobody does anything, causes sexy waves.[19]

Most of us will be content to let other people do the swimming and just enjoy the waves ourselves. No law against that.

NOTES

1. Allyson Sherman Grossman, "Almost Half of All Children Have Mothers in the Labor Force," *Monthly Labor Review*, vol. 100, no. 6 (June 1977), pp. 41-48.

2. Elizabeth M. Almquist, "Sex Stereotypes in Occupational Choice: The Case of College Women," *Journal of Vocational Behavior*, vol. 5, no. 1 (August 1974), pp. 13-21.

3. Phyllis Schlafly, quoted in Barbara Burke, "ERA Debate Like Cartoon Strip," *Ithaca (N.Y.) Journal*, January 26, 1978, p. 3.

4. George Milkovich, "A Few Overlooked Research Issues on the Way to Equal Opportunity," Working Paper 76-04, Industrial Relations Center, University of Minnesota, August 1976.

5. Nora Harlow, *Sharing the Children: Village Child Rearing Within the City* (New York: Harper & Row/Colophon, 1975).

6. Jennie Farley, "Women Going Back to Work: Preliminary Problems," *Journal of Employment Counseling*, vol. 7, no. 4 (December 1970), pp. 130-136.

7. Helena Znaniecki Lopata, "The Life Cycle of the Social Role of Housewife," in Marcello Truzzi (ed.), *Sociology in Everyday Life* (Englewood Cliffs, N.J.: Prentice-Hall, 1968), pp. 11-124.

8. Rosabeth Moss Kanter, *Men and Women of the Corporation* (New York: Basic Books, 1977), pp. 105-115.

9. Georgette Jasen, "Ma Bell's Daughters," *The Wall Street Journal*, February 28, 1978, p. 1.

10. *Phillips* v. *Martin Marietta*, 400 U.S. 542 (1971).

11. Irving Bieber et al., *Homosexuality: A Psychoanalytic Study of Male Homosexuals* (New York: Vintage Books, 1962), pp. 17 ff.

12. "Supreme Court Permits Firing of Gay Teacher: Refuses to Hear Case Involving Homosexual Status, Not Conduct," *Civil Liberties*, No. 320 (November 1977), pp. 1, 7.

13. Gilbert J. Ginsburg and Jean Galloway Koreski, "Sexual Advances by an Employee's Supervisor: A Sex-Discrimination Violation of Title VII?" *Employee Relations Law Journal*, vol. 3 (Summer 1977), pp. 89-93.

14. Robert E. Quinn, "Coping with Cupid: The Formation, Impact, and Management of Romantic Relationships in Organizations," *Administrative Science Quarterly*, vol. 22, no. 1 (March 1977), pp. 30-45, p. 44.

15. Virginia E. Schein, "Women Managers: How Different Are They?" paper presented to the American Psychological Association, Washington, D.C., September 1976.

16. Terry Wetherby, "Up Close with Women Who Hold 'Men's Jobs,'" *New*

Woman, January-February 1978, p. 41.

17. "When the Boss Is a Woman," *For Your Information* (Public Affairs Section, General Electric), vol. 1, no. 4 (December 1977), p. 3.

18. "Sex Bias Cases to Cut Schools' Aid," *Ithaca (N.Y.) Journal*, March 9, 1978, p. 10.

19. Helen Gurley Brown, *Sex and the Office* (New York: Pocket Books, Inc., 1965), p. 181.

3. Coping with Cupid: The Formation, Impact, and Management of Romantic Relationships in Organizations*

ROBERT E. QUINN

Romantic relationships between two members of the same organization are explored in this study and answers to three questions are provided: what aspects of organizations facilitate the formation of romance; what is its organizational impact; and how do superiors, coworkers, and subordinates perceive and cope with the phenomenon?

IMPORTANCE OF THE STUDY

Social psychologists have noted that affiliation is a prerequisite of attraction (Rubin, 1973: 48; Shaw, 1971: 95). Organizations are thus a natural environment for romantic relationships. Murstein (1970) pointed out that the organization is a closed field in that it provides routine interaction over time and allows people to discover the deeper, attractive aspects of others. While the actual incidence of romantic entanglements at work is unclear, they are often feared and such fears influence policies and decisions about women at work (Bradford, Sargent, and Sprague, 1975: 53). It has also been argued that the frequency of romantic relationships in organizations will increase (Bradford, Sargent, and Sprague, 1975: 54). The reasons cited are a rise in the number of women in the work force, more opportunities for interaction, and the erosion of traditional social controls. There has been, however, no attempt to analyze the phenomenon systematically and little is known about the formation, impact, and management of organizational romance.

RESEARCH DESIGN

Organizational romance is defined as a relationship between two members of the same organization that is perceived by a third party to be characterized by sexual attraction.[1] The focus of this exploratory study is on people in white-collar positions. The topic does not readily lend itself to rigorous research methods. From whom, for example, does the researcher get data? Actual participants—the romantically involved male and female—are not only difficult to locate, but, once located, are difficult to approach. Many are unable to talk about the organizational impact and management of their romance. For these reasons, a third-party approach was adopted. People were asked to describe romantic relationships between pairs of their present or former associates. This approach also presents difficulties. A third party may have limited information, dislike or resent one or both participants, be influenced by his or her own

---

1. The degree of perceived intimacy may vary. Eighty-five percent of respondents in this study believed that the relationship they described was sexually intimate.

---

*Source: From Administrative Science Quarterly, vol. 22 (March 1977), pp. 30-45. Copyright © 1977 Administrative Science Quarterly. Reprinted by permission.

romantic fantasies, or have still other biases. The conclusions from such data must be seen as tentative.

The study was carried out in two phases. The purpose of phase one was to gain an understanding of the dynamics of organizational romance through the gathering of qualitative data. The purpose of phase two was to describe more fully and accurately the dynamics of the phenomenon through a questionnaire based on the phase one analysis.

In the first part of the study, a large class of graduate students collected 132 descriptive case studies. Pairs of interviewers went to professional acquaintances and asked them if they had ever witnessed a romantic relationship in an organization. Using open-ended questions, the respondents were asked to describe the organization and the specific departments or work groups that were involved; the participants; the nature of the romantic relationship; the impact on the organization; the strategies evolved by subordinates, colleagues and superiors to cope with the situation; and the way in which the situation was resolved.

The two interviewers independently evaluated each case and indicated obvious or potential biases of the interviewee or the interviewer. After all 132 cases were written up in a uniform format, the descriptions were reviewed, and 12 cases were eliminated because of obvious biases. The remaining cases were then analyzed for content to discover variables, patterns, and typologies that could be operationalized in a quantitative format. Based on the results of this analysis, an extensive questionnaire was designed.

In a pretest, the questionnaire was distributed to classes of part-time graduate students who also held full-time professional positions. The questionnaires were to be picked up one week after distribution. Despite continual follow-up, the response rate never rose above 25 percent. From discussions with students, it became apparent that the nature of the subject matter made them hesitant to respond.

What was needed at this point was a large sample of white-collar employees, working in different organizations, who would be willing to take the time to share their observations of organizational romance. The answer to the problem came from a study carried out in the waiting areas of the Logan Airport in Boston (Rubin, 1973: 171). Rubin reported that people from outside of Boston made more intimate disclosures than Bostonians. People waiting at the Albany and at the LaGuardia Airports were therefore approached and 70 percent accepted and completed questionnaires.[2] One item on the questionnaire asked the respondent to indicate the number of times he or she had ever been closely associated, as a third-party observer, with a romantic relationship between two members of the same organization. If the answer was never, they were told to stop. If the answer was once or more than once, they were asked to select the case with which they were most thoroughly familiar and describe it in the remainder of the questionnaire. One hundred thirty of the 211 respondents indicated that they knew of at least one relationship.

When people returned the questionnaire, they were often anxious to recount the details of the case they described. In no instance was there any indication of intentional distortion or of manufacturing a case. One question about the impact of romance was repeated in two places on the questionnaire. Respondents never reversed the two responses. The patterns that

2. The respondents were told—and the promise repeated on the cover of the questionnaire—that no questions would be asked about the respondents' personal lives. This is one of the reasons why there is no data on the frequency of occurrence in this study. While there is some slight evidence (Johnson, 1974) on frequency, it remains a major question for future research.

Table 1

RESPONDENT CHARACTERISTICS (N = 130)

Marital Status	Single	Married			
	29%	70%			
Race	Black	White	Other		
	2%	96%	2%		
Sex	Female	Male			
	28%	71%			
Education	High School	Bachelors	Masters	Ph.D.	
	15%	51%	25%	5%	
Organization	Public	Private	Voluntary	Other	
	53%	35%	2%	8%	
	Professional-				
Occupation	Technical	Managerial	Sales	Clerical	Other
	49%	23%	7%	5%	15%
		Standard			
	Mean	deviation	Range		
Age	33 yrs.	10 yrs.	18-62 yrs.		
		Standard			
	Mean	deviation	Range		
Income	$20,339	$13,784	$600-80,000		

emerged from the analysis of the quantitative data were consistent with those from the qualitative data.

The reader should again be cautioned about the nature of the data. First, the data were gathered from third-party observers; there are numerous factors that may influence and filter the perceptions of third parties. Second, the airport setting was partially selected because it would tend to produce a middle-class sample. (See Table 1 for sample characteristics.)

FINDINGS

FORMATIVE ASPECTS OF
ORGANIZATIONAL ROMANCE

● *Proximity.* An analysis of the cases in phase one shows that proximity is a major factor in the development of romantic relationships in organizations. Three types of proximity are identified: on-going geographical proximity, proximity due to on-going work requirements, and occasional contact. (Behavioral characteristics at each stage of the romance—formation, impact, and management—are outlined in Table 2.)

On-going geographical proximity is based on the position of the participants' work stations. It is a factor in the development of 63 percent of all romances. Such proximity occurs when a boss and a secretary work in adjoining offices or when two people are assigned to adjoining cash registers in a supermarket. In one case, a boss and a secretary shared the same small office. They worked together for an uneventful year, and then the woman experienced a number of personal problems. She began to spend long periods of time at work obtaining advice from her sympathetic boss. As a result, their relationship became more and more personal. After several months, they became romantically involved.

On-going work requirements include such activities as training, consulting, supervising, business trips, and attendance at organizational social activities. They are a factor in 77 percent of all romances. Geographical and work requirements may be, but are not normally, mutually exclusive. Two systems analysts, for example, had worked together on a number of assignments be-

Table 2

IMPORTANT CATEGORIES OF BEHAVIOR IN THE FORMATION, IMPACT, AND MANAGEMENT OF ORGANIZATIONAL BEHAVIOR

I. Formative Aspects

A. Proximity
1. On-going geographical
2. On-going work requirements
3. Occasional contact

B. Perceived motives
1. Job (advancement, security, power)
2. Ego (excitement, ego satisfaction, sex)
3. Love (sincerity, companionship, spouse)

C. Types of relationships
1. The fling (male ego, female ego)
2. Sincere love (male sincere, female sincere)
3. The utilitarian relationship (male ego, female job)

D. Work group characteristics
1. Rules and expectations
2. Closeness of supervision
3. Closeness of interpersonal relationships
4. Intensity or criticalness of the work or mission

II. Impacts of the Relationship

A. Visibility of the relationship
1. Signals and tip-offs (observed when away from work station, chatting, lunches)
2. Impact (sensitizing, discussion-avoidance, legitimizing)

B. Behavior changes in the participants
1. Positive changes (easier get along with, more productive)
2. Competence changes (lost respect, preoccupied)
3. Power changes (favoritism, eyes-ears, flaunt)

C. Reactions of the members
1. Approve
2. Tolerate
3. Cope (advise, complain, undermine, ostracize)

D. Overall impact on the system
1. Positive (teamwork, productivity)
2. Negative (gossip, hostility, productivity)

III. Management

A. No action (ignore, resolve self)
B. Punitive action (reprimand, warn, transfer, terminate)
C. Positive action (openly discuss, counsel)

---

fore being sent to a week-long job in a distant city. Being alone at night in a strange city led to a romantic relationship that continued after their return home.

Continued proximity and on-going interaction are not always factors in the development of organizational romance. In a small number of cases, relationships were facilitated by temporary proximity stemming from mutual membership in the same organization. This category of proximity has been labeled occasional contact. In one case, for example, the vice president of a bank became romantically involved with a receptionist. While he seldom saw the woman, he one day struck up a conversation on an elevator and then invited her to lunch. She accepted and soon a romance was initiated. While he was not in close organizational proximity to her, and while he had no structured on-going organizational relationship with her, the romance was made possible by their mutual membership in the same organization.

• *Perceived motives.* Affiliation with others satisfies certain needs. The question arises as to what types of need the participants in an organizational romance are trying to fulfill.

The empirical literature on affiliation is fairly clear and consistent in pointing out that physical attraction (Berger, 1952; Walster *et al.*, 1966) and similarity of attitudes, beliefs, personality, race, sex, and economic level (Shaw, 1970: 95) are important factors in determining relationships. These findings also tend to agree with the theoretical models of reinforcement and exchange developed by Newcomb (1956), Thibaut and Kelly (1959), Blau (1964), and Kuhn (1974).

While there are many myths and stereotypes about organizational romance, most are based on a transactional model. These are best reflected by Veblen (1934: 34) who argued in terms of conspicuous consumption. He felt that female attractiveness is seen as a valued commodity which allows powerful men to evidence their success. From an organizational viewpoint, Mechanic (1962) hypothesized that attractiveness is one of the characteristics that can be used as a source of power by individuals in lower-level positions. The belief in the exchange of female attractiveness for male wealth and power also has some empirical foundation (Elder, 1969).

Based on physical attractiveness, 94 percent of the female participants were rated at the midpoint or above on a seven-point measure.[3] In addition, 74

---

3. On the same scale, 84 percent of the males were rated at the mid-point or higher.

percent of the cases were characterized by a male in a higher-level position than his female counterpart. Of the female subordinates, 48 percent were secretaries, 26 percent were some other type of direct subordinate, and the remainder were in positions two or more levels below the male. While these data are somewhat supportive of the conspicuous consumption argument, there are a number of other reasons for involvement in organizational romance.

The descriptions provided in phase one were filled with statements about the motives and the character of the participants. These statements or the observer's perceptions of the motives and characteristics of the participants were each broken down into three types. Measuring motives and characteristics of people is a difficult job at best. Such is not the intent here. Instead, the categories are intended to describe how participants are viewed by members of the work group. These perceptions are important because they assign meaning to the relationship and help to define how people in the organization should react to the relationship. For example, when two participants are perceived as being sincerely in love, the relationship has a different meaning than when the male is perceived as always looking for his next conquest and the female is thought of as being on her way up the organization, no matter what the cost.

When the cases were analyzed for content, three types of perceived motives emerged: job, ego, and love. These motives and their components appear in Table 3. People with job motives are perceived as being after advancement, job security, increased power, financial rewards, and other organizational payoffs. The only time that such motives were attributed to males were in the few cases—3.4 percent—in which a male was involved with a female superior. People with ego motives were perceived to be after such personal rewards as excitement, ego satisfaction, adventure, and sexual experience. The people

Table 3
THREE TYPES OF PERCEIVED MOTIVES AND THEIR COMPONENTS

Job Motives	Ego Motives	Love Motives
Advancement	Excitement	Sincere love
Job security	Ego satisfaction	Companionship
Increased power	Adventure	Spouse
Financial rewards	Sexual experience	
Easier work		
Job efficiency		

who were perceived as having sincere motives were described as being sincerely in love, and seeking companionship or a spouse. The existence of these three types of motives was later substantiated by a factor analysis of the questionnaire data.

When perceived motives of men are compared to those of their female associates, six types of relationships are possible. Using factor scales for each type of motive, the zero-order correlations between male and female motives were computed and they appear in Table 4. The results from the statistical analysis are consistent with the conclusions from the phase one data in that three types of relationships emerge. The fling is usually characterized by high excitement on the part of both participants and is often accompanied by the belief that the relationship is going to be temporary in duration. True love reflects sincerity on the part of both partici-

pants. It usually, but not always, involves two unmarried people and tends to end in marriage. The utilitarian relationship is one in which the male is perceived as seeking such things as excitement, ego satisfaction, adventure, and sexual experience, while the female is viewed as in search of organizational rewards.

● *Work group characteristics.* The characteristics of the work group are as important as proximity and the motives and characteristics of the participants in the formative aspects of organizational romance. The more important work group characteristics are rules and expectations, closeness of supervision, closeness of interpersonal relationships, and intensity or criticalness of the work or mission. These are often interrelated. A group, for example, might be characterized by strict rules, close supervision, close interpersonal relationships, and intense working conditions.

Table 4
MOTIVES AND THREE DOMINANT PATTERNS OF ORGANIZATIONAL ROMANCE (*N* = 126)

	Female Job	Female Ego	Female Sincere
Male ego	Utilitarian relationship .23*	The fling .61**	−.09
Male sincere	.00	−.15	True love .50**

*p.01   **p.001

Rules and expectations were often mentioned in the initial descriptions. In some organizations, there are explicit rules against fraternization. In others there are none, but there are powerful unexpressed expectations that mediate against romantic involvement. In still other settings, there are no rules or expectations or there are expectations that actually encourage romantic involvement. In one political organization, for example, romantic relationships were common. The interviewee stated, "It was expected that when you hired a secretary, you weren't looking for a typist. In fact, hardly anyone could type."

In a number of cases, it was reported that participants had to be cautious because of the scrutiny of a demanding supervisor. Intimate relationships were also deterred because of other close interpersonal relationships. When the work group began to express disapproval, the participants felt pressure to break off the relationship or to become more discreet. Pressure was often exerted when the reputation or image of the work group was threatened. In two illicit cases that occurred in public schools, for instance, word quickly passed from faculty to students to parents. In a short time parents were exerting pressure on administrators to take action. In four similar cases, it was pointed out explicitly that the participants were especially discreet because they were sensitive to the possibility of such reactions.

Intensity or criticalness of the work or mission is generally, but not always, a deterrent to organizational romance. There were many cases in which the respondents described one or both participants as bored because there was little work to be done. A nurse, employed during the summers in a state park, became involved with a male employee "because they simply had little else to do." In three phase one cases, great pressure was observed to be a facilitator of romance. In all three, this pressure led males and females to work long hours overtime. Being alone in the office night after night and the close working relationships that developed under such circumstances eventually led to romantic involvement.

THE IMPACT OF ORGANIZATIONAL ROMANCE

Romantic relationships can be a serious practical problem because they sometimes distort the smooth functioning of organizations. Proximity, participant characteristics and motives, and work group characteristics have a bearing on the impact of relationships. There are also a number of other variables that are important in explaining the impacts of an organizational romance: visibility, behavior changes in the participants, reactions of other members, and the overall impact on the system.

• *Visibility of the relationship.* Visibility is defined as the degree to which the participants behave so that members of the work group are aware of the existence of the romance. According to respondents, about two-thirds of the couples involved in an organizational romance initially attempted to keep the relationship a secret. In some organizations, there are explicit or implicit rules against fraternization and disclosure could lead to some form of punishment. In other cases, there is the fear of gossip or general disapproval among members of the organization. In cases where one or both participants are married, often the predominant fear is that family will find out.

Despite efforts to keep a relationship secret, participants often fail. Most work groups are especially sensitive to even minor changes in behavior of their coworkers. It takes little to tip off other members that something is going on (see Table 5). Among the most common activities that alert members of the organization are being observed together away from work, longer or more frequent chats, long lunches together, long discussions behind closed doors, and

Table 5

VISIBILITY OF THE RELATIONSHIP: FREQUENCY OF AGREE RESPONSES

Items	F	N	% of Total
1. Seen together away from work	88	113	77.9
2. Initially tried to keep it a secret	82	123	66.7
3. Spent unusual amount of work time chatting	71	124	57.3
4. Took long lunches together	54	115	47.0
5. Even after others knew, still thought the relationship was secret	55	120	45.8
6. Had long discussions behind closed doors	45	108	41.7
7. Sometimes physically displayed their affections at work	40	122	32.8
8. Went on business trips together	13	120	10.8

joint business trips. Less subtle, but surprisingly common tip-offs involve the physical expression of affection. In about a third of the cases, participants are seen embracing in closets, kissing in supply rooms, or fondling in the parking lot.

Not all cases are revealed by accident. In some instances, despite a desire for secrecy, one of the participants will have an equally strong desire to reveal the fact that the relationship exists. This stems from the conspicuous consumption phenomenon (Veblen, 1934: 34). If an individual's motive in establishing a romantic relationship partially stems from the need to demonstrate his or her social worth, the person also needs to let others know of the accomplishment.

In several of the phase one cases, the revelation of the relationship was achieved with great subtlety. In one, shortly after the start of the romance, the male, who was described as being proud of several earlier conquests, approached a female member of his department and asked her to pick out a nice woman's dress of a certain size and type. Thinking that the dress was a surprise for his wife, the woman complied. Two days later, another female member of the organization showed up wearing the dress.

Three of the most frequent results of the visibility of a relationship are sensitizing members to further changes in the participants, discussion-avoidance, and the legitimizing of other relationships. Once members of the work group detect signals that a romantic relationship might exist, nearly every aspect of both participants' behavior is analyzed and passed through informal communication channels. Work groups become sensitized. The more blatant or exciting the behavior, the more quickly it is transmitted.

Even after members become aware of the relationship and the participants know that the members are aware, there is still a tendency in many cases to avoid an open discussion or to make a recognition of the existence of the romance. This happens almost 50 percent of the time (Table 5). Despite the fact that everyone knows, and everyone knows that everyone knows, the participants continue to act as if the relationship was a secret and members continue to act as if they were unaware of it.

Finally, the establishment and visibility of one relationship can lead to the establishment or the public emergence of others. In a Catholic college that turned coeducational, a brother became involved with a female student. As the faculty member defied warnings by spending ever-increasing amounts of time with the student in public, two of his colleagues soon established similar relationships. According to the respondent, who claimed to know all three participants well, the decisions of the latter participants were influenced by the presence and visibility of the first relationship. In other words, some relationships have a legitimizing effect in that they give other members the courage to experiment with similar behaviors. This observation is supported by the fact that 22 percent of the respondents to the questionnaire agreed or strongly agreed with the statement, "The romantic relationship resulted in other people having romantic relationships."

• *Behavior changes in the participants.* Once a romance emerges, the participants often signal others that the romance is present through such means as being seen together away from work,

engaging in longer or more frequent chats, and taking long lunches together. There are also many other changes in the participants: positive changes, competence changes, and power changes (see Tables 6 and 7). Their presence or absence has a great deal to do with the reactions of others and also with the overall impact of the romance.

Sometimes one or both participants change for the better. They may become more productive or easier to get along with. In several cases, for example, a secretary was suddenly willing to do large amounts of extra work for the male, or female subordinates were willing to work overtime and on weekends to be with the male. In one case, a male supervisor, described as sloppy and disorganized, began to improve both physically and managerially when he be-

Table 6

BEHAVIOR CHANGES IN THE MALE: FREQUENCY OF AGREE RESPONSES

Items	F	N	% of Total
Male: Competence behavior changes			
Lost respect of members	39	117	33.3
Became preoccupied	30	110	27.3
Covered mistakes of the female	29	111	26.1
Began to arrive late, leave early	27	114	23.7
Did less work	25	114	21.9
Began missing commitments, and meetings	17	112	15.2
Lower quality work	16	114	14.0
Made costly errors	11	113	9.7
Became incompetent	10	117	8.5
Male: Power behavior changes			
Showed favoritism to the female	84	117	71.7
Became eyes and ears of the other	36	113	31.9
Ignored complaints about the female	30	112	26.8
Promoted the other	28	119	23.5
Isolated the female from members	22	119	18.15
Gave female more power	21	120	17.5
Became inaccessible	19	119	16.0
Began to flaunt new power	5	119	4.2
Male: Positive behavior changes			
Was easier to get along with	29	115	25.2
Became more productive	19	111	17.1
Changed for the better	15	115	13.0

Table 7
BEHAVIOR CHANGES IN THE FEMALE: FREQUENCY OF AGREE
RESPONSES

Items	F	N	% of Total
Female: Competence behavior changes			
Lost respect of members	42	115	36.5
Became preoccupied	40	111	36.0
Did less work	30	111	27.0
Began to arrive late, leave early	28	115	24.3
Covered mistakes of the male	25	110	22.7
Lower quality work	20	114	17.5
Ignored complaints about the male	19	110	17.3
Began to miss meetings and commitments	13	112	11.6
Made costly errors	11	109	10.1
Became incompetent	10	117	8.5
Became inaccessible	10	120	8.3
Female: Power behavior changes			
Showed favoritism to male	69	114	60.5
Assumed more power in the organization	26	118	22.0
Isolated the male from members	21	118	17.8
Began to flaunt new power	16	118	13.6
Gave the male more power	8	118	6.5
Female: Positive behavior changes			
Was easier to get along with	33	116	28.4
Changed for the better	19	112	17.0
Became more productive	17	111	15.3

came involved with one of the social workers he supervised. A number of times, individuals who had reputations for being hard to work with underwent dramatic changes for the better after a romantic relationship was initiated.

Participants may also become less competent, making costly errors, missing meetings and commitments, being generally preoccupied, producing a lower quantity or quality work, arriving late or leaving early, and losing the respect of others. A supervisor, after becoming involved with a female subordinate, established the habit of calling her into his office each afternoon after lunch. He then became unavailable for the rest of the day. In another case, a romantically preoccupied male began to turn major legal decisions over to his secretary. One such decision, on the part of the unqualified secretary, led to a major suit against the organization. In many other instances, one of the participants would be absent from his or her normal work station for extended periods of time to be with the other, thus necessitating that coworkers do all or portions of the person's duties.

The third category of participant responses, alteration of power, occurs most often in romances involving a superior and a subordinate. For the male in a higher position than the female such changes involve showing favoritism to the female, ignoring complaints about her performance, promoting or giving a raise to the female, formally or informally increasing her power, and being inaccessible. For the female, favoritism, the assumption of power, isolating the male, and the flaunting of power are especially prominent. A corporation president hired an attractive and competent young secretary. After they became romantically involved, he began to delegate tasks that he normally disposed of himself to his secretary. Anxious to accomplish this work, she began to demand necessary kinds of information from vice presidents. Resenting demands and instructions from a secretary, the vice presidents openly resisted her efforts. They soon found, however, that it was more difficult to get access to their boss. The secretary delayed or blocked appointments, calls, and memos. She also became an extended set of eyes and ears for the boss by reporting comments and actions that normally would not have reached him.

• *Reactions of the members*. In many cases, the emergence of a romantic relationship is met with little more than gossip or attempts on the part of members to define the meaning of the new situation. Sometimes subordinates and colleagues approve of the relationship and other times they simply tolerate it. As competence and power changes be-

come more pronounced, subordinates and colleagues soon begin to develop strategies for coping with the relationship (see Table 8).

Deciding how to cope with a problem romance is not easy, and, as a result, arguments sometimes occur about what actions should be taken. The most frequent is simply going to one of the participants and advising him or her about the relationship. Usually this is done with a friendly and positive posture. Should the situation get worse, members tend to complain to a superior in the organizational hierarchy. Some people, however, feel that going to a superior is risky or will do little to resolve the difficulty. As a result, more severe strategies are developed. Members may try to undermine or sabotage one or both of the participants. By taking such actions, it is often hoped that the severity of the situation will be exposed and that superiors will be forced to take corrective actions. For example, members of a steno pool stole files and hid parts of projects that one romantically involved secretary was working on. In another case subordinates leaked damaging information about the work of their boss to a regulatory agency.

Table 8
THE ROMANTIC RELATIONSHIP: PERCENTAGE OF AGREE RESPONSES

Items	Male's Subordinates	Male's Colleagues	Female's Subordinates	Female's Colleagues
Approval or toleration				
Tolerated their involvement	66.7	57.9	61.4	63.3
Approved of their involvement	23.5	29.4	12.5	19.4
Stood by and defended them	17.9	18.3	17.1	17.3
Coping				
One or more advised them about the relationship	32.1	55.1	31.4	54.9
One or more complained to a superior	31.0	24.7	26.3	31.8
Argued about what should be done	17.7	18.0	27.0	19.2
Tried to undermine them	13.2	11.2	16.3	15.6
One or more quit or left because of them	15.9	5.8	9.5	9.2
One or more tried to sabotage their work	6.3	5.8	5.1	9.3
Ostracized them	4.2	4.6	7.3	8.3
One or more threatened to or actually blackmailed them	1.8	2.2	3.0	7.5

Other severe strategies include blackmail, ostracism, and quitting. In one case, a romantically involved manager began to reprimand a subordinate for inadequate work. The subordinate interrupted and threatened to tell the man's wife about the manager's romantic involvement. In a number of cases, especially among the subordinates of a male superior, they ostracized him for involvement in the informal work group. Interactions were solely limited to required, formal exchanges. The final, and most drastic reaction is quitting. In the few cases in which someone quit, the people who chose to leave were considered the better or more qualified members of the work group. They had more alternatives and were less willing to stay in an unacceptable situation than were others.

• *Overall impact.* The impact of organization romance may be positive, negative, or nonexistent (see Table 9). A little more than 10 percent of the cases are characterized by such positive re-

sults as increased coordination, lower tensions, improved team work, improved productivity, and improved work flow. Two departments in an organization had a long history of intergroup conflict. The female head of one of the departments was considered to be especially difficult to get along with. When she became romantically involved with a member of the other department, a dramatic increase in interdepartmental cooperation occurred. One participant may also be willing to work harder and longer for the other.

Negative results vary in intensity. About one-third of the cases are characterized by only increased gossip and perceptions of favoritism. A third, however, are characterized by serious negative features, the most frequent being complaints, hostilities, and distorted communications. These are followed by the perception that the image or reputation of the unit is being jeopardized, there is slower decision making, a redistribution of work, client or customer

Table 9

OVERALL IMPACT OF THE ROMANTIC RELATIONSHIP: FREQUENCY OF AGREE RESPONSES

Items	F	N	% of Total
Negative impacts			
Caused much gossip	88	126	69.8
Complaints and gripes	41	120	34.2
Caused hostilities	41	124	33.1
Distorted communication	30	122	24.6
Threatened image or reputation of unit	27	124	21.8
Redistributed work	26	120	21.7
Client awareness	25	116	21.6
Lowered morale	25	120	20.8
Lowered output or productivity	21	118	17.8
Slowed decision making	18	121	14.9
Positive impacts			
Increased coordination	16	120	13.3
Lowered tensions	14	119	11.8
Improved teamwork	14	122	11.5
Improved productivity	10	121	8.3
Improved the work flow	9	124	7.3

awareness, lower morale, lower productivity, and someone loses a job. As a university administrator in a large non-academic division became involved with a very competent and aggressive secretary, he delegated authority to her and she soon was in conflict with the four men who reported directly to her boss. What had once been known as an exemplary organization was racked with intense hostility. Afraid to approach their boss about the romantic relationship itself, the four department heads tried several times to expose his secretary as an incompetent. When the administrator turned a deaf ear to their complaints, they began to spend hours complaining to each other, and then to people outside the division. Decision processes practically ground to a halt and complaints from students increased dramatically.

THE MANAGEMENT OF
ORGANIZATIONAL ROMANCE

Once superiors know about a romantic

relationship, they may do three things: take no action at all, take punitive action, or take positive action. In several of the cases with the most negative results, the male's superior chose to ignore the problem (see Table 10). Frequently, there was no response.

In some cases, such as that of the corporation president, the participant had no superior. Often the superior is reticent to take action because of the highly personal nature of the problem. A few respondents indicated that it was embarrassing to tell a subordinate that his personal life was out of hand and that he must change. Managers were also slow to take action because, as one person put it, "If the guy denies that a relationship exists, what do you say then?" Finally, it was felt that the situation would soon resolve itself. For example, a participant might already be scheduled for a transfer or the relationship was seen as a temporary fling by the male's superior. In a few cases, the male's superior took such punitive ac-

Table 10

SUPERIORS MANAGEMENT OF THE ROMANTIC RELATIONSHIP:
FREQUENCY OF AGREE RESPONSES

Item	Male's F	N	Superior %	Female's F	N	Superior %
No action						
1. Decided to ignore	60	97	61.9	58	101	57.4
2. Felt problem would resolve itself	48	90	53.3	49	97	50.5
3. Did not want to risk taking action	36	97	37.1	40	101	40.0
4. Did not know what to do	31	94	33.0	38	99	38.4
Punitive action						
1. Reprimanded	11	90	12.2	6	94	6.4
2. Warned to change or leave	9	92	9.8	8	100	8.0
3. Transferred	7	104	6.7	7	111	6.3
4. Terminated	5	104	4.8	12	112	10.7
Positive action						
1. Openly discussed situation	28	85	32.9	7	111	6.3
2. Counseled about what to do	18	82	22.0	14	91	15.4

tion as issuing a reprimand or warning to change or leave, transfer, and termination. Positive action includes openly discussing the situation and counseling the participant about what to do.

The female is twice as likely to be terminated as is the male. Because the male is usually in a higher position, he apparently is seen as less dispensable than the female. The female is also thought to be much less likely to benefit from an open discussion or from counseling by superiors. The latter two conditions, however, are mediated by the fact that the female's superior is often the other participant in the relationship.

DISCUSSION

The model of organizational romance presented here is theoretically important because it emphasizes a natural but, at least according to the Weberian model (Weber, 1947), deviant behavior pattern in organizations. It points to the models developed by Barnard (1938), Georgiou (1973), Kuhn (1974), and others in which the organizations are seen as "market places whose structures and processes are the outcomes of complex accommodations made by actors exchanging a variety of incentives and pursuing a diversity of goals" (Georgiou, 1973). The organizational romance is perceived as an exchange or transaction between two people. In some cases, the transaction is of little organizational consequence. This is especially so if no one else incurs any costs as a result of the romance. In other cases, especially those perceived to be utilitarian, there are impacts and organizational consequences. For example, in many utilitarian relationships, the lower organizational participant, who is usually the woman, is able to then influence the transactional relationships of others as a result of the romantic relationship or new transactional position. Because she provides ego rewards to the male in exchange for organizational rewards, she is able to influence the

contracts and transactional positions that others have established in such potent areas as organizational identity, communication, and power. Because others tend to operate with Weberian belief systems in which particularistic relationships are deemed inappropriate, the transaction is seen as unfair and their sense of justice or social equity (Adams, 1965) is violated. As the negative effects of the romantic relationship increase, the coping strategies become more extreme and the negative impact tends to be greater.

The model should be of value to researchers because it provides an initial, but tentative, statement about the problem. It needs to be tested, modified, and elaborated upon. It would be especially helpful in future work to gather reliable data on the frequency of occurrence.

The model should be of value to administrators because it serves as a lens through which a complicated phenomenon can be viewed. While the present data are not suited for the generation of principles or guidelines, the model should serve to sensitize the administrator to the complicated dynamics of organizational romance, and thus provide a greater understanding of a phenomenon with which he or she may have to deal.

NOTES

J. Stacy Adams, "Inequity in social exchange." In L. Berkowitz (ed.), *Advances in Experimental Social Psychology* (New York: Academic Press, 1965), pp. 276-299.

Chester I. Barnard, *The Functions of the Executive* (Cambridge, Mass.: Harvard University Press, 1938).

E. Berger, "The relation between expressed acceptance of self and expressed acceptance of others," *Journal of Abnormal and Social Psychology* 47 (1952): 778-782.

Peter M. Blau, *Exchange and Power in Social Life* (New York: Wiley, 1964).

David I. Bradford, A. G. Sargent, and M. S. Sprague, "The executive man and woman:

the issue of sexuality." In Francine Gordon and Myra Strober (eds.), *Bringing Woman into Management* (New York: McGraw-Hill, 1975), pp. 39-58.

Glen Elder, "Appearance and education in marriage mobility," *American Sociological Review* 34 (1969): 519-533.

Petro Georgiou, "The goal paradigm and notes towards a counter paradigm," *Administrative Science Quarterly* 18 (1973): 291-309.

H. J. Johnson, *Executive Life Styles*. A Life Extension Institute Report on Alcohol, Sex, and Health (New York: Crowell, 1974).

Alfred Kuhn, *The Logic of Social Systems: A Unified, Deductive, System Based Approach to Social Sciences* (San Francisco: Jossey-Bass, 1974).

David Mechanic, "Sources of power of lower participants in complex organizations," *Administrative Science Quarterly* 7 (1962): 349-362.

Bernard I. Murstein, "Stimulus-value-role: a theory of marital choice," *Journal of Mar-*
riage and the Family 32 (1970): 465-481.

T. M. Newcomb, "The prediction of interpersonal attraction," *American Psychologist* 11 (1965): 575-586.

Zick Rubin, *Liking and Loving: An Invitation to Social Psychology* (New York: Holt, Rinehart and Winston, 1973).

Marvin E. Shaw, *Group Dynamics: The Psychology of Small Group Behavior* (New York: McGraw-Hill, 1971).

J. W. Thibaut and H. H. Kelly, *The Social Psychology of Groups* (New York: Wiley, 1959).

Thorstein Veblen, *The Theory of the Leisure Class* (New York: Modern Library, 1934).

E. Walster, V. Aronson, D. Abrahams, and L. Rottman, "Importance of physical attractiveness in dating behavior," *Journal of Personality and Social Psychology* 4 (1966): 508-516.

Max Weber, *The Theory of Social and Economic Organization* (New York: Oxford University Press, 1947).

4. A Proposal: We Need Taboos on Sex at Work*

MARGARET MEAD

What should we—what can we—do about sexual harassment on the job?

During the century since the first "type writer"—that is, the first young woman clerk who had mastered the operation of the mechanical writing machine—entered a business office and initiated a whole new female-male work relationship, women have had to struggle with the problem of sexual harassment at work. And we still are at a loss as to how to cope with it successfully.

Certainly no one of us—young or old, single or married, attractive or homely, naïve or socially skilled—has escaped entirely unscathed. True, actual sexual assaults—rape and seduction—have been less common in almost any work situation than fathers and brothers once feared and predicted. But who among us hasn't met the male kiss-and-tell office flirt, the pinching prankster, the man in search of party girls or the man who makes sex a condition for job promotion? Who has not known the man who thinks no task is too tedious, unpleasant or demeaning for his "girl" to do in or out of office hours, the gossipmonger and—perhaps most dangerous—the apparently friendly man who subtly undercuts every direction given by a woman, depreciates every plan she offers and devalues her every accomplishment? Some women get discouraged and give up; most women learn to be wary. But as long as so many men use sex in so many ways as a

weapon to keep down the women with whom they work, how can we develop mature, give-and-take working relationships?

As I see it, it isn't more laws that we need now, but new taboos.

Not every woman—and certainly not every man—realizes and acknowledges that the mid-1960s marked a watershed in the *legal* treatment of women in the working world. Beginning with the Equal Pay Act of 1963 and the Civil Rights Act of 1964 (especially Title VII), legislation has been passed, executive orders have been issued, official guidelines have been established and decisions in a great many court cases have set forth a woman's right to be a first-class working citizen. Slowly but surely, using the new laws, women are making progress in their fight to gain what the law now so clearly defines as the right of every working person. And today almost half of all adult women are working persons.

But there are serious discrepancies. At home and at school we still bring up boys to respond to the presence of women in outmoded ways—to become men who cannot be trusted alone with a woman, who are angry and frustrated by having to treat a woman as an equal—either as a female with power who must be cajoled or as a female without power who can be coerced. But at the same time we are teaching our daughters to expect a very different

*Source: Reprinted by permission from Redbook Magazine (April 1978), pp. 31, 33, 38. Copyright © 1978 Mary Catherine Bateson and Rhoda Metraux.

working world, one in which both women and men are full participants.

In keeping with this we are insistent that the rights women have gained must be spelled out and that women use every legal device to ensure that new rules are formulated and translated into practice. Why, then, do I think that the new laws will not be sufficient to protect women—and men too, for that matter—from the problems of sexual harassment on the job? Why do I think we need new taboos?

I realize that this must sound strange to a generation of young women who have felt the need to break and abandon taboos of many kinds—from taboos against the inappropriate use of four-letter words to taboos against petty pilfering; from taboos against the use of addictive drugs to taboos against the public display of the naked human body; from the taboo against the frank enjoyment of sex to the taboos against full sexual honesty.

In some circles it has even become fashionable to call incest taboos—the taboo against sex with close family members other than husband and wife—out of date and unimportant. Yet incest taboos remain a vital part of any society. They insure that most children can grow up safe in the household, learn to trust, to be loved and to be sexually safe, unexploited and unmolested within the family.

When we examine how any society works, it becomes clear that it is precisely the basic taboos—the deeply and intensely felt prohibitions against "unthinkable" behavior—that keep the social system in balance. Laws are an expression of principles concerning things we can and do think about, and they can be changed as our perception of the world changes. But a taboo, even against taking a human life, may or may not be formulated in legal terms in some societies; the taboo lies much deeper in our consciousness, and by prohibiting certain forms of behavior also affirms what we hold most precious in our human relationships. Taboos break down in periods of profound change and are re-created in new forms during periods of transition.

We are in such a period now. And like the family, the modern business and the modern profession must develop incest taboos. If women are to work on an equal basis with men, with men supervising women in some cases and women supervising men in others, we have to develop decent sex mores in the whole working world.

In the past, when women entered the working world as factory workers or clerks in shops, as typists or chorus girls, they entered at the bottom; their poverty and their need for the job were part of their helplessness. Like women in domestic service, they were very vulnerable to sexual advances and seduction by men in positions of power over them. But sex also presented a precarious ladder by which a girl just might climb to become the pampered mistress or even the wife of the boss, the producer, the important politician.

For a long time after women began to work away from home, people made a sharp distinction between women who virtuously lived at home and limited "work" to voluntary efforts and other women who, lacking the support and protection of a father, brother, husband or son, were constrained to work for money. Wage-earning women were sexually vulnerable, and it was generally believed that the woman who was raped probably deserved it and that the woman who was seduced probably had tempted the man. By leaving home a woman did not merely move beyond the range of the laws that protected her there, but beyond the areas of living made safe by the force of taboos.

In the primitive societies in which I worked and lived as a young woman and as an older one, women who obeyed the accepted rules of behavior were not molested. But a woman who broke the rules—went out in the bush at night, worked alone in a distant garden or followed a lonely path without even a child companion—was asking for trouble. In general, women and men knew what was expected of them—until their lives were shaken up by change through the coming of strangers and the introduction of new kinds of work and new expectations. Then, along with other sorts of confusion, there was confusion about the sex relations of men and women. Cases of sex molestation, attack and rape reflected the breakdown of traditional security.

Everywhere and at all times, societies have developed ways of stylizing relations between women and men. Though the rules might be cruel and exploitative, they defined with clarity the posture and gait, the costume and the conversation, that signaled a woman's compliance with the rules as well as the circumstances in which a woman defined herself as a whore. In our own society, when women first became nurses their costume, reminiscent of the dress of nuns, at once announced the virtue of their calling. When a young American woman went away from home to teach children in one of the thousands of one-room schoolhouses that abounded in the countryside, the local community took charge of her virtue. Sometimes the rules were broken—on purpose. But the rules that protected men as well as women were known and agreed upon.

Today, with our huge and restless mobility from country to city, from one city to another, from class to class and from one country to another, most of the subtle ways in which women and men related to each other in a more limited setting have broken down. And now a new element has entered into their working relations with the demands that women must be employed in unfamiliar occupations and at higher executive and professional levels. Almost without warning, and certainly without considering the necessity for working out new forms of acceptable behavior, men and women are confronting each other as colleagues with equal rights.

And suddenly there is an outburst of complaints from women who find themselves mistreated in ways to which they are quite unaccustomed, as well as complaints from women who have suddenly discovered that sexual harassment on the job no longer is part of the expected life of a working woman. By banding together, organizing themselves and counseling one another, women are beginning to feel their strength and are making themselves heard, loud and clear, on the job, in the media and in the courts. Harassment on the job and wife beating at home have become part of our public consciousness.

Now, how to deal with the problems, the social discord and dissonance, in the relations between women and men? The complaints, the legal remedies and the support institutions developed by women all are part of the response to the new conception of women's rights. But I believe we need something much more pervasive, a climate of opinion that includes men as well as women, and that will affect not only adult relations and behavior on the job but also the expectations about the adult world that guide our children's progress into that world.

What we need, in fact, are new taboos that are appropriate to the new society we are struggling to create— taboos that will operate within the work setting as once they operated within the household. Neither men nor women should expect that sex can be used either to victimize women who need to keep their jobs or to keep women from advancement or to help men advance their own careers. A taboo enjoins. We need one that says clearly and unequivocally, "You don't make passes at or sleep with the people you work with."

This means that girls and boys will have to grow up together expecting and respecting a continuous relationship, in season and out, alone together or in a mixed group, that can withstand tension and relaxation, stimulation and frustration, frankness and reserve, without breaking down. It will have something of the relationship of brothers and sisters who have grown up together safely within a household, but it also will be different. For where brother and sister have a lifelong relationship, women and men who work together may share many years or only a few weeks or days or even hours.

In the way in which societies do develop new ways of meeting new problems, I believe we are beginning to develop new ways of working together that carry with them appropriate taboos—new ways that allow women and men to work together effortlessly and to respect each other as persons.

The beginning was made not at work but in our insistence on coeducation in the earliest grades of school, and gradually at all levels. This has made it possible for women to have much greater freedom wherever they go—so much so that we take this almost wholly for granted. We know it is not always wholehearted, but it is a beginning we know well.

And now, in line with new attitudes toward sex and equality, many students have demanded, and obtained, coeducational dormitories. Their elders mistook this as a demand for freer sexual access; but student advocates said firmly that, as young men and women, they wanted to meet under more natural circumstances and get to know one another as friends.

Today, wherever there is coeducation with a fairly even ratio between the sexes and several years' experience of living in coeducational dormitories, a quiet taboo is developing without the support of formal rules and regulations, fines or public exposure, praise or censure—a taboo against serious dating within the dormitory. Young women and young men who later will have to work side by side, in superordinate and subordinate relations as well as equals and members of a team, are finding their way toward a kind of harmony in which exploitative sex is set aside in favor of mutual concern, shared interests and, it seems to me, a new sense of friendship.

This is just a beginning, and one that is far from perfect. But one of the very good things is that women are discovering they can be frank and outspoken without being shrill, just as men are discovering there are pleasures in friendships without domination.

It is just a beginning, but students can set a style that will carry over into working relations in which skill, ability and experience are the criteria by which persons are judged, and appreciation of a woman or a man as a whole person will deeply modify the exploitation and the anguish of sexual inequality. Laws and formal regulations and the protection given by the courts are necessary to establish and maintain institutional arrangements. But the commitment and acceptance that are implied by taboos are critical in the formation and protection of the most meaningful human relations.

II

Sexual Harassment: The Problem

Introduction. Sexual harassment may be one of the most pervasive problems facing working women. If so, it is centrally involved in the issue of women's equality or, to be more precise, their lack thereof. Unfortunately, few if any papers have addressed the topic from the perspective of men.

Catharine MacKinnon's piece on "Women's Work," describes the work experiences of women as characterized by horizontal segregation, vertical stratification and income inequality. Horizontal segregation is defined to mean that women are limited to certain jobs because of their gender. Vertical stratification means that women occupy lower-ranking positions in the labor force and are dependent upon men for their initial hirings and advancements. Income inequality includes the fact that as active participants in the labor force, women still suffer from economic insecurity and economic dependence. Sexual harassment, according to MacKinnon, is a major factor contributing to this disadvantaged work status. The question MacKinnon poses is a subtle one: Does the sexual harassment of women occur because women occupy less prestigious and powerful positions, and are they, therefore, likely targets for this type of behavior? Or, do women tend to occupy positions of lower status because they are being sexually harassed? In other words, the question is: Which is the cause and which the effect?

Peggy Crull, after surveying 92 women who had experienced sexual harassment on the job, noticed a pattern that helped explain how women's self-confidence and their ability to perform at work are undermined. Sexual harassment—repeated, intrusive and uninvited sexual overtures—appeared again and again as the cause, regardless of the woman's age, marital status or salary. The effects of sexual harassment ranged from women being fired or pressured into resigning, to a diminished ability to perform effectively on the job, to an undermining of self-confidence, to health problems similar to those resulting from high job stress. Crull concludes that sexual harassment is a significant barrier to the professional and economic advancement of women.

No book on sexuality in organizations would be complete without addressing "The Other Side of the Coin: Women Who Exploit their Sexuality for Gain." Backhouse and Cohen, two Canadian researchers, write sensitively about the motivations of women who presumably use their sexuality for personal and professional gain. Anger, financial need and social conditioning are three major reasons. The authors conclude that the prevailing myth—that women can and do use their sexuality in the workplace—is less real than presumed and that the risks associated with calculated sexual behavior are infinitely greater than the rewards.

5. Women's Work*

CATHARINE A. MACKINNON

Women work "as women." The American workplace and work force are divided according to gender. Compared with men, women's participation in the paid labor force[1] is characterized by horizontal segregation, vertical stratification, and income inequality.[2] Women tend to be employed in occupations that are considered "for women," to be men's subordinates on the job, and to be paid less than men both on the average and for the same work.

Sexual harassment on the job occurs in this material context and is directly related to it. Horizontal segregation means that most women perform the jobs they do because of their gender, with the element of sexuality pervasively implicit. Women who work at "men's jobs" are exceptions. By virtue of the segregation of most women into women's jobs, such women are residually defined as "tokens." So even women who are exceptional among their sex remain defined on the job according to gender, with sexuality a part of that definition. Vertical stratification means that women tend to be in low-ranking positions, dependent upon the approval and good will of male superordinates for hiring, retention, and advancement. Being at the mercy of male superiors adds direct economic clout to male sexual demands. Low pay is an index to the foregoing two dimensions. It also deprives women of material security and independence which could help make resistance to unreasonable job pressures practical.

This is not to suggest that sexual harassment alone explains these characteristics of women's position in the labor force. But very little is known about the day-to-day processes by which women's disadvantaged work status is attained.[3] This chapter takes the view that the sexual harassment of women can occur largely because women occupy inferior job positions and job roles; at the same time, sexual harassment works to keep women in such positions. Sexual harassment, then, uses and helps create women's structurally inferior status.

HORIZONTAL SEGREGATION

Most working women are employed in jobs which mostly women do: this is horizontal segregation. In 1960, 47 percent of employed women worked at occupations in which women comprised 80 percent or more of the workers; only 2 percent of working women were employed in occupations in which they represented less than 33 percent of the total workers at that job. Almost 90 percent of employed men worked at jobs which had fewer than 33 percent women doing them.[4] By 1970, the picture had changed little: 72.6 percent of all employed women remained in occupations which were 45-100 percent female.[5] This segregation of women into certain types of jobs characterizes occupational categories both as a whole and subdivided by industry and firm. In 1974, 35 percent of working women

*Source: From Sexual Harassment of Working Women by Catharine A. MacKinnon, chapter 2, pp. 9-16. Copyright © 1979 by Yale University Press. Reprinted by permission.

had clerical jobs, occupying 77 percent of those jobs; 43 percent of women workers held service jobs, constituting 58 percent of all service workers.[6]

Women represent 98.5 percent of private household workers (paid) and 41.7 percent of all sales workers. By contrast, women comprised 4.2 percent of craft and kindred workers, 18.6 percent of managers and administrators and 15 percent of all farm workers.[7] Thirteen percent were operatives (factory workers,* and 6.8 percent were sales workers.[8] Taken together, this means that over 75 percent of working women are employed in "women's jobs," that is, in job categories noted for their sex-typing and in workplace settings characterized by sex segregation. Women who work are typically secretaries, typists, file clerks, receptionists, waitresses, nurses, bank tellers, telephone operators, factory workers (especially as dressmakers and seamstresses), sales clerks in department stores or cashiers in supermarkets, kindergarten or elementary school teachers, beauticians or cleaning women.[9] This distribution of occupations by sex leaves everything else—including both blue collar and high-status jobs—for men. In 1970, half of all women workers were employed in seventeen occupations of uniformly low status and pay, while half of all male workers were employed in sixty-three occupations which included a full range of pay and status.[10] In 1973, more than 40 percent of all women workers were employed in ten occupations, while the ten largest male occupations employed less than 20 percent of all working men.[11]

Women's jobs are usually "dull, re-

petitive, routine or dead-end."[12] So are many men's jobs. The difference is that women are almost universally restricted to a limited range of jobs at the bottom of the socioeconomic spectrum *because of their sex.* The remaining range of employment possibilities is open to men by comparison with other men (not, as a rule, by comparison with women) according to factors *other than sex,* race and class (or its proxy, education) being the most common. To grasp the precise interaction that keeps women defined by sex either in women's work or as token women and men doing everything that is considered either beyond women's capacities or sex-neutral would be to define a major dynamic of the socioeconomic system. But a single equivalence, at least, is clear: women's work is defined as inferior work, and inferior work tends to be defined as work for women.

Moreover, work that is considered inferior is often so defined on the basis of the same standards that define it as suitable for women: low interest or complexity, repetition and tediousness, little potential for self-direction, predominantly service-oriented, high contact with customers, involvement with children, and keeping things clean. These are tasks which men tend to shun unless there is no other job—or woman—around. Some of the most pointed documentation of the correlation of women's work with inferior work is revealed in explanations given for the shift in specific jobs from "men's jobs" to "women's jobs" between 1953 and 1961 in a large New Jersey county. Several typical explanations were:

[Most] technological changes were of a type that would tend to increase the percent of women. For example, we have broken down the alignment of components and simplified [the] job and as the jobs called for less skill, they became women's work." "In assembly we have one job . . . which was formerly performed by men. We decided that the job was simple enough so that there was no point in con-

---

*Factory work is not generically women's work, unlike, for example, service or clerical work. But women who are employed as factory workers are overwhelmingly employed in sex-defined sectors or subsets of factory jobs, such as in small electronics assembly, garment production, food packaging, and the like.

tinuing to recruit men for it. So we made it a woman's job. We couldn't redesign it; it was already too simple." "We feel that jobs requiring manual dexterity call for women. Also this work is particularly tedious and painstaking—definitely a woman's job.[13]

These observations are supported by studies which, taken together, suggest that as work becomes degraded by mechanization and routinization, it becomes defined as "women's work."[14] Given the qualities of jobs that make them considered women's work, it should be no surprise that many are easily replaced by machines.[15] At the same time, automation sometimes increases the available women's jobs by reducing to an unskilled operative level (for women) tasks that were formerly performed by a skilled worker (a man). This partly explains how women's labor force participation rate can increase while the overall unemployment rate, and the rate for women, also increases.

Another way of documenting the equivalence of women's work with inferior work is dynamically: the pay and status of whole occupations decline over time as women enter them. Clerical work,[16] primary and secondary education, and medicine in the Soviet Union are striking examples. As Andrea Dworkin synthesizes these trends, "when women enter any industry, job or profession in great numbers, the field itself becomes feminized, that is, it acquires the low status of the female."[17]

VERTICAL STRATIFICATION

Differentiation by sex holds as true within occupations as between them: this is vertical stratification. Women are generally men's subordinates on the job, with men in the position to do the hiring, firing, supervising, and promoting of women.

Only about 5 percent of all women workers occupy managerial or administrative jobs, accounting for only about 18 percent of all managers and adminis-

trators. As we have seen, women are overwhelmingly in positions that other people manage, supervise, or administer. Even in women's jobs, the managers are men.[18] A large percentage of professional women are teachers or health workers, yet they do not occupy the same proportion of the top positions in these fields.[19] The same is true in the federal civil service, where hierarchy is easy to observe. Compared with men, women are overwhelmingly concentrated in the lower-level civil service grades.[20]

Thus women work as men's workplace inferiors, either at inferior work or at inferior positions in the same work. Sex differentiation on the job need not be expressed in overt segregation, although often it is. Equally disadvantageous can be the gender-integrated situation where women do the same kinds of work as men but systematically occupy an inferior rung on the job ladder, dependent upon and vulnerable to male employers' or supervisors' approval for job security and career advancement. And at a certain point, especially when the prospects for upward mobility are limited, to do a lower-level version of the same job is to do a different job. Where the reason is sex, vertical and horizontal segregation tend to converge.

INCOME INEQUALITY

One particularly telling reflection of the foregoing two dimensions is women's income inequality with men. In 1974, women who worked full time earned 57¢ for every dollar earned by men. In 1976, the median earnings of year-round, full-time workers were only 60 percent of men's.[21] Computed by occupational group, adjusted for age and education, professional and technical women in 1974 made an average of 64 percent of the salaries of their male counterparts, woman nonfarm laborers, 72 percent. On the other end of the scale, female sales personnel made an average of 41 percent of the salary of salesmen. Broken down further, and stated differently, in 1974 the difference between women's and men's salaries was smallest for professional and technical workers and laborers, where women occupy the smallest proportion of the occupational category; the difference was highest in those jobs occupied mostly by women.[22]

This earnings differential was wider in 1974 than in most previous years, and the gap is increasing. In 1955, men's median earnings exceeded women's by an average of 56.4 percent, in 1974, by 74.8 percent.[23] Education does not proportionately improve women's status. In 1974, women with four years of college had lower salaries than men who had completed the eighth grade, and only 59 percent of the income of their male counterparts. This was a lower wage than was earned by fully employed men who did not complete elementary school.[24] Poor women tend to be substantially better educated than equally poor men.[25]

This means that the higher the job status, the more likely a woman is to be paid marginally closer to a man's wage-rate, and the less likely women are to occupy these positions at all, regardless of educational preparation. The more women there are in an occupation, the greater the likelihood that the few men in that profession will be paid disproportionately higher wages—and the lower-paid the job category as a whole tends to be when compared with jobs occupied mostly by men. Controlling for differences in education, skills, and experience (factors which themselves could be created by discrimination), studies have found a remaining difference between men's and women's salaries of between 20 and 43 percent, a difference which can be explained only as discrimination.[26] In 1976 the Women's Bureau concluded, after discussing the possible contribution of many factors to wage differentials, including concentration in low-paying occupations, working less overtime, dif-

ferences in education, training and work experience, age, region, and degree of industrial concentration:

> These differences between the earnings of men and women suggest that women are being paid less for doing the same job. . . . Studies have shown . . . that even after adjusting for some of these and other factors . . . much of the male-female earnings differential remains unexplained—representing a maximum measure of discrimination.[27]

A comparison of sex discrimination with race discrimination—a comparison which will be pursued throughout this discussion—completes the dismal statistical picture of women at work. The law has long based its efforts to alleviate discrimination upon the assumption that racial discrimination is the more critical and widespread and damaging social evil. Yet the President's Task Force on Women's Rights and Responsibilities concluded, "Sex bias takes a greater economic toll than racial bias."[28] Black women make less than white women, but white women make less, on the average, than black men. Since women's incomes are so low, it would follow that many women would be poor. Poor women outnumbered poor men by more than 4 million in 1975. Data for 1976 indicate that nearly two out of every three poor persons were women.[29] Black women are much more likely to be poor than white women, although poor white women outnumber their black counterparts by nearly two to one.[30] The conclusion is unquestionable: women, as a definable social group, are disadvantaged in employment.

Nor can working women be ignored as economically unimportant because they are supported by a man. Women work because they need the money. Close to three quarters are either single (23 percent), divorced, widowed or separated (19 percent), or have husbands who earn less than $10,000 a year (29 percent).[31] Many working women are heads of households and the sole support of their families. They cannot typically afford to risk loss of work. In March 1974, approximately 12 percent of all families, or one out of eight, were headed by a woman.[32] In 1976, women headed 14 percent of all families.[33] Families headed by women also tend to be poor, further restricting women's job flexibility. While the labor force participation rate of women household heads is substantially higher (54 percent) than that of all women (45 percent), their income is lower than for families headed by men,[34] and their unemployment rate is higher (6.4 percent) than that for husbands in husband-wife families (2.7 percent).[35] As a result, in 1976, 48 percent of all poor families were headed by women. About one-third of all families headed by women were poor, more than five times the rate for male-headed families.[36]

Contributing to low pay, as well as to vulnerability to employer capriciousness and victimization, is working women's comparative lack of unionization. Unionized women's pay is closer to unionized men's than nonunionized women's pay is to nonunionized men's. But in the United States, women belong to unions far less often than men do, which is another way of saying that women's occupations tend to be less unionized than the rest of the labor force. In 1970, only 10.4 percent of all working women were unionized, compared with 27.8 percent of all working men. Among white collar workers, 7.4 percent of women were in unions, 12.5 percent of men; among blue collar workers, which includes relatively few women, 27.8 percent of women were unionized, compared with 42.1 percent of men. For factory operatives and like workers, 29 percent of women belonged to unions, while 46.2 percent of men did. The disparity is also impressive in service work, where an overwhelming majority of workers are women: in 1970, 5.7 percent of women service workers were unionized, compared with 20.1 percent of men. As with

pay rates, the disparity in unionization is greatest in those jobs occupied mostly by women, and by most women.[37]

Taken together, these dimensions describe but do not explain sex segregation, one of the most tenacious rigidities of the labor market. It is clear that the current economic system requires some collection of individuals to occupy low-status, low-paying jobs; it is unclear whether there is any economically determinate reason why such persons must be biologically female. The fact that male employers often do not hire qualified women, even when they could pay them less than men, suggests that more than the profit motive is implicated.[38] Various reasons have been suggested for such unusual behavior by allegedly profit-maximizing businesses. One view is that money losses are overruled by psychological gains: "It feels so good to have women in their 'place.'"[39] Another view is that men *see women as less profitable even when they are paid less:*

> Sex role stereotypes pervasive in our culture may lead employers to believe that women would be such inefficient workers in traditionally male jobs that they would not be worth hiring, even at low wages.[40]

Still another view is that capitalists as a whole

> profit from discrimination and few if any individual capitalists lose money in the process, while many gain; . . . probably none see themselves as losing money from it.[41]

The reason is the structure of monopoly in industry. The mostly highly monopolized industries, less affected by competition, can afford to sex-segregate jobs (that is, pay men more to do the work) because they pass on higher wages to consumers. The most competitive, less profitable industries almost universally employ exclusively female workers.[42] A contributing explanation might be that few men apply for women's jobs because they have options to these low-paying, dead-end positions, which, moreover, affront their manhood, while

few women apply for men's jobs because they believe (with reason) they
will not be hired. The employer may
seldom be presented with two persons
of different sexes for the same job, that
is, with an opportunity to discriminate.[43]
The contextual aspects of women's
work that an examination of sexual
harassment highlights may also contrib-
ute to explaining sex segregation. A defining element of women's jobs may be
the subtle or blatant sexual prerogative
afforded the (almost universally) male
employer by having women employees
perform certain jobs.

NOTES

1. Women's labor force participation has
been increasing dramatically and continu-
ously since 1940 both in rate and in numbers. In 1975, 35 million women participated
in the labor force, representing 39.3 percent
of all workers, 45 percent of all women. In
March 1940, 25.4 percent of workers were
women, 28.9 percent of all women; in 1960,
33.3 percent and 37.4 percent, respectively.
Women's Bureau, *1975 Handbook on
Women Workers* (hereinafter, *1975 Handbook*), Bulletin 297, U.S. Department of
Labor, Employment Standards Division
(1975), table 2, at 11. See also Valerie Kin-
cade Oppenheimer, ''The Female Labor
Force in the United States: Demographic and
Economic Factors Governing its Growth and
Changing Composition'' (Berkeley, Califor-
nia: Institute of International Studies, Univer-
sity of California, 1970), and Lise Vogel,
''Women Workers: Some Basic Statistics''
(Boston: New England Free Press, 1971).

2. Lapidus uses these analytic dimen-
sions. Gail Warshofsky Lapidus, ''Occupa-
tional Segregation and Public Policy: A
Comparative Analysis of American and
Soviet Patterns,'' *Signs: Journal of Women in
Culture and Society*, vol. 1, no. 3, part 2
(Spring 1976), at 120.

3. In a good review of recent studies of
women's labor force particiaption Elizabeth
M. Almquist concludes:

The major recommendations, then, are
that research should become less

generalized and more specific, less concerned with outcomes and more concerned with the process of status attain-
ment, less attentive to the decisions
women make and more attentive to the
decisions employers make, less abstract in
orientation and more focused on the day-
to-day transactions between workers and
boss.

''Women in the Labor Force,'' *Signs: Journal
of Women in Culture and Society*, vol. 2, no.
4 (Summer 1977), at 854. Research on sexual
harassment meets all these requirements.

4. U.S. Census, 1960 Occupational
Characteristics, quoted and discussed at table
5.1 by Harriet Zellner, ''Determinants of Occupational Segregation,'' in Cynthia Lloyd,
ed., *Sex, Discrimination and the Division of
Labor* (New York: Columbia University Press,
1975), at 126.

5. Barbara B. Bergmann and Irma Adelman, ''The 1973 Report of the President's
Council of Economic Advisors: The Economic Role of Women,'' *American Economic Review*, vol. 68 (September 1973), at
510: See also *Statistical Abstract of the
United States*, 1971, ''Employed Persons, by
Major Occupation and Sex: 1950-1971,'' at
222.

6. These calculations are based upon
data in 1975 *Handbook*, at 84 and 86. For a
sensitive analysis of these dimensions of
working women's lives, see Nancy Seifer,
''Absent from the Majority: Working Class
Women in America'' (New York: Institute of
Human Relations, National Project on Ethnic
America of the American Jewish Committee,
1973). See also Nancy Seifer, *Nobody
Speaks for Me! Self-Portraits of American
Working Class Women* (New York: Simon
and Schuster, 1976), for oral histories on the
subjects discussed statistically in this chapter.

7. *1975 Handbook*, at 86-87.

8. *1975 Handbook*, table 36 (Manpower
Report of the President, April 1974), at 84. As
shown in this table, 15.6 percent of working
women are in a ''professional, technical''
category. Depending upon its precise param-
eters, given the miniscule representation of
women in the professions and the lack of
congruence in status between professionals
and particularly lower level technicals, this
category seems inapt. The vast majority of
these women are probably lower level technical workers, with more in common with
clericals, service workers, and factory workers than with women professionals.

9. *1975 Handbook*, at 89-91, table 38,

"Employed Persons in Selected Occupations by Sex, 1973 Annual Averages."

10. Janice N. Hedges, "Women-Workers and Manpower Demands in the 1970's," *Monthly Labor Review* 93 (June 1970), at 19.

11. *1975 Handbook*, at 91-92.

12. Seifer (1973), *supra*, note 6, at 29.

13. Georgina Smith, "Help Wanted—Female: A Study of Demand and Supply in a Local Job Market" (1964), quoted in Babcock, Freedman, Norton, and Ross, *Sex Discrimination and the Law: Cases and Remedies* (Boston: Little, Brown, 1975), at 209. See Babcock et al. for supportive materials on "sex stereotypes that make sex discrimination acceptable," at 208 ff.

14. Harry Braverman, *Labor and Monopoly Capital: The Degradation of Work in the Twentieth Century* (New York and London: Montly Review Press, 1974), especially at 293-358; Margery Davies, "Woman's Place is at the Typewriter: The Feminization of the Clerical Labor Force," *Radical America*, vol 8, no. 4 (July-August 1974).

15. Seifer (1973), *supra*, note 6, at 31-32; see also *1975 Handbook*, at 64 ff.

16. See C. Wright Mills, *White Collar* (New York: Oxford University Press, 1956), at 192-193.

17. Andrea Dworkin, "Phallic Imperialism: Why Economic Recovery Will Not Work For Us," *Ms.*, vol 5, no 6 (December 1976), at 104. For data, see Ester Boserup, *Woman's Role in Economic Development* (New York: St. Martin's Press, 1970).

18. Data from *1975 Handbook*, at 97. Rosabeth M. Kanter, *Men and Women of the Corporation* (New York: Basic Books, 1977), at 17, draws a similar conclusion.

19. *1975 Handbook*, at 94-96.

20. *1975 Handbook*, at 115. For further empirical documentation of the existence, depth, and dimensions of sex segregation, see Bergmann and Adelman, *supra*, note 5, at 509-514; Francine D. Blau, "Pay Differentials and Differences in the Distribution of Employment of Male and Female Office Workers," (Ph.D. diss., Harvard University, 1975); Francine Blau Weiskoff, "Women's Place in the Labor Market," *American Economic Review* 62 (May 1972), at 161-166; John E. Buckley, "Pay Differences Between Men and Women in the Same Job," *Monthly Labor Review* 94 (November 1971), at 36-39; Edward Gross, "Plus ça change. . . ? The Sexual Structure of Occupations Over Time," *Social Problems* 16 (Fall 1968), at

198-208; Oppenheimer, *supra*, note 1; Elizabeth Waldman and Beverely J. McEaddy, "Where Women Work—An Analysis by Industry and Occupation," *Monthly Labor Review* 97 (May 1974), at 3-14; and Francine Blau and Carol L. Jusenius, "Economists' Approaches to Sex Segregation in the Labor Market: An Appraisal," *Signs: Journal of Women in Culture and Society*, vol. 1, no. 3, part 2 (Spring 1976) at 181-199. See generally the entire volume of *Signs: Journal of Women in Culture and Society* devoted to "The Implications of Occupational Segregation," based on a conference on occupational segregation held at Northampton, Massachusetts, May 21-23, 1973, vol. 1, no. 3, part 2 (Spring 1976 Supplement).

21. Women's Bureau, U.S. Department of Labor, Employment Standards Administration, "Women with Low Incomes" (November 1977) (hereinafter, Women's Bureau, 1977), at 1.

22. U.S. Department of Commerce, Bureau of the Census, *Current Population Reports*, P-60, No. 101 (1974), issued January 1976.

23. U.S. Department of Commerce, Bureau of the Census, "Money Income of Families and Persons in the U.S.," *Current Population Reports*, 1957-1975. U.S. Department of Labor, Bureau of Labor Statistics, *Handbook of Labor Statistics*, 1975. One man's experience attempting to apply for such a "woman's job" illustrates the reality behind these data:

> Galvan Pool and Sauna needs a "Gal Friday," and you can type, file, and transcribe from a dictaphone. The woman on the phone apologizes, "We're only offering $95 a week, so we only want a woman."

Rik Myslewski, "But can he type?" *Sister: Connecticut's Feminist Publication*, vol. 5, no. 10 (New Haven, November 1976), at 10.

24. Women's Bureau, U.S. Department of Labor, Employment Standards Administration, "The Earnings Gap Between Women and Men" (1976), at 2-3.

25. Women's Bureau, 1977, at 5.

26. Six recent econometric studies reviewed by Bergmann and Adelman, *supra*, note 5. Larry Suter and Herman Miller, in "Income Differences Between Men and Career Women," demonstrate that women receive smaller increments of income for equal increases in educational level and oc-

cupational status. In Joan Huber, ed., *Changing Women in a Changing Society* (Chicago: University of Chicago Press, 1973), at 21-22. The Carnegie Commission on Higher Education reveals a similar pattern, concluding that women faculty members earn an average of $1,500-$2,000 per year less than men in comparable positions with comparable qualifications. *Opportunities for Women in Higher Education* (New York: Carnegie Commission, 1973). See also Myra Strober, "Lower Pay for Women: A Case of Economic Discrimination," *Industrial Relations* II (May 1972), at 279-84.

27. *1975 Handbook*, at 2. Congress noted the "profound economic discrimination against women workers" at H. Rep. No. 238, 92d Cong., 1st Sess., *reprinted in* [1972] *U. S. Code Cong. & Ad. News* 2137, *et seq.*

28. The median earnings of white men employed year-round full-time is $7,369, of Negro men $4,777, of white women $4,279, of Negro women $3,194. Women with some college education both white and Negro earn less than Negro men with 8 years of education. Women head 1,732,000 impoverished families, Negro males head 820,000. One-quarter of all families headed by white women are in poverty. More than half of all headed by Negro women are in poverty. Less than a quarter of those headed by Negro males are in poverty. Seven percent of those headed by white males are in poverty.

This was in 1970. "A Matter of Simple Justice, The Report of the President's Task Force on Women's Rights and Responsibilities," U.S. Government Printing Office (April 1970), at 18. See also Robert Stein, "The Economic Status of Families Headed by Women," *Monthly Labor Review* 93 (December 1970), at 7. The figures had changed little by 1972. See Women's Bureau, U.S. Department of Labor, Employment Standards Administration, "Facts About Women Heads of Households and Heads of Families" (April

1973), at 8, and *1975 Handbook*, at 141-142. Data for 1976 can be found in Women's Bureau, "Women with Low Incomes" (November 1977).

29. Women's Bureau, 1977, at 1.

30. *Id.*, at 5.

31. *1975 Handbook*, at 124.

32. *1975 Handbook*, at 19-21.

33. Women's Bureau, 1977, at 6.

34. *Id.*, at 8.

35. *1975 Handbook*, at 21.

36. Women's Bureau, 1977, at 6.

37. All data from Edna E. Raphael, "Working Women and their Membership in Unions," *Monthly Labor Review* (May 1974); see especially table 3, "Union Membership of Private Wage and Salary Workers, by occupation of longest job, industry and sex, 1970." (The author attributes her data to the Bureau of Labor Statistics.)

38. See Janice Madden, *The Economics of Sex Discrimination* (Lexington, Mass.: Heath, 1973), chap. 2.

39. Barbara Bergmann, "Economics of Women's Liberation," *Challenge*, vol. 16 (May/June 1973), at 14.

40. Mary Stevenson, "Women's Wages and Job Segregation," *Politics and Society*, vol. 4, no. 1 (Fall 1973), at 93.

41. Barbara Deckard and Howard Sherman, "Monopoly Power and Sex Discrimination," *Politics and Society*, vol. 4, no. 4 (1974), at 477.

42. A review of the growing empirical literature in this field is provided by Andrew I. Kohen, *Women and the Economy: A Bibliography and a Review of the Literature in Sex Differentiation in the Labor Market* (Columbus, Ohio: Center for Human Resource Research, Ohio State University, 1975).

43. For a specific review of theoretical approaches to sex segregation, see Francine D. Blau and Carol L. Jusenius, *supra*, note 20, at 181-199.

6. The Impact of Sexual Harassment on the Job: A Profile of the Experiences of 92 Women*

PEGGY CRULL

INTRODUCTION

Over the last four years Working Women's Institute has become a nationally recognized research/resource/action center focussing on the issue of sexual harassment on the job. The issue and the Institute's work have received widespread attention in national and local media. As a result women from across the United States write the Institute. Many of them ask for concrete assistance on how to handle a sexual harassment problem. Others are simply seeking a sympathetic audience to listen to their story. Still others see their letters as a contribution to the effort to eliminate sexual harassment.

After reading scores of these letters we noticed patterns which helped to explain how sexual harassment undermines women's ability to take their rightful place in the labor force and earn a decent living. In order to organize the rich information contained in the letters and document these patterns, a short questionnaire was constructed and mailed to each of 325 women whose letters indicated they had personally experienced sexual harassment on the job.[1] The questionnaire asked for information on the woman's age, occupation, marital status, and salary at the time of the harassment experience, a description of the incident, the ramifications for her job, job performance, subsequent employment, and attitudes toward work. Ninety-two women responded with a completed questionnaire describing an experience which fits the Institute's definition of sexual harassment.[2]

The results of the analysis of the responses provide a vivid profile of the sexual harassment experience and its negative consequences for the women who encounter it.

WHO RESPONDED TO THE QUESTIONNAIRE?

All of the people who filled out the questionnaire were women. At times men have written to get assistance for wives, daughters, and friends, but none have sought help for themselves. The respondents were from every region of the country, and from both large and small cities, with the heaviest concentrations in the most populous states— New York, New Jersey, Ohio, and California. They work in every kind of setting—factories, restaurants, schools, offices, hospitals. Their average age at the time of the sexual harassment experience was 30 years, but some were as young as 16 and others as old as 65.[3]

This group of women depended on their jobs and had little economic leeway when the incident happened. More than three-quarters of them were single, separated, divorced or widowed, and over half of them were the sole support of their families and/or themselves.

*Source: Reprinted by permission from Peggy Crull, Ph.D., Research Director of Working Women's Institute, Research Series Report No. 3 (Fall 1979). Copyright © 1979 Working Women's Institute. All rights reserved.

Fig. 1

OCCUPATIONAL DISTRIBUTION OF STUDY POPULATION AND EMPLOYED WOMEN

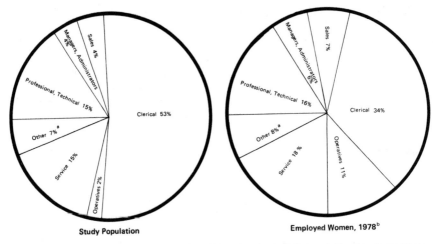

Study Population

Employed Women, 1978[b]

a. *Other:* Craft workers; transport equipment operatives; laborers (non-farm); private household workers; farm workers.
b. *Source: Employment and Unemployment During 1978: An Analysis* (U.S. Department of Labor, Bureau of Labor Statistics, 1979).

Their incomes were low: 51 percent of those working full-time made $150 or less per week before taxes. This income level is consistent with the occupations held by the group; the greatest proportion (53 percent) were clerical workers (secretaries, bookkeepers, etc.), followed by a substantial proportion (15 percent) of service workers (waitresses, hospital aides, etc.), both of which are low-paying occupations with limited opportunity for advancement (see Figure 1 for the complete occupational distribution of this group and a comparison with the occupational distribution of employed women in the United States.)

WHAT KINDS OF INCIDENTS PROMPTED THEM TO WRITE

The incidents described by the respondents were not harmless passes or mutual flirtations; they involved uninvited, invasive and often embarrassing behaviors, which were usually repeated despite the woman's expressed dis-

pleasure. The most common mode of harassment was verbal—comments on the woman's body, jokes about sex, invitations to go to bed, which persisted over a period of time. However, more than half of the women were also subjected to repeated physical advances such as touching and kissing. In 39 percent of the incidents sexual parts of the woman's body were fondled or grabbed without her consent and in 12 percent of the situations the harasser restrained the woman with physical force.

Not only were the situations unpleasant and embarrassing, but they were inherently coercive. Seventy-nine percent of the men involved had the power to fire or promote the woman; 79 percent of them were married and their average age was 14 years greater than the woman's. In 16 percent of the cases women were explicitly threatened with repercussions if they did not cooperate. Sometimes the sheer numbers of men rather than their status created a coercive atmosphere; in 18 percent of the cases several men were harassing one woman.

HOW DID SEXUAL HARASSMENT AFFECT THEM?

The women attempted to resolve their dilemmas in a variety of ways, but regardless of their efforts, the outcome was usually detrimental. Even though they were often uncertain about what to do, most of the women took direct action to stop the harassment. Seventy-six percent of them explained to the harasser or to someone in authority that they wanted the behavior to stop. (As we have seen, more often than not the person in authority is also the harasser.) This tactic was generally useless. In only 9 percent of the cases did it stop the harassment altogether, and in another 17 percent it resulted in a slight reduction of the behavior. Frequently (49 percent of the cases), the women were not taken seriously and nothing changed.

Even worse, the situation sometimes backfired (26 percent) and her complaint led to retaliation such as increased work loads, withheld raises, poor references.[4] About one-third of the women took their complaints to their union, a lawyer, or to a state or local human rights division.

Once the sexual harassment had begun, the jobs of the majority of women were in serious jeopardy, whether or not they complained. Twenty-four percent of the respondents were fired (see Figure 2). In some cases the harasser was angered simply because the woman refused his advances, and in others she was fired for being a troublemaker after she complained. Prior to termination the employer often began to find fault with her work in an apparent attempt to justify the firing. Even when not officially fired, women were often pressured into leaving their jobs. Forty-two percent of the respondents eventually resigned as a result of the intolerable working condi-

Fig. 2

EFFECTS OF SEXUAL HARASSMENT ON EMPLOYMENT STATUS

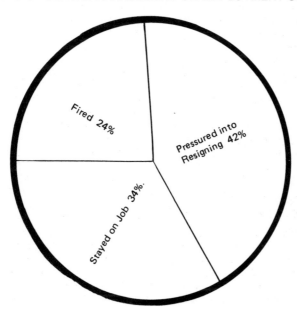

tions created by the sexual harassment and the retaliatory harassment that followed their refusals to cooperate (see Figure 2).

Sexual harassment did not have to lead to the retaliation or the termination of the women's jobs to have damaging effects on their economic security and advancement; it also held them back by diminishing their ability to work efficiently and destroying their ambition. Most of the respondents expressed pride at being able to handle their jobs despite the annoyance and embarrassment of having to fend off sexual advances. However, 83 percent of them conceded that the situation had in some way interfered with their job performance (see Figure 3). Not surprisingly, the presence of someone who repeatedly forced sexual attentions on them prevented them from concentrating on their work. They spent valuable time and energy looking for ways to steer clear of the offending parties. As a result, their work suffered and they began to question their ability

to handle themselves socially and professionally. For some the end result was that they dreaded going to work and began to lose their enthusiasm for working altogether.

Being trapped in a situation where they were not free to reject sexual advances without risking their jobs created health problems similar to those which develop in other kinds of stressful working conditions. (See Figure 3.) Almost all (96 percent) of the respondents reported suffering some type of emotional stress. Nervousness, fear, anger, and sleeplessness were mentioned most often. A majority of the women (63 percent) also developed physical reactions as a result of the tension of the situation. Most common were headaches, nausea, and weight losses and gains. In 12 percent of the cases the stress symptoms were so severe that the women sought therapeutic help to alleviate them. In short, sexual harassment became a hidden occupational hazard.

Women who were fired or pressured

Fig. 3
EFFECTS OF SEXUAL HARASSMENT ON PRODUCTIVITY AND HEALTH

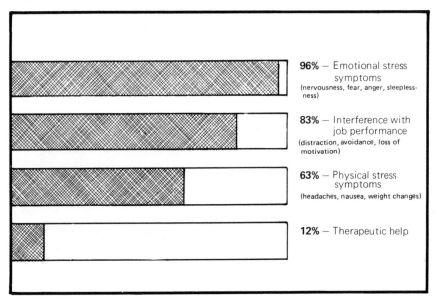

96% — Emotional stress
symptoms
(nervousness, fear, anger, sleeplessness)

83% — Interference with
job performance
(distraction, avoidance, loss of
motivation)

63% — Physical stress
symptoms
(headaches, nausea, weight changes)

12% — Therapeutic help

to leave their jobs had special difficulty getting back on their feet economically. Employers whose advances were rebuffed often refused to write letters of recommendation. Prospective employers were skeptical of the women's explanations of why they left their previous jobs. When they tried to collect unemployment they were met with the same skepticism. Eighteen of the respondents who lost their jobs applied for unemployment benefits. Many of those, fearing they would not be believed, opted to give some other reason than sexual harassment for their job termination. Of the 12 women who gave sexual harassment as the reason, only 7 received benefits.

HOW DOES SEXUAL HARASSMENT HINDER WOMEN'S ECONOMIC PROGRESS?

These results show that sexual harassment kept this group of women underpaid, underemployed, and unemployed in both direct and indirect ways. They were directly denied the opportunity to work and advance routinely, based on their job skills. They were fired and passed up for raises and promotions for reasons that clearly were not job-related. They received poor work evaluations and references, which damaged their chances for new and better jobs. Unemployment Insurance officials were skeptical of their claims and refused them benefits to tide them over while they looked for other work. Even when they were not directly denied jobs or advancement, their ability to work productively was diminished by the strain of the harassment. They had to spend valuable time and energy appeasing and fending off the harassers, rather than concentrating on their work. Their self-confidence was shaken and their emotional and physical health was impaired by the stress of the situation. Many who were not willing or able to tolerate the harassment had to quit and take the risk that they would not be able

to find comparable work. A number felt that the experience had eroded their ambition and motivation to work at all.

This study is a first attempt to pinpoint the specific mechanisms through which sexual harassment directly and indirectly creates economic hardships for working women. Although research with more random samples is needed to determine the extent to which this profile is typical of women who are sexually harassed, a vast range of anecdotal evidence and results from informal surveys indicate that sexual harassment is widespread and the effects described here pervasive. It appears that sexual harassment in conjunction with other discriminatory conditions such as unequal pay, inadequate job training, and sex segregation of jobs is a major force in maintaining the low status of all women in the workforce.

NOTES

1. A number of these questionnaires probably did not reach their destinations since many of the addresses were old. We do not know how many were received, since the bulk mailing arrangement did not allow for undeliverable pieces to be returned to us.

2. The Institute's definition of sexual harassment is "any repeated and/or unwanted sexual attention, jokes, innuendoes, touching, or propositions from someone in the workplace that make you uncomfortable and/or cause you problems on your job." Some of the returned questionnaires recounted experiences which did not fit this description of sexual harassment, but referred to some other types of job problems. They were not included in the analysis.

3. All of the age, salary, and other demographic data refer to the time of the harassment incident, not to the time at which the questionnaire was filled out. Most of the incidents occurred between 1970 and the present.

4. Many women volunteered stories about retaliation in response to the question "What happened when you complained." But since they were not specifically asked if retaliation took place, the figure given here is probably a low estimate.

7. The Other Side of the Coin: Women Who Exploit Their Sexuality for Gain*

CONSTANCE BACKHOUSE
LEAH COHEN

THE WIDESPREAD VIEW

At a recent Ontario government conference on sexual harassment, the first question raised by a member of the audience was: "What about women who exploit their sexuality?" The answer given by one of the panelists was: "I don't think women gain from trading on their sexuality in the workplace." A small chorus of obviously angry women in the audience retorted, "Oh, come on!"

After an American newspaper covered the results of a study in San Antonio, Texas, on sexual harassment, an irate male reader shot back the following in a letter to the editor:

Why protect only working women from sexual harassment? Should not all women be protected from the harassment of flowers, dinners, theatre tickets, trips and such like? And what about the silent majority of women harassed by being neglected and ignored by the men who chase the resident blonde, and totally ignore the plump pulchritude of brunettes? Why should the inconsiderate brutes not be thrown in jail for discrimination? After all, scorn is much more annoying to women than unsolicited advances.

It is only too clear that in most sectors of our society, there is a widespread view that women can and frequently do exploit their sexuality for gain in the workplace.

At the outset we should point out that we are not speaking of office romances, which are mutual affairs. Both parties have willingly decided to enter into a liaison and no element of coercion is present. Such relationships are not instances of sexual harassment. However, in any discussion of sexual harassment the question of whether women are trading on their sexuality for unfair job advantages is inevitably raised.

Certainly, if you took office gossip at face value, you would be forced to admit that successful women owed most of their promotions to the liberality with which they dispense their sexual favours. One high-ranking corporate manager we interviewed openly voiced his firmly held conviction that any woman who has achieved success in business has used sexual relations to get to her position of power.

To some extent such attitudes are a smokescreen which serves to obfuscate what is, in reality, a reluctance to attribute competence to women. Many men and women are uncomfortable with the notion of an able, powerful, economically independent woman. They assume she has been sleeping with powerful men. After all, they reason, what other way could she have done it?

*Source: From The Secret Oppression: Sexual Harassment of Working Women by Constance Backhouse and Leah Cohen, chapter 8, pp. 166-73. Copyright © 1978 by The Macmillan Company of Canada Limited. Reprinted by Permission.

women really don't have anything else to offer.

WHY DO WOMEN USE THESE TACTICS?

To be fair, however, one must admit that some women in our society do try to exploit their sexuality for gain.

Some do so out of anger. They recognize that the workplace is saturated with discriminatory attitudes and policies. For women who have assessed that hard work and competence are not enough to break into the upper echelons of the work world, the notion of trading on one's sexuality becomes an alluring option.

Many women build up a tremendous internal rage when they realize that the odds are stacked against them in the workplace. This rage translates into an attitude of "I'll get even"—namely by exploiting my sexuality. Unconsciously or consciously these women decide to reap whatever advantages they can from their sexuality. One powerful and well-known Canadian trade-unionist freely admits that she has to be seductive in order to get what she wants. "It's all fair in this game," she says.

Other women try to trade on their sexuality because of financial need. In Victorian times women's wages were set so low that many were forced to supplement their incomes through prostitution to survive. Today, although their situations may be less desperate, the vast majority of women have to come to an accommodation with a husband or a boss in order to maintain their economic livelihood. One American female sociologist sees it as the inevitable extension of low wages. She told us:

In a society where the male is the fundamental breadwinner, you're going to have office romances, and some women will try to use their sexuality. But women who exploit their sexuality, in some cases, are looking for sexual attention as a means of income-supplement. One woman I know had to ensure she was asked out for dinner every night, just in order to make ends meet.

SOCIAL CONDITIONING

Still other women try to curry favour in the workplace with sexual attention because they have accepted the roles forced upon them by a society that defines a woman as nurturer, mother, wife, and the helpmate of men. Magazines such as *Cosmopolitan* openly counsel women to adopt a strategy of sexual manipulation, advising them to use this technique for their own advantage. It is difficult to place the blame on individual women who are merely acting out the patterns of behaviour they are encouraged by society and the media to utilize.

MARRY THE BOSS

The peculiarities of North American life prepared the social-psychological ground for the mass sex market, and the mass competition among females.

Just as the Horatio Alger stories became the handbook for men on how to rise from rags to riches, so the romance stories for women told them how to get and marry the boss's son or even the boss himself.[1]

The majority of working women quickly learn that the possibility of rising on their own to a position of prominence which would afford them both power and financial independence is extremely unlikely. Rather than remain a marginal worker in a dead-end, low-paying job, the prospect of marriage, especially to a man who by comparison has the trappings of power and money, becomes an obvious way out.

In effect women who aspire to marry the boss are only complying with the social mores of our society. They are encouraged from childhood on to cultivate their physical attributes with the objective of "catching" a man. Most of society does not condemn this type of trading on one's sexuality. If anything it is considered perfectly legitimate, particularly when it leads to marriage.

With all of this outright encouragement of sexual interplay in the workplace, it is not surprising that some women do attempt to gain promotions, pay raises, and other benefits by virtue of their sexual attractions. The obvious question becomes whether they find this tactic successful in the long run.

THE UNWRITTEN RULES OF THE CORPORATION

Although you will never find company policies on office affairs written in personnel manuals, a comprehensive code of ethics exists in all organizations. These rules are patterned after the customs and standards of a male-dominated society where male-female relationships are viewed as a male conquest, an indication of power, virility, and domination.

Michael Korda, in *Male Chauvinism: How It Works,*[2] acknowledges this:

> On a basic male chauvinist level an office affair is a badge of status, always provided that it's handled well; that is, with the minimal amount of emotional disturbance and with its course and direction firmly controlled (or thought to be firmly controlled) by the male partner. Any display of emotion on the part of the man, or suggestion that the woman either initiated the affair or decides when and how it will end, loses the man his status in his peer group.

While all organizations will strenuously disclaim in public that they have a corporate policy on male-female sexual relationships, in fact, office affairs are a male assertion of superiority in corporate gamesmanship. A man who sleeps with an employee or co-worker is instantly superior in game terms, while the woman is downgraded to inferior status. As a general rule, a woman augments the status of any and every man she sleeps with in the office, while lowering her own. Betty Lehan Harragan, author of *Games Mother Never Taught You,*[3] cautions women as follows:

> What this unwritten and unverbalized canon of male ethics adds up to for women is clear: any corporate woman employee who engages in intercourse has jeopardized her chances of significant advancement within that particular corporate structure. She is irrevocably labeled "inferior" and must go elsewhere to move upward with a clear path.

> Women can't win this game. They must not play the game with any male member of their particular business community if they want to remain viable activists in the impersonal master game of corporate politics where the goal is money, success, and independent power.

The double standard stands out clearly in any discussion of whether women derive unfair gains based on their sexuality. Even presuming a woman has made substantial job gains from an office liaison, the anger and hostility from fellow-employees and the world at large focuses exclusively on her. The role of the male partner in granting promotions or job benefits for sexual favours he has been bribed with is surely just as reprehensible. Yet his actions are rarely scrutinized and reprisals against such men are virtually unheard of.

Robert E. Quinn, a thirty-two-year-old professor of public administration at the State University of New York, recently completed a comprehensive study of the office affair. His study, entitled *Coping with Cupid: The Formation, Impact and Management of Romantic Relationships in Organizations,* revealed that "women who put their sexuality to work for them in the workplace are playing a dangerous game that, statistically, leads them to be fired for fooling around twice as often as men." Professor Quinn observed that "because the male is usually in a higher position, he is seen as less dispensable than the female, if superiors feel an affair is getting out of hand." As he said, "If people are stepping out of line, sexually, there seems to be a compulsion on the part of the upper hierarchy to do something about it. Unfortunately, it's the woman who has to go."

Despite this deterrent, women, according to Professor Quinn, do "use their sexuality to attempt to accomplish organizational ends." In 74 per cent of the affairs that he studied the male held a higher position in the office than the female partner. Co-workers, he discovered, reacted with disapproval, cynicism, and hostility—all of which was particularly directed at the woman, who they perceived as engaging in sexual exchange for career advantage and favouritism. The women who evoked these negative responses from their co-workers became depressed and defensive.[4]

MALE GOSSIP

Talking about one's conquests—real or imagined—is a favourite male pastime. Harragan cautions working women that "as long as sexual conquests of female employees are male status symbols, the trophies must be publicized." She estimates that 80 per cent of conversation in all-male groups is about sex, specifically the availability of women and the sexual prowess of men in "making" those women. Furthermore, she points out that "male-initiated propositions and consummations would have no status value if nobody knew about them, so office affairs are the most public personal relationships there are."

Successful women are particularly the butt of male gossip, be they subordinates, peers, or superiors. With so many men threatened by the notion of job equality, lewd insinuations about women achievers offers an easy, but vicious, way of discharging anxiety. Whether a woman is engaging in office romances or not, she may become the target of this insidious male gossip, which is often a gross exaggeration or a fantasy. Harragan strongly urges women "to refuse to talk about other women disparagingly." By doing so, she concludes, "they play right into men's hands and help reduce all women (including themselves) to the contemptible level of cunts."[5]

EXCEPTIONS TO THE RULE

There are two kinds of office affairs that generally do not result in reprisals to the woman. You can marry the man in question or be his secretary.

Marriage legitimizes you as part of a couple and places you outside the realm of office politics. You survive and may even thrive, since you have conformed to society's notion of an upstanding, moral member of the community. You are a wife, not a temptress or a seductress. As a wife, other men are loath to pursue you or gossip about you, since your husband may be a co-worker or superior. Furthermore, territorial imperatives are involved. As another man's wife in the same workplace you are viewed as his exclusive property, his conquest.

The only other instance in which a woman's office affair does not place her in job jeopardy is the long-term affair between a secretary and her boss. As Harragan points out, this exemption only applies to those secretaries "who remain in their subservient, noncomplaining role of the dutiful doormat." These sexual relationships, she continues, are only possible because secretarial jobs have no place in the hierarchy as presently constituted. They are extraneous servant positions. A secretary has no upward mobility. A secretary-boss sexual liaison is degrading to the woman, but it affects nobody else in the hierarchy, so nobody really cares— as long as she "behaves herself" and is completely under the man's controlling thumb.[6]

HOW HIGH ARE THE STAKES?

With such obvious risks facing any woman who enters into an office affair, it becomes important to examine how lucrative the potential gains may be. Do women gain in a significant way from sexual liaisons on the job?

What we are asking, essentially, is whether women who exploit their sexuality receive substantial payoffs. Since these women are, in effect, selling sex indirectly, it is helpful to look to the example of women who are selling sex directly: the prostitutes. Prostitutes are women who are exploiting their sexuality in a forthright manner. Consequently one would assume they would derive greater financial rewards than women who merely exploit indirectly.

However, the vast majority of the most elegant call-girls find themselves old at thirty, bitter, and broke. Prostitution is not a profession in which one moves up through the ranks. Experience is no asset, and it is all downhill as one gets older. Although the top call-girls earn between $30,000 and $100,000 a year, taxfree, their expenses are monumental. They require costly clothes and plush apartments in the most exclusive districts. A large proportion of their income goes to pay off pimps, madams, building superintendents, landlords, doormen, prostitution lawyers, politicians, the police, and in some cases even the Mafia. In 2,000 interviews conducted over ten years, Charles Winick and Paul Kinsie found no more than 100 older prostitutes who had any money left.[7]

With such a dismal picture facing prostitutes, it should not be surprising to discover that women who try to use sex indirectly, for job-related gains, have little success. These women may be able to improve their job title or pay *over other women,* but they are never able to compete with men on such a basis.

SERIOUS PITFALLS

Women who do "buy" promotions, raises, etc., with sexual payoffs, almost always find they are left with nagging doubts about their abilities and job skills. Whether or not they are in fact competent to handle the work they are doing, their crises of self-confidence often jeopardize their job performance.

Furthermore, they are faced with a complete absence of job security. Office affairs, like all male-female relationships, have a disturbing propensity to shift with the winds of time. When the relationship goes on the rocks, or another more tantalizing woman comes along, the cozy setup could be called off in a hurry.

The "love 'em and leave 'em" routine can quickly turn to "love 'em and fire 'em" in the work setting. One clearcut example of the devious lengths to which this scenario can be taken was related to us by an affirmative action specialist from a multinational manufacturing concern.

"The executive director of our all-male marketing department did everything he could to forestall the introduction of our affirmative action program in his department," she told us. "When he realized he would have to bow to the inevitable," she continued:

In keeping with his childish personality, he devised a sneaky plan to subvert the program. He agreed to hire women, all right. But he hired them not on the basis of their ability to do the job, but because he found them sexually appealing. He would have a short and swift affair with each of them, and when it was over he would try to fire them. He would point out, quite correctly, that they were not qualified to fill the positions and that their work was not up to standard. He used this to create an outcry about the affirmative action program, arguing that it was forcing him to hire unacceptable women. I was left in the intolerable position of trying to defend these poor women, trying to protect them from losing their jobs. After all, they certainly were qualified for the jobs they were really hired for—to be the sexual playthings of the executive director. Unfortunately, the president of the company did not believe me, and all the women were fired. The affirmative action program was effectively scuttled by these outrageous tactics.

Another critical obstacle facing women who try to trade on their sexuality is the hostility and frustration felt by other employees, who inevitably react against what they perceive to be an unfair advantage. A woman who is handed a promotion as a return for sexual favours will find her work so sabotaged by her fellow-workers that she will rarely be able to function. Subordinates and superiors of both sexes will undermine her work and belittle her authority. They will all assume she holds her position not on an independent basis, but only so long as her male paramour can protect her. She will never be able to take control or build up satisfactory working relationships with her fellow-workers. Inevitably the performance of the operation will suffer, and no matter how powerful her male protector is, she will be removed because of her inability to get the job done in an acceptable manner.

The prevailing mythology is that women can sell sex to men and receive adequate or spectacular financial, professional, or emotional rewards. In fact, upon closer examination, it becomes clear that most women do not receive adequate or spectacular financial, professional, or emotional rewards whether they sell sexual services or refuse to do so.

NOTES

1. Evelyn Reed, *Problems of Women's Liberation* (New York: Pathfinder Press Inc., 1972), p. 81.
2. Michael Korda, *Male Chauvinism: How It Works* (New York: Random House, 1973). Reproduced by permission of Random House, Inc.
3. From *Games Mother Never Taught You* by Betty Lehan Harragan (New York: Rawson Associates Publishers, Inc., 1977), pp. 289-93. Copyright © 1977 by Betty Lehan Harragan. Reprinted by permission of Rawson Associates Publishers, Inc.
4. *Toronto Star*, June 5, 1978.
5. Harragan, *op. cit.*, p. 299.
6. *Ibid.*, p. 297.
7. Charles Winick and Paul Kinsie, *The Lively Commerce* (New York: Quadrangle, 1971).

III

Organizational Responses to Sexual Harassment

Introduction. Sexual harassment is clearly becoming a significant management concern. Until recently, no governmental or private sector policies have existed that prohibit sexual harassment as an unfair or discriminatory labor practice. Since 1978, however, there have been some important positive steps taken.

"Responses of Fair Employment Practices Agencies to Sexual Harassment Complaints: A Report and Recommendations," prepared by the Working Women's Institute, provides the context for the articles in this section. It suggests that despite the concerns expressed by many fair employment practices agencies, most of these organizations had not established policies or procedures to deal with the special requirements of sexual harassment cases—at least until 1978. There is no cause to presume that other public or private agencies would have responded very differently to such a survey.

Faucher and McCulloch in "Sexual Harassment in the Workplace: What Should the Employer Do?" offer a prescription for organizations faced with the possibility of sexual harassment complaints. They state clearly that "intelligent" employers should attend to developing personnel policies that will protect them from litigation in this field, protect employees from unfair allegations and allow the work environment to be a protected place for potential victims of sexual harassment. Mechanisms to handle complaints of sexual harassment and formal procedures for investigation and remedial action are suggested and a flow chart that outlines steps that employers might take to both prevent and handle these issues is provided.

Backhouse and Cohen, in "Action Plans for Management and Unions," outline a "Ten-Point Plan for Management," which details steps available both to prevent sexual harassment and to insure positive intervention. The authors then address the topic from the perspective of unions and offer a "Ten-Point Plan for Unions" as well. These pragmatic suggestions serve as a useful guide to managers sensitive to the potential problems posed by sexual harassment complaints.

The most significant organizational response to sexual harassment is perhaps the "Memorandum to Heads of Departments and Independent Agencies on the Subject of Sexual Harassment," from the U.S. Office of Personnel Management. This brief policy statement and definition of sexual harassment provides a mandate to all federal agencies to insure that merit principles are enforced, so that employees may work in an environment free from sexual harassment. The regulatory authority of the Office of Personnel Management serves to underscore the significance of this document as the chief operating policy of the federal government.

Atkinson and Layden provide an excellent overview of the "Federal Response to Sexual Harassment: Policymaking at Johnson Space Center, NASA." After describing the federal government's activities in the field, they describe the actions undertaken by one federal agency to achieve the federal government's intent.

Finally, as a local government counterpart to the federal guidelines, "The District of Columbia Mayor's Order 79-89" translates and broadens the federal government's policy on sexual harassment. Mayor Marion Barry, Jr., establishes, without question, that the policy of the District of Columbia prohibits sexual harassment of District employees in any form. The order goes on to mandate District agencies to establish procedures for filing, investigating and adjudicating complaints of sexual harassment, as well as to design affirmative action programs that insure a working environment free from sexual harassment. Presumably, other local governments, as well as state governments and private sector organizations, will follow suit.

8. Responses of Fair Employment Practices Agencies to Sexual Harassment Complaints: A Report and Recommendations*

WORKING WOMEN'S INSTITUTE

Since 1975 Working Women's Institute has served as a national research/resource/action center devoted to combatting the problem of sexual harassment on the job. One of the Institute's major activities is monitoring legal developments on this issue. As a part of this effort, we mailed a questionnaire to state and local civil rights enforcement agencies throughout the country in the spring of 1977, inquiring about their practices and observations with regard to sexual harassment complaints. On the whole, the survey results showed that despite the genuine concern expressed by many fair employment practices agencies, most had not established policies and mechanisms to deal with the special requirements of sexual harassment cases.

Based on the survey responses and the Institute's own experience as a national information and referral center, we have been able to pinpoint some ways that fair employment practices agencies can be more responsive to women who approach them with sexual harassment in employment complaints. The following is a summary of our findings and recommendations.

DOCUMENTATION OF SEXUAL HARASSMENT COMPLAINTS BY AGENCIES

Responses to the questionnaire reflected a laissez-faire attitude toward the issue on the part of many agencies. Only 74 of the 540 agencies which received the questionnaire returned it. (See Table 1 for a state-by-state breakdown.) While there are undoubtedly many reasons why agencies had difficulty completing the questionnaire, this small number of responses indicates that, for the vast majority, the issue is a low priority.

Most of the 74 agencies who did fill out the survey were unable to document the numbers and types of sexual harassment complaints they had received because they could not easily locate them. Only two had kept track of sexual harassment complaints in any systematic way. More often than not, agencies simply included sexual harassment in the general category of "sex discrimination" (45 agencies) or in some category not specifically related to sex (14 agencies). The remainder of the responding agencies had not yet estab-

*Source: The survey of fair employment practices agencies was prepared for Working Women's Institute by Sherry Lederman. This report was written by Peggy Crull, Ph.D., the Research Director of Working Women's Institute. Research Series Report No. 2, Fall 1978. Copyright © 1978 Working Women's Institute, 593 Park Avenue, New York, N.Y. 10021. All rights reserved; reprinted by permission.

Table 1

NUMBER OF AGENCIES RESPONDING BY STATE[a]

	State	Number Responding		State	Number Responding
1.	Alaska	1	17.	Missouri	5
2.	Arizona	1	18.	Montana	1
3.	California	6	19.	Nebraska	1
4.	Colorado	1	20.	New Jersey	2
5.	Connecticut	2	21.	New York	7
6.	Florida	1	22.	Ohio	5
7.	Georgia	2	23.	Oklahoma	1
8.	Illinois	4	24.	Oregon	1
9.	Indiana	4	25.	Pennsylvania	2
10.	Iowa	2	26.	South Dakota	1
11.	Kansas	1	27.	Tennessee	2
12.	Kentucky	1	28.	Texas	1
13.	Maine	1	29.	Vermont	1
14.	Maryland	4	30.	Washington (State)	2
15.	Michigan	6	31.	Wisconsin	2
16.	Minnesota	1	32.	Cannot Tell	2

[a]Includes both state and local agencies as well as local offices of some state agencies

lished any practice at all for handling such complaints. *(See Table 2.)* Another reason for the difficulty in locating sexual harassment complaints is that in a majority of cases sexual harassment complaints is that in a majority of cases sexual harassment was not the primary cause of action, but was included in a broader complaint.

The absence of easily retrievable information results in sketchy and incomplete data on the incidence of sexual harassment complaints. Only 15 of the responding agencies were able to provide actual or even estimated figures on the number of complaints they had received between 1974 and 1977 (February). Forty-one agencies were aware of receiving complaints, but were unable to provide any statistics because there was no way to trace complaints. Eighteen agencies did not remember receiving any sexual harassment complaints in those years. *(See Table 3.)*

Table 2

CATEGORIES IN WHICH SEXUAL HARASSMENT COMPLAINTS ARE FILED

Category	Number of Agencies Using
Sexual harassment	2
Sex discrimination	45
Other (employment complaints, harassment, grievances, etc.)	14
No practice established	13
TOTAL AGENCIES	**74**

Table 3

AGENCY EXPERIENCE WITH COMPLAINTS

Method of Calculating Number of Complaints	Number of Agencies
Counted or estimated number	15
Recalled receiving complaints but could not estimate	41
TOTAL OF AGENCIES RECEIVING COMPLAINTS	56
Remember receiving no complaints	18
TOTAL AGENCIES	**74**

Because they did not keep specific records on sexual harassment complaints, most agencies were not able to report how many they had received. Consequently, we were not able to estimate the volume of complaints in out total sample.

FORMS OF HARASSMENT AND DEMOGRAPHIC CHARACTERISTICS OF COMPLAINANTS

The forms of harassment reported to agencies ranged from offensive comments to outright assault. The form most frequently described was somewhere in the middle of this range; women were most likely to complain about explicit sexual advances or persistant invitations. Although the harasser in these complaints was sometimes a co-worker, he was more often the boss or someone in authority. In the instance of harassment by a boss, the sexual come-ons were often accompanied by the threat of losing a job or being passed up for a promotion, a threat often carried out.

Of the approximately 25 agencies that were able to characterize the typical occupation and/or income level of their sexual harassment complainants, almost all agreed that they were concentrated in low-paying jobs. Perhaps this is, in part, a reflection of the income level of the clients of fair employment practices agencies in general, but it is also characteristic of the income level of the women who seek help from Working Women's Institute. This may indicate that a great proportion of victims of harassment are in low-income jobs or that harassment affects low-income women more severely because of their economic vulnerability. Higher income occupations in the professional and managerial categories were listed about one-fourth as often as lower income jobs.

There was little agreement among the agencies as to which *type* of occupation produced the most complaints. The category of jobs most often mentioned was clerical/secretarial, the category in which the largest number of women are employed and from which Working Women's Institute most often receives complaints. Other service jobs like waitress, cashier, bar maid, and sales clerk were listed with some frequency. Factory workers were complainants in several instances.

DISPOSITION OF CASES

Only one agency was able to provide concrete and detailed information on the disposition of its sexual harassment cases. Others did not have a way of retrieving information on this specific topic. As a result, we were not able to obtain data on the outcomes of cases, but only general impressions of what happens to complainants.

A majority of the agencies (58 out of 74) felt that hesitancy to talk about sexual harassment keeps women from contacting fair employment practices agencies in the first place. Many reported that women often make an initial call but are reluctant to file an actual complaint because they fear nervous husbands, sensational publicity, ridicule, and possible loss of jobs. One official said she suspected that the manner in which her own staff had handled some case had inadvertently discouraged some women from pursuing complaints.

Uncertainty about whether sexual harassment in employment was within the jurisdiction of fair employment practices agencies diminished the number of complaints filed. Several agencies turned away complaints because they were of the opinion that sexual harassment is not a form of sex discrimination "under the law." Among those agencies which recognized sexual harassment as sex discrimination, several commented that they thought their constituents did not file complaints because they were unaware that legal protection against sexual harassment was available.

The most complete documentation of

the disposition of cases came from the New York State Division of Human Rights. In 1976 this agency began tagging sexual harassment complaints with the intention of doing a study at a later date. In that year they counted 65 complaints, a dramatic increase over the 8 recorded in the two previous years. The Division's experience with these complaints has alerted it to the special problems of sexual harassment cases. Because the incidents tend to take place in private there are usually no witnesses, so that the case becomes the complainant's word against the respondent's. Even when there are witnesses, they may refuse to come forward for fear of losing their jobs or because they think sexual harassment is a problem "between two individuals." When the complainants are pressed for details they often feel embarassed about providing them. Because personal dynamics between people who work together are often complex, charges of sexual harassment tend to be treated with skepticism and, thus, not seriously pursued by investigators. These difficulties have convinced the Division of the need for careful examination of the procedures for handling such cases.

RECOMMENDATIONS

It is evident from this survey that agencies with civil rights enforcement responsibilities had not focussed much attention as of the spring of 1977. There are several compelling reasons for fair employment practices agencies to re-examine their current attitudes and practices with regard to sexual harassment.

There have been changes in the law; court decisions have begun to define sexual harassment as a form of sex discrimination. Studies show that sexual harassment is widespread and is a significant threat to the employment opportunities and job security of millions of working women. With increased publicity about the issue, requests for assistance from Working Women's Institute have multiplied; we expect that state and local fair employment practices agencies will face a similar situation. They need to be prepared to deal with these complaints adequately and responsibly.

One of the first steps is to better understand sexual harassment and the ways it differs from more traditional forms of sex discrimination. Sexual harassment is still widely misunderstood. Because it touches on people's concepts of sexuality, it is a highly charged, emotional issue. It also presents more difficult proof problems than usual, since the incidents are likely to occur in private and since women's credibility is frequently questioned where sexuality is concerned.

The following recommendations stem from Working Women's Institute experience in providing direct service to sexual harassment victims over the last three years and from results of the present survey. Our hope is that fair employment practices agencies will institute new procedures to enable them to be more responsive to the needs of their complainants.

1. Research indicates that sexual harassment typically and systematically happens to and disadvantages women as a group. The Federal courts, moreover, are finding it to be a violation of Title VII of the 1964 Civil Rights Act. We recommend that fair employment practices agencies follow the lead of the federal judiciary and take the initiative to include sexual harassment within their jurisdiction.

2. As the foregoing report indicates, while sexual harassment is a form of sex discrimination, it is unique in many ways. For this reason, we recommend that fair employment practices agencies devise a system for keeping separate track of sexual harassment complaints, both in those cases where it is the primary allegation and in those when it emerges as a contributing factor. This will make it possible to retrieve information readily for general research purposes and to evaluate agency procedures for handling sexual harassment cases.

3. The public needs information about some of the common forms of sexual harassment, the reasons why it is illegal, and the kind of evidence that is needed to substantiate a claim. Agencies should take on the responsibility of informing employers and employees that sexual harassment in employment is discriminatory, and of explaining to them how a claim can be filed.

4. Because sexual harassment complainants frequently feel uncomfortable when they report an incident, we recommend that agency staff, especially in-take personnel, be educated to the problem. Such training is meant to help staff be as sensitive and impartial as possible. The staff should also be trained to use new investigatory procedures, as they are adopted, to meet special needs of these types of complaints.

Until recently, women have had few places to turn where their complaints would be received with understanding. Since the time when the survey was begun, Working Women's Institute has been encouraged to hear from several agencies who have shown increased interest in this issue. The four measures we are suggesting are only a first step toward policies which will enable agencies with civil rights responsibilities to give proper attention to this long-overlooked abuse of women's right to equal employment opportunities.

9. Sexual Harassment in the Workplace—What Should the Employer Do?*

MARY D. FAUCHER
KENNETH J. McCULLOCH

The "casting couch" on which aspiring actresses enhance their chances of becoming stars may soon become a thing of the past. Producers, instead of enjoying a "fringe benefit," may find themselves being sued for sex discrimination when they suggest that the road to stardom entails a detour into the bedroom. This is because several courts have recently determined that when a supervisor makes sexual advances and conditions a promotion or the retention of a job on the acceptance of these advances, he[1] may be liable for sex discrimination under Title VII.[2] Title VII makes it an unlawful employment practice for an employer to discriminate against any individual with respect to conditions or privileges of employment on the basis of sex.

Sexual harassment on the job may take several forms. When do these various forms of sexual harassment on the job constitute sex discrimination? A supervisor may condition a promotion on fulfillment of his sexual desire, he may simply make a sexual advance, or he may verbally harass the employee by making repeated references to physical characteristics of women or use phrases like "women are illogical." The courts that have addressed the problem of sexual harassment have faced only the issue of a superior's sexual advances, acceptance of which was made the condition of a promotion or job reten-

tion. This discussion will examine those court decisions, but it will also include an analysis of other forms of sexual harassment and will offer employers faced with the problem of sexual harassment suggestions including preventing, investigating, and avoiding corporate liability for it.

Prefatory to analyzing the court decisions, it is necessary to understand problems facing the judiciary. On the one hand, courts have not desired to increase the EEOC's backlog by making every complimentary remark or flirtatious approach to a member of the opposite sex the basis for a cause of action under Title VII. On the other hand, in recent decisions the courts are increasingly recognizing that there is a point beyond which a person in a supervisory position should not be permitted to abuse his power by making a sexual demand on an employee. Thus far, in all cases that have been the subject of judicial opinion, a supervisor-subordinate relationship was involved, there was present the potential for retaliation by the supervisor whose approaches were rejected, and actual retaliatory action by such supervisor was alleged to have occurred. Apparently, as the law now stands, employees who make sexual advances to a co-worker, and thus are not in a position to retaliate should their advances be rejected, are in a much better position to continue such

*Source: From EEO Today, vol. 5 (Spring 1978), pp. 38-46. Copyright © 1978 Executive
Enterprises Publications Company, Inc. Reprinted by permission.

advances immune to the strictures of Title VII. However, for such employees we anticipate that there will develop a body of law equating their conduct to situations in which co-workers use racial epithets or make derogatory ethnic or racial remarks. In such situations, once the employer is put on notice of such conduct and is apprised of the fact that such remarks are objectionable, there arises the legal requirement for the employer to prevent such conduct. While this is not the state of the law at present, we anticipate that it will be, and that employers should administer their personnel policies now to protect themselves from liability for such conduct.

The courts initially determined that sexual propositions made by a supervisor do not give rise to a cause of action under Title VII. In *Corne v. Bausch & Lomb, Inc.*, 390 F. Supp. 161, 10 FEP Cases 289 (D. Ariz. 1975), *vacated and remanded on other grounds*, 562 F.2d 55, 15 FEP Cases 1370 (9th Cir. 1977), the plaintiffs' alleged that their supervisor's sexual advances made working conditions so onerous that they were forced to resign from their jobs. The court held that there was no cause of action under Title VII against either the supervisor or the employer, because the supervisor was satisfying a personal urge and there was no employer policy involved. The employer had no responsibility for the "verbal and physical advances of the supervisor" because these advances had no relationship to the nature of employment.[3]

In all cases following *Corne*, however, the courts have determined that the employee does have a cause of action under Title VII where the supervisor conditions career enhancement on sexual submission *and* an employer policy or employer acquiescence is involved. What constitutes an employer practice or employer acquiescence has been the central issue with which the courts have wrestled in addressing the sexual advances problem.

In *Williams v. Saxbe*, 413 F. Supp. 654, 12 FEP Cases 1092 (D.D.C. 1976), *appeal pending*, the court made a distinction between a pattern or practice of imposing a condition of sexual submission on female employees and a non-employment-related personal encounter. The court went on to state that any policy or practice of a supervisor was automatically a policy or practice of the employer. In *Miller v. Bank of America*, 418 F. Supp. 233, 13 FEP Cases 439 (N.D. Cal. 1976), *appeal pending*, the court held that the employer was not liable for the supervisor's actions because the employer had a stated policy against such conduct, the employer had a formal department to which an employee could complain about such conduct, and the plaintiff had never complained to that department. In *Barnes v. Costle*, ____ F.2d ____, 15 FEP Cases 345 (D.C. Cir. 1977), the court stated that an employer generally is chargeable for discriminatory practices of a supervisor, but where the supervisor contravenes employer policy without the employer's knowledge, and the employer rectifies the consequences when the conduct is discovered, the employer may be relieved from liability. In *Tomkins v. Public Service Electric & Gas Co.*, ____ F.2d ____, 16 FEP Cases 22 (3d Cir. 1977), the court determined that where an employer has actual or constructive knowledge of a supervisor's conduct and does not take prompt and appropriate remedial action, Title VII is violated. The Fourth Circuit agreed with that approach. *Garber v. Saxon Business Products*, ____ F.2d ____, 15 FEP Cases 344 (4th Cir. 1977).

The cases demonstrate that the plaintiff must show that the sexual advances of the supervisor were a condition of employment and were not personal, non-employment-related encounters. In all cases other than *Corne*, the plaintiffs eventually were terminated after refusing their supervisors' propositions. All courts other than the *Corne* court required actual or constructive knowledge by the employer of the supervisor's conduct, through either a direct complaint, knowledge of other supervisory personnel, or acquiescence in the termination. The courts have determined that it is not necessarily sexual advances that violate Title VII, but the retaliatory measures taken once these advances are refused, that make the conduct a condition of employment that violates Title VII.

While the law is relatively clear regarding a direct sexual proposition by a supervisor, it is less clear regarding the remarks that usually precede the direct proposition. In *Tomkins*, the plaintiff also suggested to the court that Title VII mandates that employees be afforded "a work environment free from the psychological harm flowing from an atmosphere of discrimination." The plaintiff made an analogy to EEOC decisions where violations of Title VII were found when employees were subjected to racial and ethnic epithets. The court, in a footnote, determined that because it held that the facts as alleged constituted a sex-based condition of employment, it did not need to reach this alternative theory.

Other forms of sexual harassment, such as referring to women as "girls," maintaining that "women are dumb" or that they "can't take pressure," or remarking on physical characteristics, can be analogized to situations in a racial or ethnic context where employees refer to co-workers in derogatory terms. Although one court has recently determined that the use of derogatory comments must be "excessive and opprobrious" to become discriminatory, *Caradidi* v. *Kansas City Chiefs Football Club, Inc.*, ____ F.2d ____, 15 EPD ¶ 8014 (8th Cir. 1977), most courts have generally held that such conduct does constitute racial or ethnic harassment, but that where the employer makes a diligent effort to eliminate such conduct, it is not responsible. Where the employer is on notice of the existence

of such conduct, it must at least take some positive action to avoid liability. Moreover, one court has determined that where a supervisor, in his supervisory capacity, has knowledge of the conduct, this constitutes knowledge to the employer, *Anderson* v. *Methodist Evangelical Hospital*, 4 FEP Cases (W.D. Ky. 1971), aff'd, 4 FEP Cases 987 (6th Cir. 1972), and another court has adopted the rationale that an employer is presumed responsible for any actions of its supervisory personnel. *Ostapowicz* v. *Johnson Bronze Co.*, 369 F. Supp. 522, 7 EPD ¶ 9211 (W.D. Pa. 1973), aff'd in part, rev'd in part, 541 F.2d 394 (3d Cir. 1976).

The EEOC, in making reasonable-cause determinations, has been more liberal in imposing employer liability where supervisors use racial or ethnic epithets or employ religious intimidation. For example, where a supervisor constantly preached to employees, the EEOC found reasonable cause and maintained that the employer was responsible for actions of its supervisors and that the employee had no obligation to inform higher-level management of the intimidation. The EEOC has also maintained that, at the very least, positive action is required where such action is necessary to redress the harassment, and that where such positive action is taken the supervisor's conduct will not be imputed to the employer. Generally, according to the EEOC, an employer is obliged to maintain a working environment free of racial intimidation or insult.

Repeated references to women in a derogatory manner ("girls," "women are dumb") would appear to constitute a Title VII violation where the employer takes no action, as in the racial-epithet context mentioned above. The EEOC has determined that constant referral to women as "girls" is sufficient for a reasonable-cause determination that Title VII has been violated. EEOC Decision No. 72-0679, 1973 CCH EEOC Decisions, ¶ 6324 (Dec. 27, 1971).

However, no court has discussed the applicability of this analogy, and courts would probably be reluctant to apply it. In the sexual-advances cases, courts have demonstrated their reluctance to address the issue of verbal harassment because "flirtations of the smallest order would give rise to liability." *Miller, supra*, at 441.

Nonetheless, in the racial-epithet context, the cases and EEOC determinations demonstrate that an employer is under a duty to investigate and eradicate such intimidation where it knows or should know that such conduct is occurring. Thus sexual harassment in the form of verbal abuse or sexual propositions could require the same employer action. In any event, recent case law addressing the problem of sexual harassment in the form of sexual advances as a condition of employment does imply that positive action on the part of the employer is required to avoid liability.

What constitutes positive action is not clear. The racial-epithet cases have held that a diligent investigation of complaints by the employer is sufficient. Certainly, the employer must do something. In *Miller*, the employer maintained a policy of preventing and prohibiting moral misconduct, including sexual advances, and calling for suspension, dismissal, and/or reprimand where this policy was contravened. The company also had an employee relations department to which complaints could be made and through which investigations were conducted. The court appeared to approve of this system, and because the employee alleging the advances did not take advantage of it, the court dismissed her complaint.

Moreover, the concurring opinion in *Barnes* suggests preventive measures by which the employer can avoid derivative liability: (1) post its policy against sexual harassment, (2) provide a workable mechanism for the prompt reporting of complaints, (3) include within this mechanism a rapid warning for the supervisor involved, and (4) afford the

opportunity for the complainant to remain anonymous.

All the foregoing suggests that the intelligent employer should set up some kind of mechanism to handle complaints of sexual harassment. This need not be a separate apparatus, but could be made part of a department addressed to complaints of discrimination generally. Most companies already have at least informal procedures for processing complaints of employee mistreatment, but the development of a formal system appears warranted, in the discrimination area in general and in the area of sexual harassment in particular. Sometimes a sexual advance may not be offensive, and sexual liaisons between employees may not necessarily originate in the workplace. Nevertheless, complaints may arise from such situations, and a formal mechanism for handling such complaints will serve to weed out unfounded charges.

The investigatory and remedial action of an employer also raises problems that warrant a formalized procedure. Apart from the investigation, what form should the reprimand take—a warning, a note in the personnel file, or something else? If, after the investigation, the charges appear supported, the warning might be coupled with a determination that a second charge would mandate immediate suspension or dismissal. Alternatively, a demotion might be in order. The cases and EEOC decisions emphasize that a diligent investigation is required, but what if the investigation fails to reveal anything? This situation is very likely to arise where the case boils down to the word of the employee against the word of the supervisor. Where the investigation shows no foundation for the charge, other than the complaint itself, should the supervisor still receive a reprimand in some form? Obviously, some standard procedures should be set up to afford consistency and to demonstrate diligence on the part of the employer, but if an investigation cannot confirm the allegation, no reference to the allegation should be included in the personnel file of the accused employee, and no dissemination of the accusation should take place.

It should be reiterated that the cases involving sexual harassment have alleged a sexual advance by a supervisor to a subordinate and retaliatory action by the supervisor for refusal. This is a separate problem from the situation where an advance is made by one employee to another. In that situation it is unclear whether a sexual advance, in and of itself, constitutes sex discrimination. Courts have maintained that it is not the sexual advance, but the retaliatory action, that constitutes sex discrimination. However, in the case of advances by employees, an analogy can be made to those cases where co-workers used racial epithets or derogatory ethnic remarks. The authors feel that the courts eventually will apply such an analogy to sexual harassment by co-workers, and thus it would be wise to include in the investigatory mechanism the opportunity to complain of sexual advances alone. This would allow complaints to be made before damaging retaliatory action could be taken. Also, where co-workers are involved, it would allow the employer to put an end to the offensive conduct. As an example of such a comprehensive policy, the company in *Miller* prohibited sexual advances between *any* employees, not just between supervisors and employees working under them.

Obviously, problems peculiar to the individual fact situation may arise that require tailor-made remedies short of suspension or dismissal, such as transfer, warning, or some other kind of reprimand. Formal procedures, however, will help to create a fair system for addressing the problem and allow for reasonable resolution of complaints. What should be emphasized is that some mechanism should be developed, because sexual harassment, at least in the form of sexual advances by supervisors and retaliatory action for refusal, is a

violation of Title VII, and therefore an employer is under an obligation to attempt to prevent it and to remedy it if it occurs.

There follow a sample notice that incorporates the philosophy of the courts in this legal area, and a flow chart [p. 91] that delineates the manner in which, at least for the present, employers might react to problems in this area.

Poster

OUR COURTS HAVE DECIDED THAT RACIAL, ETHNIC, RELIGIOUS, OR SEXUAL HARASSMENT ON THE JOB IS AGAINST THE LAW. THIS COMPANY PROHIBITS VERBAL AND PHYSICAL HARASSMENT OF ITS EMPLOYEES BASED ON RACE, NATIONAL ORIGIN, RELIGION, OR SEX.

Any employee subjected to such harassment should file a complaint with the Supervisor of Personnel.

NOTES

1. The male pronoun is used simply for convenience. This discussion is equally applicable to the case where a female supervisor makes sexual advances to a male employee.

2. Title VII of the Civil Rights Act of 1964, *as amended,* 42 U.S.C. §§ 2000e *et seq.*

3. The authors believe that the *Corne* decision will be reversed when the Ninth Circuit reviews the case on the merits. The case was remanded to the District Court to correct a jurisdictional defect in the plaintiff's case, and the Ninth Circuit would not have done this had it intended to affirm. See *Crosslin* v. *Mountain States Tel. & Tel. Co.,* 4 EPD ¶ 7577 (D. Ariz. 1971).

CHART

Possible Procedure for Processing Complaints:
1. Post notice of policy (including prohibitions of harassment by ANY employees)
2. Complaint —— made to proper department/party
       made to supervisory pesonnel and referred to proper department/party

Re: advances/harassment by supervisors   Re: advances/harassment by co-workers (based on racial-epithet cases)

3. Investigation
  a. Interview with complainant
  b. Interview with accused
  c. Check of personnel files
    i. Evidence of prior friction between parties
    ii. Previous complaints
    iii. Work records
  d. Interviews with witnesses/possible witnesses

4. Action to be taken
  a. No foundation other than complaint

No record in accused's file; no dissemination of charge   Reiteration of policy against harassment; general announcement

  b. Some foundation

Warning/notation in file   Warning/disciplinary slip
  —Warning coupled with automatic suspension upon second complaint
  —Reprimand coupled with automatic suspension upon second complaint
  —Reprimand/threat of suspension
  c. Solid foundation for charge
  —Demotion
  —Suspension
  —Dismissal
  —Restoration of work record of complaining employee

10. Action Plans for Management and Unions*

CONSTANCE BACKHOUSE
LEAH COHEN

A. MANAGEMENT AND SEXUAL HARASSMENT

A CASE FOR ACTION

Most male managers we interviewed either denied that sexual harassment was a problem or were aware of only a few isolated incidents. All of the female managers acknowledged that sexual harassment was a definite occupational hazard for women in the workplace. Most of the female managers had had first-hand experience with sexual harassment during their careers. Their success in dealing with it was uniformly limited, since their senior management was not prepared to take any action, unless it involved transferring or firing the female victim. With a few exceptions they concluded that a female victim of sexual harassment was in a "no-win" situation. Her only real option, they believed, was to look for another job at the first signs.

Since female managers are few and far between in most organizational structures, it is understandable that their influence is marginal. There is also an element of fear—fear that if they push too hard, their own jobs may be in jeopardy.

What we are left with is male indifference and female sympathy mingled with justifiable fear. However, management as a whole has a definite vested interest in addressing itself to the problem of sexual harassment. Women are and will increasingly become an integral part of the workplace. They are irrevocably in the workplace as fullfledged participants. Their own perceptions of how they are victimized and discriminated against will become crystallized in the next while.

In order to achieve the over-all organizational objectives of high productivity and continual expansion, a stable, relatively contented workforce is a prime prerequisite. If sexual harassment is a rampant feature within a hierarchy, the result is a high female turnover and a poisoned working environment. Office morale as a whole suffers, and with it follows a definite plunge in productivity.

Even if the victims of sexual harassment do not have the option of quitting their jobs, our research indicates that they lose a considerable amount of time due to sickness. Sexual harassment syndrome, as we have mentioned previously, manifests itself in a variety of physical and psychological ailments. Nervous, unhappy employees eventually lose interest in their jobs and may ultimately grow to hate work itself.

Most institutions today are aware that they have an obligation to promote what is commonly called "corporate responsibility." The public and the media are constantly scrutinizing corporate practices and have been known to switch products and services when a business enterprise is exposed as a per-

*Source: From The Secret Oppression: Sexual Harassment of Working Women by Constance Backhouse and Leah Cohen, chapter 10, pp. 184-93. Reprinted by permission of Macmillan of Canada.

petrator of unfair practices. But on a more immediate level, good corporate policy demands the promotion of amiable employer-employee relations.

Employees must trust that their organization will administer corporate justice. If not, the victims of sexual harassment may choose a legal remedy outside the corporation. Then the corporation is almost assuredly open to the glare of publicity. The press will paint a picture of corporate complicity in female exploitation. Once a corporation is labelled with this image, it will become difficult to attract female employees seeking long-term careers.

If female employees are so dispensable that this is hardly an organizational concern, consider the cost to the corporation in key male employees. As women begin to speak up about sexual harassment, the male perpetrators' careers become at risk. The organizational investment in male harassers can be considerable. Management would be wise for this reason alone to take issue with sexual harassment.

Sexual harassment is an incendiary issue, smouldering beneath the surface. Avoidance is always a disastrous approach. There are a number of definite steps that management can take to ensure that the incidence of sexual harassment is dramatically reduced. Coupled with this is the need to devise tactical measures to deal effectively with perpetrators of sexual harassment. We have prepared a ten-point plan for management. This plan incorporates both the principles of prevention and positive intervention.

TEN-POINT PLAN FOR MANAGEMENT
1. *Corporate blue letter.* As with all corporate policies, a corporate statement condemning the practice of sexual harassment must have the strong endorsement of *all* the chief officers. The corporate blue letter should define sexual harassment and clearly state that such behaviour is *unacceptable.* This letter should be posted on all bulletin

boards, reprinted in any in-house publications, and placed in the manager's manual.

2. *Management training sessions.* Companies are beginning to respond to occupational hazards such as alcoholism and drug addiction with educational programs. Sexual harassment is a problem of the same magnitude. A special educational program should be designed for the benefit of management to explain more fully the corporation's stance on sexual harassment. The emphasis should be that sexual harassment is disastrous behaviour for managers, constituting a case of coercion which could cost the manager his career.

3. *Branch meetings.* To supplement the special training sessions and to demonstrate the seriousness with which the corporation views acts of sexual harassment, special branch meetings should be held where the branch director or supervisor issues the corporate directive in more precise terms and invites a dialogue to avoid any misconceptions.

4. *Conduct an employee survey.* Since sexual harassment is such a secretive and potentially explosive issue, consider conducting a survey amongst your employees. Promise employees anonymity and confidentiality. Be careful to word the survey in such a way that you cover the whole range of behaviour and the consequences that flow from sexual harassment to the victim. The results of the survey should be posted and printed for distribution.

5. *Orientation sessions for new employees.* New employees should be advised of company policy on sexual harassment at their orientation session. They should also be made aware that their complaints will be treated seriously.

6. *Establish an investigative procedure.* The first step in dealing with a complaint of sexual harassment is to assure the victim that her job is not in jeopardy and that she is not on trial.

Advise the victim to document all incidents relating to the sexual harassment. Encourage her to enlist the support of witnesses, if she has any. Search for other victims, particularly if the harasser has a history of firing female subordinates or his female subordinates regularly resign.

The moment you approach the harasser, the victim is in greater jeopardy. So if you choose to proceed this way, warn the harasser that a complaint has been lodged and he is under surveillance. Make it very clear that sexual harassment is coercive and deeply offensive to the victim, as well as an invasion of her civil liberties.

7. *Protect the victim.* Sexual harassment by its very nature does not lend itself to normal rules of investigative procedure. The victim, if left unprotected, is open to reprisals from her harasser. He is in a position to make her working environment intolerable. As a result she may become both physically and psychologically ill.

Offer the woman the use of the corporation's counselling facilities; assure her that her job is secure; and determine if it is possible to move her harasser. If not, try to transfer her.

8. *Set out a disciplinary agenda.* There are a range of disciplinary measures that management has at its disposal. Consideration should be given to whether or not this is the first complaint, to the seriousness of the offense, to the length of service, and to the job performance of the harasser. The following seven steps are progressively harsh, ultimately leading to the harasser's dismissal.

1. Issue a warning.
2. Insist on counselling for the harasser.
3. Transfer the harasser.
4. Withhold a promotion or work assignment.
5. Lower performance rating.
6. Put on probation.
7. Fire.

9. *Utilize outside consultants.* Try to avoid the pitfalls of conducting a sexist investigation where the victim is put on trial. Consider the use of outside consultants. Since sexual harassment is a hierarchical, power-based problem, the victim will feel more comfortable with an outside consultant who is not a part of the organizational structure. She will also be more confident that she will receive a fair hearing.

10. *Deal with the harasser in a productive fashion.* When you issue your first warning to the perpetrator of sexual harassment, explain the implications of his behaviour to him. By the time you approach him, be prepared to move him or his victim. Try to isolate the man, if possible. Failing this, do not attempt to solve the problem by replacing the victim with a plain or older woman. Our research indicates that the perpetrators of sexual harassment are exercising their power, not expressing desire. Warn the new woman of her boss's proclivities and encourage her to report any further incidents of sexual harassment.

If your warning fails and all subsequent deterrents fail, fire him. Not doing so leaves the corporation open to lawsuits, public inquiries, and bad press.

B. UNIONS AND SEXUAL HARASSMENT

A FIRST-RATE ORGANIZING TOOL

Historically unions have fought courageously to improve the lot of working men and women. Striving to obtain a fair share of the profits generated by the labour of the workers, they stood in the forefront of progressive social change. Unions have clearly defined their role to protect workers from exploitation, and have taken aggressive action to fulfil their mandate.

Sexual harassment is an exploitative practice which creates intolerable working conditions for women. The issue of sexual harassment is no less important than the traditional issues unions have fought for—wages, benefits, occupational health, and safety. Sexual harassment is a pervasive problem which dramatically affects vast numbers of rank and file workers. If unions are to accomplish their goal of ending exploitation and injustice in the workplace, they must address this matter.

In the past there have been some incidents within the trade union movement of discrimination against women members. Many union officials today sincerely wish to redress these wrongs. In both Canada and the United States legislation stipulates that unions have a duty to represent all of their members fairly. A number of unions are now openly encouraging their women members to play a more active role in union affairs. Dealing with the problems of sexual harassment in the workforce may prove an effective way of catching and holding the interest of female union members.

Trade unions are not completely free of sexual harassers themselves. Many sexual harassers are not managers, but male union members. By taking swift and direct action to oppose sexual harassment from supervisors and managers, unions will set an instructive example for their own membership. Where they develop educational programs and strict policies condemning sexual harassment, this will help to purge sexual harassment from within their own ranks.

Finally, sexual harassment provides a unique tool in aid of union organizing campaigns. Nearly nine out of ten working women report they have experienced sexual harassment; almost half state they or a woman they know have quit a job or been fired because of sexual harassment on the job. The tragedy is that until recently, although so many women were adversely affected by sexual harassment, there was little discussion between victims. Now that sexual harassment is becoming a topic of common conversation, women on the job will be able to communicate more frankly about their problems. As they meet to discuss their mutual frustrations with sexual harassment, they will natu-rally begin to share their concerns about wages, job benefits, etc. Unionization is an obvious vehicle they can use to improve their situation.

Unions have had difficulties organizing women employees. Large sectors of the female workforce remain unorganized. Sexual harassment could be the key issue to foster communication amongst women workers and collective action to redress the manifold injustices inflicted on women at work.

TEN-POINT PLAN FOR UNIONS

1. *Discuss sexual harassment in union organizing campaigns.* Train union organizers to recognize sexual harassment and what it means. Design campaign literature to deal with sexual harassment, and indicate how a union can help victims. Use discussions of sexual harassment to begin the communication process about the need for unions. Union representatives should develop expertise in this area, and endeavour to sit on public panels and in all public forums where sexual harassment is discussed. The benefits a union can provide working women should be pointed out, and the unionization process should be outlined to all such audiences.

2. *Education of union personnel.* It is critical to provide comprehensive education about sexual harassment to union officials and members. The topic can be addressed at union meetings and conferences and in union publications and brochures. Sexual harassment should be defined, strategies for prevention should be examined, and a full discussion should be held of remedies for sexual harassment victims and the union's role in obtaining such remedies. Special educational sessions can be held for new female union members outlining the protections that the union can provide in this area. The union can demand that management be required to undergo similar education campaigns.

3. *Contract negotiations.* When it comes time to bargain for a new con-

tract, the existing union contract should be examined carefully to determine whether it prohibits sexual harassment and provides adequate remedies. Clauses which outlaw discrimination on the basis of sex and provide that there can be no discharge or discipline without just cause go some way toward providing protection, but a comprehensive clause dealing with sexual harassment specifically is more satisfactory.

Consider whether the normal grievance procedure is adequate for sexual harassment complaints or whether special requirements should be set out. For example, it might be better to have a reverse onus of proof in sexual harassment cases. Due to the problems of proving sexual harassment, it could be stated in the contract that once a woman employee complained of sexual harassment, the onus shifted to the alleged harasser to disprove the complaint.

During the contract negotiations, bargain for provisions which specifically prohibit sexual harassment and provide protection to victims of such behaviour. Since many women are forced to quit their jobs, the contract should extend protection to these women in addition to women who are fired—a carefully worded constructive dismissal clause should be included in the contract. These clauses provide that women do not have to wait to be fired before they can seek redress. If working conditions are made intolerable, women are entitled to interpret them in the same manner as a firing, and leave the job. The arbitrator who interprets the contract clause will evaluate the woman's story. If she can prove that working conditions were made intolerable, the arbitrator will "construct" a dismissal and provide a remedy for sexual harassment.

4. *Utilize the grievance procedure.* Once the contract covers sexual harassment, encourage victims to come forward with grievances. Actively solicit these complaints in union publications and at union meetings. Once a griev-

ance is lodged, treat it seriously and make it a priority to argue the case, acting as the woman's advocate throughout the various stages of the grievance process, to arbitration if necessary. Encourage sexual harassment victims to make grievance as groups. A number of sexual harassment victims grieving against one manager will have a much greater chance for success than will an individual grievor. Since many sexual harassers are repeaters, when an isolated complaint is made, investigate to determine whether there have been any previous victims. If so, urge them to support the initial grievance. In acting with management to select arbitrators to hear sexual harassment grievances, use caution in choosing arbitrators who are unlikely to be guilty of sexual harassment themselves.

5. *Assist women in fighting sexual harassment in other forums.* If the contract does not deal adequately with sexual harassment, women victims may be better advised to take their complaints to government agencies (such as human rights commissions, the EEOC, etc.) or the courts, rather than to utilize the grievance procedure. Unions can take an active role in assisting women who are willing to pursue these outside remedies. They can act as an advocate, helping women to put together a compelling case with as much evidence as can be marshalled. Unions have traditionally provided these kinds of services to members seeking unemployment insurance, workmen's compensation, etc. This assistance should be extended to victims of sexual harassment seeking compensation from government tribunals and courts. Unions can provide legal counsel or perform a referral service by referring women victims to sympathetic, knowledgeable lawyers.

6. *Other tactics.* There are a variety of more informal techniques that can be employed where women employees are reluctant to pursue a grievance or outside legal remedies. These women can be encouraged to make confidential, in-

formal complaints to union officials. The union representatives can then warn other union members about such harassers and solicit the assistance of the membership in reporting further incidents. In some cases it may be beneficial to put the harasser on notice that his actions have not gone ignored and that further harassment will result in formal grievances.

Where the formal grievance procedure and these other informal tactics fail to provide relief, the union can consider making the problem public. Publicity in the media about sexual harassment at a specific organization would raise corporate eyebrows far and wide and could result in the organization's being forced to take immediate corrective action.

7. *Lobbying.* Legislative change is needed to address the problems of sexual harassment. Political pressure will be required to push such reforms through the legislatures. Unions can pass local resolutions advocating legal reforms and direct these to the attention of public officials and politicians. Letterwriting campaigns, media gimmicks, and other lobbying techniques can be employed to apply pressure upon elected officials for amendments to the appropriate legislation.

8. *The trades: a special work environment.* Women are increasingly moving into nontraditional work areas—construction, mechanics, electronics, and other trades. There they are facing extreme and virulent forms of sexual harassment. Most trade occupations are unionized, and the unions in this field hold a great degree of control over the operations of contractors. The union leadership could take a special role in protecting women from sexual harassment on nontraditional worksites. Incoming women employees could be given strategic training on sexual harassment, and union officials could furnish them with active support and assistance in coping with the problems caused by this adverse defensive reaction by male supervisors and co-workers. Contract language should be tightened up to deal with sexual harassment, educational programs could be directed at female and male employees and managers, and union hiring-hall procedures could be utilized to enforce sanctions against notorious harassers.

9. *Encourage women to participate in union affairs.* Experience indicates that unions which have an active female membership, with women in positions of authority inside the union structure, have a better record on sexual harassment cases. Such unions tend to understand the problem more clearly and to act more effectively on complaints. In an effort to root out this coercive behaviour, unions should actively seek greater participation in their internal affairs from women members.

10. *Conduct research.* For years sexual harassment has remained a hidden, secret oppression. Out of fear and a realization that complaints would not be treated fairly, women have been reluctant to speak up. Unions are in a unique position to bring forward detailed information concerning the nature and extent of this problem. Extensive surveys and indepth research could be conducted amongst union members to uncover the reality of sexual harassment facing working women. Case studies could be explored to determine which strategies proved successful in dealing with sexual harassment. Those findings could be incorporated into educational documentaries and written material for distribution to union members and the public at large.

11. Policy Statement and Definition on Sexual Harassment*

U.S. OFFICE OF PERSONNEL MANAGEMENT

December 12, 1979

MEMORANDUM TO HEADS OF DEPARTMENTS AND INDEPENDENT AGENCIES

SUBJECT: Policy Statement and Definition on Sexual Harassment

This memorandum transmits the Office of Personnel Management's policy statement on sexual harassment which is applicable to each Federal agency and department. The policy statement also includes the specific definition of sexual harassment which should be utilized in addressing this issue.

The Subcommittee on Investigations of the Committee on Post Office and Civil Service has held hearings on the problem of sexual harassment within the Federal sector. The Office of Personnel Management was requested by Chairman James M. Hanley to assist in the effort to curtail sexual harassment by issuing a policy statement which made clear that sexual harassment undermines the integrity of the Federal Government and will not be condoned. Merit system principles require that all employees be allowed to work in an environment free from sexual harassment.

I am recommending that each of you take a leadership role by initiating the following actions:

    1. Issue a very strong management statement clearly defining the policy of the Federal Government as an employer with regard to sexual harassment;

    2. Emphasize this policy as part of new employee orientation covering the merit principles and the code of conduct; and

    3. Make employees aware of the avenues for seeking redress, and the actions that will be taken against employees violating the policy.

ALAN K. CAMPBELL
DIRECTOR

---

*Source: U.S. Office of Personnel Management, "Memorandum to Heads of Departments and Independent Agencies—Subject: Policy Statement and Definition of Sexual Harassment" (December 12, 1979).

POLICY STATEMENT AND DEFINITION ON SEXUAL HARASSMENT

Federal employees have a grave responsibility under the Federal code of conduct and ethics for maintaining high standards of honesty, integrity, impartiality and conduct to assure proper performance of the Government's business and the maintenance of confidence of the American people. Any employee conduct which violates this code cannot be condoned.

Sexual harassment is a form of employee misconduct which undermines the integrity of the employment relationship. All employees must be allowed to work in an environment free from unsolicited and unwelcome sexual overtures. Sexual harassment debilitates morale and interferes in the work productivity of its victims and co-workers.

Sexual harassment is a prohibited personnel practice when it results in discrimination for or against an employee on the basis of conduct not related to performance, such as the taking or refusal to take a personnel action, including promotion of employees who submit to sexual advances or refusal to promote employees who resist or protest sexual overtures.

Specifically, sexual harassment is deliberate or repeated unsolicited verbal comments, gestures, or physical contact of a sexual nature which are unwelcome.

Within the Federal Government, a supervisor who uses implicit or explicit coercive sexual behavior to control, influence, or affect the career, salary, or job of an employee is engaging in sexual harassment. Similarly, an employee of an agency who behaves in this manner in the process of conducting agency business is engaging in sexual harassment.

Finally, any employee who participates in deliberate or repeated unsolicited verbal comments, gestures, or physical contact of a sexual nature which are unwelcome and interfere in work productivity is also engaging in sexual harassment.

It is the policy of the Office of Personnel Management (OPM) that sexual harassment is unacceptable conduct in the workplace and will not be condoned. Personnel management within the Federal sector shall be implemented free from prohibited personnel practices and consistent with merit system principles, as outlined in the provisions of the Civil Service Reform Act of 1978. All Federal employees should avoid conduct which undermines these merit principles. At the same time, it is not the intent of OPM to regulate the social interaction or relationships freely entered into by Federal employees.

Complaints of harassment should be examined impartially and resolved promptly. The Equal Employment Opportunity Commission will be issuing a directive that will define sexual harassment prohibited by Title VII of the Civil Rights Act and distinguish it from related behavior which does not violate Title VII.

12. A Federal Response to Sexual Harassment: Policy-Making at Johnson Space Center, NASA*

JOSEPH D. ATKINSON, JR.
DIANNE R. LAYDEN

Sexual harassment at the American workplace has received minimal attention until recently, perhaps because it has been regarded only as "business as usual," and perhaps because of the absence of protests by women, whose participation in the civilian labor force was 28 percent in 1947, 32 percent in 1955, and 37 percent in 1967.[1] It is likely that contemporary concern is the result of a continuing increase in female participation in employment—42 percent in 1979,[2] the passage of the Civil Rights Act of 1964, as amended, which provides redress for women, minorities, and others in the event of discriminatory acts by employers, and, generally, increased awareness of those personnel practices which have an adverse impact on members of the protected groups. As its victims seek enforcement of the civil rights laws, call attention to its direct impact on the rights of women, and succeed in securing redress, social views on sexual harassment will also change and, hopefully, diminish the tacit social support which once sanctioned, if not encouraged, its practice in American employment.

As the nation's largest single employer, the Federal government often perceives itself as having the obligation to demonstrate exemplary conduct to other employers. The Federal government employs more than two and one-half million full-time civilians, of whom 876,000, or 32 percent, are women.[3] As Ruth T. Prokop, Chairperson, Merit Systems Protection Board, points out,

> [i]f sexual harassment in the Federal Government is found to be as pervasive a practice as informal studies indicate, the potential for abuse is enormous.[4]

CONGRESSIONAL INTEREST

During recent months, the subject of sexual harassment in Federal employment has received considerable attention from the news media, unions, human rights organizations, Federal managers, and from Congressman James M. Hanley's Subcommittee on Investigations, which conducted hearings on this issue in October and November, 1979.[5] Chairman Hanley initiated an investigation of the problem in the Federal workplace as a result of allegations of its widespread existence within the Department of Housing and Urban Development (HUD). These allegations, based on an unofficial survey conducted by a HUD employee, were made public July 27, 1979.[6] The HUD incident may be viewed as merely prologue, inasmuch as the hearings resulted in allegations of violations in other agencies.

To manage this problem effectively, it became apparent that certain critical

*Source: Written specifically for this book. Copyright © 1980 Moore Publishing Company, Inc.

administrative mechanisms were necessary which were lacking in the existing Federal personnel management system, as follows:

1. A clear definition of sexual harassment and a declaration that it is a prohibited practice as well as a violation of merit system principles;
2. an official survey, scientifically constructed, providing data on the magnitude of the problem and assistance in determining what steps should be taken; and
3. an effective and expeditious system for administration and enforcement of the Federal laws prohibiting discrimination in employment.

Among the many witnesses who testified before the Subcommittee, three represented Federal agencies which were in a position to direct government-wide action to prevent or to remedy the sexual harassment problem—Alan K. Campbell, Director, Office of Personnel Management (OPM); Eleanor Holmes Norton, Chair, Equal Employment Opportunity Commission (EEOC); and Ruth T. Prokop, Chairperson, Merit Systems Protection Board (MSPB).

Preliminary investigations by the Subcommittee revealed that most agencies avoided issuing a policy statement on sexual harassment, as if to do so would admit that it existed.[7] In September and October, 1979, however, a few agencies released their own definitions of sexual harassment with a policy statement that it would not be condoned within their respective agencies. While their intentions and actions were commendable, the agency definitions varied so widely that their use could result only in added confusion in managing an already complex personnel problem. To correct this situation, the Subcommittee requested that Campbell develop a definition and policy statement which would be uniformly applicable to all Federal agencies and departments.[8] This would represent the initial critical step toward alleviating the problem, after which other administrative actions could take place.

POLICY FORMULATION FOR THE EXECUTIVE BRANCH

The Office of Personnel Management (OPM) is responsible for the administration of the Federal merit system, including personnel policy development and employee training, for the Executive branch of the Federal government.

On December 12, 1979, Alan K. Campbell, Director, issued a memorandum to heads of departments and independent agencies transmitting the "Policy Statement and Definition on Sexual Harassment".[9] His memo stated that the policy statement included the following specific definition which should be utilized in addressing this issue:

Specifically, sexual harassment is deliberate or repeated unsolicited verbal comments, gestures, or physical contact of a sexual nature which are unwelcome.

Regarding Federal policy, Campbell's issuance further stated:

It is the policy of the Office of Personnel Management (OPM) that sexual harassment is unacceptable conduct in the workplace and will not be condoned . . . At the same time it is not the intent of OPM to regulate the social interaction or relationships freely entered into by Federal employees.

In his testimony before the Subcommittee, he emphasized that one of the considerations in developing a definition was to make it as broad as possible to cover many forms of sexual harassment, yet narrow enough to reduce frivolous complaints.[10] Further, Campbell stated that it is premature and impractical to link specific penalties (such as admonishment, reprimand, suspension, and dismissal) to a given set of sexual harassment behaviors, the rationale being that (1) there is not sufficient experience with the application of specific penalties to specific actions in cases of sexual harassment, and (2) the Merit Systems Protection Board is the agency responsible for deciding when an action is a prohibited personnel practice.[11]

In addition to the definition and policy statement, OPM has developed a training module for the conduct of workshops for both supervisory and non-supervisory employees. The objectives of the training program are to inform employees of Federal policy, of the differing perceptions of harassing behavior, of the impact of harassment on morale and productivity, and available courses of action if harassment is experienced or observed.

THE ROLE OF THE EEOC

The mandate of the Equal Employment Opportunity Commission (EEOC) is the enforcement of the Civil Rights Act of 1964, as amended, *i.e.*, the investigation of charges alleging discrimination and the issuance of rulings on the merits of those charges, in accordance with Title VII, as amended, which prohibits discrimination on the basis of race, color, national origin, religion, age, handicap, or sex (the 1972 amendment prohibits sex discrimination).

On April 11, 1980, EEOC published in the *Federal Register* an interim amendment to the guidelines on sex discrimination, which specifically addresses sexual harassment. As Eleanor Holmes Norton, Chair, stated the issue to the Subcommittee:

[EEOC] pioneered the development of Title VII case law on sexual harassment . . . We have taken the position that sexual harassment is discrimination and violates Section 703(a) of Title VII which prohibits the imposition of an onerous condition of employment upon an individual because of that person's sex.[12]

It is important to note that sexual harassment is not classified as an additional protected category. EEOC prohibits its practice under the provisions governing sex discrimination, just as harassment on the basis of race, color, national origin, religion, or age is prohibited. Norton stated further:

We have insisted that sexual discrimination, like racial discrimination, generates a

psychologically harmful atmosphere and that Title VII guarantees female employees . . . a working environment free of (discriminatory) intimidation . . . Our position has now been generally sanctioned in the courts.[13]

EEOC believes that the additional guidelines will further clarify its position, encourage employers to take affirmative action to eliminate sexual harassment, and re-emphasize that employers have been and continue to be responsible for eliminating this practice.[14] Further, EEOC has taken the position that the employer clearly is liable for the acts of its supervisory employees or agents, regardless of whether the acts were authorized or forbidden by the employer, and regardless of whether the employer knew or didn't know of their occurrence,[15] although the Federal courts do not uniformly support the EEOC position.[16]

Under its expanded charter for affirmative action planning for all Federal agencies, EEOC is utilizing this new responsibility as a vehicle for eliminating this troublesome practice by (1) requiring that their affirmative action plans state that employees will be informed that coercive sexual advances are prohibited, and that specific steps detailed in the plan will be taken to make the work environment free of sexual intimidation; and (2) designing a training module on sexual harassment for agency Equal Employment Opportunity (EEO) personnel, and working with OPM to include this subject in training programs for new and incumbent supervisory staff.

In addition, EEOC is issuing directives specifically to agency EEO Counselors and Federal Women's Program Managers requesting the inclusion of sexual harassment information in their programmatic initiatives. Both Norton and Campbell firmly believe that the answer to eliminating sexual harassment lies in its prevention rather than its cure.[17]

In addition to the previously mentioned forms of sexual harassment which are considered sex discrimination within the meaning of Title VII, other types of behavior which could occur as a result of its practice are also prohibited, including:

- Considering any recommendation regarding an employee other than one based on the merits of the individual's performance;
- granting any preference not otherwise available by law for the purpose of improving or injuring the prospects of any particular applicant for employment;
- taking or failing to take a personnel action in reprisal for revealing a violation of law, rule, or regulation (including sexual harassment); and
- discrimination on the basis of conduct which does not adversely affect performance.[18]

DEFINING THE PROBLEM: THE MSPB SURVEY

The third key organization in the policy-making process is the Merit Systems Protection Board (MSPB). Its general mandate is to safeguard the merit system and individual employees against abuses and unfair personnel actions in its role of merit system appellate authority.

Ruth T. Prokop, Chairperson, clearly described the injurious effect of sexual harassment on the merit system, in her testimony before the Subcommittee:

When sexual harassment is permitted to dictate which employee is promoted or demoted, which employee is retained or dismissed, or whether an employee can effectively perform the job, there has been a failure to protect these merit principles. Notions of merit forbid consideration of who rejects and who submits to the unwanted advances of a supervisor.[19]

Because existing statistical surveys were informal and limited in scope, the Subcommittee requested MSPB to initiate a comprehensive survey of the Federal workforce to determine how widespread the practice of sexual harassment is. MSPB could find no indications that a scientifically constructed survey had ever been conducted at any American workplace which would enable MSPB to gauge the nature and magnitude of the problem.[20] Thus, this survey may represent the first definitive study on the subject of sexual harassment in the United States.

MSPB is now conducting (May, 1980) a random survey of approximately 20,000 female and male employees representing a cross-section of the Federal workforce on certain critical issues, including:

- The degree to which sexual harassment is occurring within the Federal workplace, its manifestations, and frequency;
- whether the victims (or perpetrators) are found in disproportionate numbers within certain agencies, job classifications, geographic locations, racial categories, age brackets, educational levels, grade levels, etc.;
- what kinds of behavior are perceived to constitute sexual harassment and whether the attitudes of men and women differ in this respect;
- what forms of express or implied leverage have been used by harassers to reward or punish their victims;
- the impact of sexual harassment on its victims in terms of job turnover, work performance, physical or emotional condition, and financial or career well-being; and
- its effect on the morale and productivity of the immediate work group.[21]

The major guidelines for the survey's development and administration are the use of the OPM definition as the basis for the formulation of survey questions, and its distribution and collection so as to assure the respondents' anonymity and privacy.

When the responses have been collected, they will be analyzed, largely by computer, to produce both quantitative information describing the magnitude of the problem, as well as descriptive information (such as agency, job classification, educational level, and age) about persons who have been subject to or who have engaged in sexual harassment. MSPB may then be able to compare trends in its occurrence to patterns of promotion and other benchmarks of job advancement or security, in order to learn more about its circumstances and effects.

The survey findings will comprise the major portion of the MSPB report. In addition, it is expected that the report will also include:

• A summary of the legal aspects of the sexual harassment issue;

• a summary of remedies currently available within the Federal government, with recommendations for change, if appropriate; and

• a detailed appendix of statistical charts and other useful data derived from survey results.

Although the MSPB study is still in progress, the general data available is sufficient to indicate that it is perceived to be a problem for some women; that, as a result, it adversely affects their employment opportunities, professional development, and sense of security at the workplace; and that women have been reluctant to complain, in the belief that such action either would be futile or would result in personal embarrassment or retaliation by the accused or the employer. MSPB anticipates that its report will be released during 1980, and that its survey will withstand the scrutiny of observers and critics as the basis for additional policy-making, if necessary to deter the practice of sexual harassment at the Federal workplace.

POLICY IMPLEMENTATION AT NASA: THE AGENCY POSITION

The National Aeronautics and Space Administration (NASA) was established in 1958 to conduct space and aeronautics activities, to include aeronautical and space research, technology, and utilization. NASA maintains Headquarters Offices in Washington, D.C., and nine major field organizations, or Centers, throughout the United States.

On April 29, 1980, Dr. Robert A. Frosch, Administrator, issued the "Policy Statement on Sexual Harassment" to Officials-in-Charge of Headquarters Offices and Center Directors,[22] which adopts the OPM definition and policy statement and directs agency-wide compliance with the EEOC interim guidelines, as follows:

I wish to reaffirm our NASA policy that discrimination on the basis of color, race, religion, sex, national origin, age or handicap is unlawful and therefore unacceptable. Sexual harassment is a form of sex discrimination and thus is a prohibited personnel practice which will not be tolerated in the NASA workplace . . . In addition, the . . . EEOC guidelines are in full effect, and NASA will use them until other guidance becomes available.

In effect, then, NASA has adopted EEOC's position that sexual harassment is sex discrimination. The NASA policy statement also directs that training be provided as necessary, as well as information regarding "established channels through which (the employees) may raise the issue of sexual harassment, including the administrative discrimination complaint procedure provided for allegations arising under Title VII, Civil Rights Act of 1964, as amended."

POLICY IMPLEMENTATION AT JOHNSON SPACE CENTER, NASA

The Lyndon B. Johnson Space Center (JSC) is located in Houston, Texas. It began its operations in 1961, and currently employs 3,500 full-time civil servant personnel.

While it is possible that instances of sexual harassment have occurred since JSC's inception, as of this writing (May 1980), there have been no documented complaints. One may theorize that this might be attributed to the general inattention to the issue throughout the Federal government, including the absence of a definition and specific policy prohibiting its practice.

On April 9, 1980, an interim policy statement patterned after the OPM policy was issued by Dr. Christopher C. Kraft, Jr., Center Director, to JSC employees. It was distributed to all employees in order to ensure their aware-ness of sexual harassment as a prohib-ited personnel practice, as well as to clarify Center objectives, demonstrate the seriousness of its intentions, and en-hance prospects for employee com-pliance. For while this practice may not be a problem for women employed at JSC, formal prohibition assures that their working conditions, employment oppor-tunities, and well-being as members of society remain free of its ill effects. It is anticipated that merely bringing the issue out in the open and establishing a prohibition will deter future occur-rences, simply because the employer has made its position known.

In adopting a policy defining sexual harassment as employee misconduct, the intention was to establish an ethical standard for behavior akin to those enumerated in the booklet, *Standards of Conduct for NASA Employees*, in that, apart from the question of sex discrimi-nation, its practice may be, in a sense, a conflict of interest in the performance of one's duties, if not an abuse of authority of one's position. At JSC, as elsewhere, management recognizes that coopera-tive working relationships are essential to productive work performance, and that platonic relationships are a social benefit of employment. Conversely, sexual harassment would be an imped-iment to the full realization of human potential which, in turn, could diminish the Center's full potential for achieving program objectives of national import.

In addition to policy adoption, JSC will provide training based on OPM and EEOC materials. Also, the JSC Equal Opportunity Office will study any re-ports or grievances alleging sexual harassment, in order to better un-derstand the nature of its practice and to discover any patterns in its occurrence; will submit any findings and recom-mendations to appropriate managers; and will be attentive to additional de-velopments in Federal policy, as well as court decisions in cases of sexual harassment in employment.

In conclusion, the authors believe that the best way to assure a workplace environment free of harassment is to declare it to be a prohibited practice, to alert employees to the nature of the problem and administrative remedies, and to train managers in the importance of both prevention and appropriate dis-ciplinary action if its practice is discov-ered. The key to preventing sexual harassment is to stress that it will not be tolerated.

NOTES

1. *Statistical Abstract of the United States,* 100th ed. (Washington, D.C.: U.S. Depart-ment of Commerce, Bureau of the Census), p. 392, No. 644.

2. *Ibid.*

3. *Employment and Earnings, March, 1980,* 27, No. 3 (Washington, D.C.: U.S. Department of Labor, Bureau of Labor Statis-tics), Table B-2. In December, 1979, the Federal government employed 2,770,000 full-time civilians, of whom 876,000 were women (31.6%).

4. *Hearings before the Subcommittee on Investigations of the Committee on Post Of-fice and Civil Service,* U.S. House of Repre-sentatives, 96th Congress, First Session, October/November, 1979, p. 164.

5. *Ibid.,* pp. 1-176.

6. James M. Hanley, Chairman, Sub-committee on Investigations of the Commit-tee on Post Office and Civil Service, U.S. House of Representatives, "Letter to Alan K. Campbell, Director, U.S. Office of Personnel Management," October 9, 1979, p. 1.

7. *Ibid.*

8. "Memorandum of Understanding be-tween the Investigations Subcommittee of the Post Office and Civil Service Committee and the Office of Personnel Management con-cerning the Problem of Sexual Harassment of Federal Employees," October, 1979.

9. Alan K. Campbell, Director, U.S. Of-fice of Personnel Management, "Memoran-dum to Heads of Departments and Inde-pendent Agencies," and "Policy Statement and Definition of Sexual Harassment," ap-pended, December 12, 1979.

10. *Hearings . . ., op. cit.,* p. 155.

11. *Ibid.*

12. *Ibid.*, p. 92.

13. *Ibid.*

14. *Federal Register*, 45, No. 72 (April 11, 1980), Rules and Regulations, 29 CFR Part 1604, pp. 25024-25.

15. *Ibid.*

16. *Vinson* v. *Taylor*, 22 EPD 30,708 (U.S.D.C., D.C., 1980). In this case, the Court ruled that in the absence of notice by the plaintiff or attempt to give notice to or file a complaint with the employer alleging sexual harassment, notice to the supervisor who was the alleged perpetrator did not constitute notice to the employer. Thus, the supervisor was not the perpretator of sexual harassment by virtue of his position alone, nor was the employer liable. The charges alleging sexual harassment and sex discrimination were dismissed with prejudice.

17. *Hearings . . ., op. cit.,* p. 91 and p. 156.

18. *Ibid.*, p. 166, testimony of Ruth T. Prokop, Chairperson, U.S. Merit Systems Protection Board.

19. *Ibid.*, p. 162.

20. *Ibid.*, p. 163.

21. *Ibid.*, pp. 163-64.

22. Robert A. Frosch, Administrator, National Aeronautics and Space Administration, "Memorandum to Officials-in-Charge of Headquarters Offices and Center Directors, Subject: 'Policy Statement on Sexual Harassment,'" April 29, 1980.

13. Policy on Sexual Harassment*

GOVERNMENT OF THE DISTRICT OF COLUMBIA

By virtue of the authority vested in me by § 422(2), (3) and (6) of the District of Columbia Self-Government and Governmental Reorganization Act, D.C. Code, § 1-162(2), (3) and (6) (Supp. V, 1978), and D.C. Law 2-38 (24 D.C.R. 2830), and in accordance with the personnel policies of the District of Columbia Government to assure fair treatment of applicants and employees in all aspects of employment without regard to political affiliation, race, color, national origin, sex, religious beliefs, age, marital status, personal physical appearance, sexual orientation or preference, family responsibilities, physical handicap or developmental disability, and to provide a proper regard for the rights of privacy and other constitutionally protected rights of citizens, it is hereby ORDERED that:

1. PURPOSE

The purpose of this order is to establish clearly and unequivocably that the policy of the District of Columbia government prohibits sexual harassment of its employees in any form, to establish procedures by which allegations of sexual harassment may be filed, investigated and adjudicated, and to require agencies to establish affirmative programs within each agency, including internal procedures and monitoring, so that work sites will be maintained free from sexual harassment.

2. AMENDMENT OF MAYOR'S ORDER 75-230

a. Section 2 of Mayor's Order 75-230, dated October 31, 1975, is amended by adding thereto the following as subsection e:

Sexual harassment shall be deemed to be a form of sexual discrimination which is prohibited under District laws and regulations, including this Order.

b. Section 3 of Mayor's Order 75-230 is amended by adding thereto the following:

Sexual harassment is defined as the exercise or attempt to exercise by a person of the authority and power of his or her position to control, influence or affect the career, salary, or job of another employee or prospective employee in exchange for sexual favors. Sexual harassment may include, but is not limited to:

(1) verbal harassment or abuse;

(2) subtle pressure for sexual activity;

(3) unnecessary patting or pinching;

(4) constant brushing against another employee's body;

(5) demanding sexual favors accompanied by overt threat concerning an individual's employment status;

(6) demanding sexual favors accompanied by implied or overt promise of preferential treatment with regard to an individual's employment status.

3. COMPLAINTS

A. GENERAL REQUIREMENTS

Allegations of sexual harassment shall

*Source: Government of the District of Columbia, Mayor's Order 79-89 (May 24, 1979).

107

be fully investigated, and corrective or disciplinary action taken as warranted. Complaining parties shall be required to swear or affirm that the facts stated in the complaint are true to the best of the person's belief, knowledge and information.

B. EMPLOYEE STATUS

Only those complaints shall be investigated which are filed by a person who at the time of filing the complaint is an employee of the District of Columbia, and which are directed against a person who at the time of the filing of the complaint is a District employee.

C. CONFIDENTIALITY

The complaint file, including all information and documents pertinent to a complaint, shall be confidential.

4. OFFICE OF HUMAN RIGHTS

The Director of the Office of Human Rights is directed to establish within the Office a unit to receive complaints and allegations involving sexual harassment directed against officers and employers of the District Government. Such complaints will be investigated and processed in accordance with the procedures and authorities set forth in Mayor's Order 75-230. In the event disciplinary action may be warranted, the pertinent complaint file or files of the Office of Human Rights shall be made available to the Director of the Office of Personnel.

5. RESPONSIBILITIES OF AGENCIES

a. Each Agency head shall within 60 days from the effective date of this Order amend the Agency's Affirmative Action Plan to indicate the procedures and authorities that will be established in the Agency for providing work sites free of sexual harassment, for monitoring working conditions so that instances

of sexual harassment will be detected soon after their occurrences, and to provide for resolution of complaints within the Agency.

b. Agency heads who have complaints of sexual harassment brought to their attention shall promptly investigate and attempt to resolve such complaints. If a resolution cannot be reached in the Agency within 60 days, the Agency head shall refer the complaint to the Office of Human Rights.

c. The bringing of a complaint or allegation of sexual harassment to an Agency shall not bar nor preclude the complainant from filing a complaint with the Office of Human Rights pursuant to Mayor's Order 75-230.

6. TIME PERIODS FOR FILING COMPLAINTS

Only complaints of sexual harassment that concern incidents which occurred within a period of one year from the time the complaint is filed shall be considered.

7. APPLICABILITY

The provisions of this Order shall be applicable to every office, agency, department, instrumentality and employee of the Government of the District of Columbia, except employees and personnel of the District of Columbia courts.

8. EFFECT UPON PRIOR MAYOR'S ORDERS

To the extent that any provision of this Order are inconsistent with the provisions of any Commissioners' Order, Order of the Commissioner or Mayor's Order, the provisions of this Order shall prevail and shall be deemed to supersede the provisions thereof.

9. EFFECTIVE DATA

The provisions of this Order shall become effective immediately.

IV

The Legal Status: Sexual Harassment Under Title VII

Introduction. The legal state of the art with respect to sexual harassment is in its infancy. The legal arguments are complex; legal precedents are being challenged and, in some cases, overturned; and the courts are relatively inexperienced in articulating and deciding the issues.

Catharine A. MacKinnon demonstrates, in "Sexual Harassment Cases," that sexual harassment is becoming a cause of action, primarily under Title VII of the Civil Rights Act of 1964. Women, primarily, are arguing that it is one form of sex discrimination and that within this context, employers should be held liable for the behaviors of employees who abuse their authority. MacKinnon outlines the various interpretations of the term "sex discrimination," in her attempt to elucidate the nuances of the law. She explores the issue of employer liability and she identifies several basic issues—power, gender and sexuality—which provide the context for the legal challenges.

Alan Goldberg's "Sexual Harassment and Title VII: The Foundation for the Elimination of Sexual Cooperation as an Employment Condition" summarizes and interprets the pertinent sections of Title VII and describes in some detail seven of the major legal cases in the field. Goldberg advances the proposition that although there is no consensus regarding the appropriateness of Title VII to cases of sexual harassment and although the facts of the individual cases are significantly different, one can argue that sexual harassment can and does result in "an adverse change in the employee's 'compensation, terms, conditions, or privileges of employment'." Terminations, demotions and reassignments due to failure to comply with sexual advances, are clear examples of adverse employment-related decisions. Assigning undesirable work and providing inadequate training and supervision are more subtle, but often no less invidious examples. Employer liability and employer responses to allegations of sexual harassment are also explored. Goldberg concludes that the courts should welcome complaints of sexual harassment as opportunities to "further Title VII's objective of eliminating invidious and arbitrary barriers to employment."

Taking a more pragmatic approach to the legalities of sexual harassment, William Seymour, in his "Sexual Harassment: Finding a Cause of Action Under Title VII," compares the potential remedies under Title VII with those which fall under state tort law. Fully aware that some courts find sexual harassment a form of sex discrimination while others do not, Seymour outlines the differences between federal and state orientations and identifies the steps a corporation should consider if it wishes to avoid liability. Does the organization have a clear and available policy statement prohibiting sexual harassment? Are there adequate mechanisms for review of personnel decisions? Are there adequate channels to air employee grievances and proper investigations of such complaints? Employers, says Seymour, must be knowledgable about ways in which they can be held liable, and they must be sophisticated with respect to how they can prevent or at least protect themselves against legal action.

The Equal Employment Opportunity Commission's interim guidelines are included so that the reader may be fully informed about the federal government's interpretation of Section 703 of the Civil Rights Act of 1964 as it applies to the issue of sexual harassment. Although these guidelines may be modified in light of solicited comments, they state clearly that an employer has the affirmative action duty to insure a workplace that is free from sexual harassment or intimidation. Furthermore, the employer is responsible for acts of employees that constitute conditions of sexual harassment, regardless of whether the employer knew or should have known about the incidents.

14. Sexual Harassment Cases*

CATHARINE A. MACKINNON

Sexual harassment, the experience, is becoming "sexual harassment," the legal claim. As the pain and stifled anger have become focused into dissatisfaction, gripes have crystallized into a grievance, and women's inner protest is becoming a cause of action. But this is not a direct process of transliteration. Life becoming law and back again is a process of transformation. Legitimized and sanctioned, the legal concept of sexual harassment reenters the society to participate in shaping the social definitions of what may be resisted or complained about, said aloud, or even felt. Similarly, when a form of suffering is made a legal wrong, especially when its victims lack power, its social dynamics are not directly embodied or reflected in the law. Legal prohibitions may arise because of the anguish people feel or the conditions they find insupportable, but the legal issues may not turn on the social issues that are the reasons they exist. Distanced from social life, yet part of its imperatives, the law becomes a shadow world in which caricatured social conflict is played out, an unreal thing with very real consequences.

Most women who have experienced sexual harassment know that it was done to them, in some sense, as women. Considerations the law requires for determining whether their treatment was based on their sex look like formalistic barriers to recognizing the obvious. Equally apparent to most sexually harassed women is that employers could rectify their situation but instead wink at it, which means that they let it happen. To the victims, employer liability comes down to holding responsible for women's situation the people with the power over it.

Legally, whether sexual harassment is sex discrimination is not nearly so straightforward. Several different interpretations of the meaning of sex discrimination have been applied in this context. In one interpretation, the variable in question must be exclusive to one gender before sex discrimination can occur. An abuse that can be visited upon either gender or upon the same gender as that of the perpetrator—as sexual harassment can—cannot be treatment based on sex.[1] In another interpretation, whenever an employment requirement, such as engaging in sexual relations as the price of a job, is fixed upon one gender that would not, under the totality of the circumstances, be fixed upon the other, the condition is seen as based on sex.[2] Another approach focuses upon whether the requirement was in fact imposed upon one gender and not the other in the case at hand.[3] Still another view might require that sexual harassment be engaged in with intent to deprive women of employment opportunities before it would be considered sex-based.[4]

A similar array of interpretations exists on the issue of whether the employer should be held liable for sexual harassment by employees. In one approach, the closest to the victim's sense of the situation, the fact that the be-

*Source: From *Sexual Harassment of Working Women* (1979) by Catharine A. MacKinnon, chapter 4, pp. 57-59. Reprinted by permission of Yale University Press.

havior occurred in the course of employment is sufficient to hold the employer responsible. Knowledge is imputed to him because if he did not know about it, he should have.[5] Another interpretation requires that the employer actually know about the abuse, and ignore it or act inadequately to remedy it, suggesting that he ratified or condoned it.[6] A variant suggests that especially stringent standards of employer knowledge should be satisfied because the behavior is sexual.[7] Not yet confronted is the extent to which *pro forma* complaint adjudication can exonerate an employer with notice who does not rectify the situation from the victim's standpoint.[8] Finally, one can imagine an approach requiring knowing acquiescence or active abetting of sexual harassment by the employer with intent to drive women out of their jobs before the employer will be held responsible.[9]

Behind the range of interpretations, basic issues are at stake. Prohibiting sexual harassment as sex discrimination implicitly defines what has been considered private and personal as another dimension of the public order. Of women by men, it suggests a relationship between individual sexual relations and the edifice of unequal gender status as a whole. If women's sexuality is a means by which her access to economic rewards is controlled, relations between the sexes in the process of production affect women's position throughout the society, just as women's position throughout the society makes her sexuality economically controllable. It also suggests that what has been considered among the most "natural" and "normal" of male urges may, in some forms, be sufficiently culturally contingent as well as onerous to give rise to discrimination against women. Boundaries between personal life and work life, the natural and the cultural, are thereby interpenetrated and confounded in the same way that they have become inseparable in women's oppression. Implicit here is whether sexuality is, in it-

self, a source, form, and sphere of social inequality or whether it is merely a sphere onto which other forms of unequal power—for example, physical force or economic clout—are displaced and imposed, a ground on which other battles (including those of gender) are fought. Behind the doctrinal arguments, conceiving of sexual harassment as unequal treatment based on sex raises fundamental questions of the definitions of, and the relations between, gender, sexuality, and power.

NOTES

1. *Corne* v. *Bausch & Lomb*, 390 F. Supp. 161, 163 (D. Ariz. 1975), *Tompkins* v. *Public Service Electric & Gas Co.*, 422 F. Supp. 553, 556 (D.N.J. 1976).
2. *Barnes* v. *Costle*, 561 F.2d 983, 989 (D.C. Cir. 1977).
3. *Williams* v. *Saxbe*, 413 F. Supp. 654, 660 (D.D.C. 1976).
4. This is one position that might be argued from *Gilbert* v. *General Electric*, 429 U.S. 125 (1976) and *Geduldig* v. *Aiello*, 417 U.S. 484 (1974). For an application of this logic to race, see *Regents of the University of California* vs. *Bakke*, 98 S. Ct. at 2748, n. 27 (1978).
5. This would be to apply the doctrine of *respondeat superior* or a strict rule of agency in the Title VII context.
6. *Barnes* v. *Costle*, 561 F.2d 983, 999-1000 (D.C. Cir. 1977); *Heelan* v. *Johns-Manville Corp.*, 451 F. Supp. 1382, 1389-1390 (D. Colo. 1978).
7. *Miller* v. *Bank of America*, 418 F. Supp. 233, 236 (N.D. Cal. 1977). *Corne* v. *Bausch & Lomb*, 390 F. Supp. 161, 163 (D. Ariz. 1975) also seems to suggest this. See also *Barnes* v. *Costle*, 561 F.2d 983, 999 (D.C. Cir. 1977).
8. *Barnes* v. *Costle*, 561 F.2d 983, 995 (D.C. Cir. 1977) (MacKinnon J., concurring). *Alexander* v. *Yale*, 459 F. Supp. 1 (D. Conn. 1977). The most recent case to address this issue, *Heelan* v. *Johns-Manville Corp.*, 451 F. Supp. 1382 (D. Colo. 1978), does not fully resolve it because the company's procedures were found inadequate to its notice of the problem's existence. *Heelan* holds that the

company's investigation was insuffiently broad, deep, or thorough to satisfy its obligation under Title VII, given that the plaintiff "did everything within her power to bring her charges to the attention of top management." *Id.*, at 1389. The court therefore does not need to reach the more difficult issue of inadequacy of result in the face of adequacy of procedure.

9. See *supra*, Note 4.

15. Sexual Harrassment and Title VII: The Foundation for the Elimination of Sexual Cooperation as an Employment Condition*

ALAN GOLDBERG

I. INTRODUCTION

Ten years after the enactment of Title VII,[1] the federal judiciary confronted its first Title VII case in which sexual harassment[2] was the primary allegation.[3] In the next three-and-one-half years, six more claims of sexual harassment reached federal district courts,[4] and three federal circuit courts of appeal reviewed lower court holdings.[5]

Neither these cases nor the considerable journalistic[6] and academic[7] attention they received reveals a consensus regarding the appropriate application of Title VII to cases of sexual harassment. This note, therefore, examines the application of Title VII to the problem of sexual harassment and suggests a coherent framework for analyzing the issues. After a brief discussion and evaluation of the cases, sexual harassment will be analyzed from the perspective of the Title VII case law of other types of discrimination. Analogies from these cases suggest that Title VII, as enacted by Congress and interpreted by the Judiciary, prohibits making sexual cooperation a condition of employment.

Since Title VII applies only to employment,[8] this note considers only those circumstances in which the alleged victim of sexual harassment is an employee and the individual allegedly making the sexual advance is either the employer or a fellow employee. Of course, except in the case of claims of discrimination in federal employment,[9] Title VII is not an exclusive remedy within the employment context.[10] Alternative causes of action for employment discrimination may be based upon the United States Constitution,[11] other federal statutes,[12] state employment laws,[13] traditional common-law contract theories,[14] and collective bargaining contracts.[15] Furthermore, statutory civil causes of action against the individual guilty of the harassment,[16] as well as criminal sanctions,[17] may be available. Nevertheless, Title VII may well provide the most direct and specific remedy for victims of sexual harassment within the employment context;[18] the presence of uniform federal statutory prohibitions and the development of more consistent precedent interpreting those provisions will furnish the courts the tools to eliminate sexual cooperation as an employment condition.

II. THE FOUNDATION: TITLE VII

The Civil Rights Act of 1964 was enacted by the United States Congress on July 2, 1964.[19] Title VII[20] of this legislation deals with equal employment opportunities. Although Title VII is broad in its coverage and content, its core is section 703(a), which provides:

It shall be an unlawful employment practice for an employer ... to ... discrimi-

*Source: From Michigan Law Review, vol. 76 (May 1978), pp. 1007-1035. Reprinted by permission of Michigan Law Review Association.

nate against any individual with respect to his compensation, terms, conditions, or privileges of employment, because of such individual's race, color, religion, sex, or national origin.[21]

For the purposes of Title VII,

the term 'employer' means a person engaged in an industry affecting commerce . . . and any agent of such a person, but such term does not include . . . the United States.[22]

To effectuate Title VII's purpose of providing a safe and effective means for resolving complaints of employment discrimination, Congress included Section 704, which prohibits employers from retaliating against employees who initiate complaints under Title VII.[23] In 1972, Congress added Section 717 to extend the coverage of Title VII to federal employees.[24]

These are the crucial provisions of Title VII. Although the legislative history of Section 703 reveals that the provisions prohibiting discrimination based on sex were added in a last-minute attempt to prevent the passage of Title VII,[25] the legislative history of the 1972 addition of Section 717 evidences Congress's commitment to eliminating employment discrimination based on sex:

Discrimination against women is no less serious than other forms of prohibited employment practices and is to be accorded the same degree of social concern given to any type of unlawful discrimination.[26]

The legislative history further reveals that Title VII is not confined to explicit acts of discrimination nor to discriminations based solely on sex,[27] any decision in which sex is a factor is discriminatory, even if other, legitimate, factors also motivated the decision. In essence, sex is to be treated like any other prohibited ground for discrimination.[28] While judicial interpretation is important, an analysis of sexual harassment must be built on this foundation of statutory language and legislative declaration.

III. SEXUAL HARASSMENT CASE LAW UNDER TITLE VII

In five of the seven cases which have created the substantive law in this area,[29] the district courts initially held that a claim alleging sexual harassment does not state a cause of action under Title VII.[30] Three of the district court decisions were reversed on appeal[31] on three different interpretations of the statute.

In one of the earliest sexual harassment cases, Corne v. Bausch and Lomb, Inc.,[32] the two plaintiffs alleged that they had to resign their jobs to avoid their supervisor's verbal and physical sexual advances. The court held that they had failed to state a claim for relief under Title VII. The court noted that the discriminatory conduct in prior Title VII sex discrimination cases arose out of company policies, and it found that the conduct alleged was not such a policy, but was "nothing more than a personal proclivity, peculiarity or mannerism" of the supervisor.[33] The court read Section 703(a) as applying only to discrimination on the part of the employer and stated that it was inapplicable to sexual advances by another employee "even though he be in a supervisory capacity where such complained of acts or conduct had no relationship to the nature of the employment."[34]

In dictum, the court commented that if Title VII were applicable, it would be "ludicrous" to find no Title VII violation when the alleged conduct had also been directed to males.[35] Furthermore, the court speculated that an employer would be forced to employ only asexual employees to avoid lawsuits every time one employee made sexual advances to another.[36]

In Williams v. Saxbe,[37] the plaintiff alleged that after she refused her supervisor's sexual advance, he harassed, humiliated, and eventually fired her. The United States District Court for the District of Columbia, taking an expansive view of Title VII, held that retalia-

tory actions of a supervisor taken because a subordinate declined his sexual
advances constitute sex discrimination
under Title VII.

The court found a cause of action
under Section 717(a), since

> the conduct of the plaintiff's supervisor
> created an artificial barrier to employment
> which was placed before one gender and
> not the other, despite the fact that both
> genders were similarly situated.[38]

The employer's argument, that the
supervisor did not discriminate against
women, but only against people who refused to accede to his sexual demands,
was summarily dismissed by the court,
as was the employer's contention that
this conduct could not be sex discrimination since application of Title VII
should not depend upon the sexual
preference of the supervisor.[39] The court
reasoned that violations of Title VII
could be found whenever a supervisor
approached only members of one sex,
but that no violation of Title VII would
occur if a supervisor made advances to
subordinates of both genders.[40]

The court concluded that there was
no cause of action unless the supervisor's conduct constituted an employer
policy or practice.[41] Echoing *Corne*, the
court implied that an employer is not liable for personal, isolated instances of
sexual harassment.[42]

In *Miller* v. *Bank of America*,[43] the
United States District Court for Northern
California dismissed a complaint in
which the plaintiff alleged that her
supervisor promised her a better job if
she would be sexually cooperative and
that he had her fired when she refused.
The court phrased the issue as "whether
Title VII was intended to hold an employer liable for what is essentially the
isolated and unauthorized sex misconduct of one employee to another."[44]
The court acknowledged that

> there may be situations in which a sex dis-
> crimination action can be maintained for
> an employer's active, or tacit approval, of
> a personnel policy requiring sex favors as a
> condition of employment,

but recommended judicial restraint absent

> specific factual allegations describing an
> employer policy which in its application
> imposes or permits a consistent, as distin-
> guished from isolated, sex-based discrimi-
> nation on a definable employee group.[45]

Concerned that under the plaintiff's
theory "flirtations of the smallest order
would give rise to liability,"[46] the court
concluded that

> the attraction of males to females and
> females to males is a natural sex
> phenomenon and it is probable that this at-
> traction plays at least a subtle part in most
> personnel decisions.[47]

The United States District Court for
Eastern Michigan held that the plaintiff
in *Munford* v. *James T. Barnes & Co.*[48]
stated a proper cause of action by alleging that she was discharged for refusing
sexual relations with her supervisor. The
court cited earlier sexual harassment
cases to show that sexual harassment is
prohibited sex discrimination under
Title VII.[49] The plaintiff's supervisor was
a proper defendant because he was an
agent of the employer and was responsible for the alleged discrimination.[50]
The supervisor's superior and the employer were also proper defendants,
since they failed to investigate the complaint of sexual harassment.[51] The court,
however, declined to hold the employer
automatically and vicariously liable for
the discriminatory acts of its supervisors.[52]

More recently, the United States District Court for the Eastern District of Virginia, in *Garber* v. *Saxon Industries,
Inc.*,[53] dismissed in a single sentence an
employee's allegation that she was fired
because she refused to engage in illicit
sexual relations with her immediate
superior. According to the court, the
plaintiff had not set forth a claim cognizable under Title VII of the Civil
Rights Act.[54] However, in an equally
brief per curiam opinion, the United
States Court of Appeals for the Fourth

Circuit reversed the district court's order to dismiss and remanded the case.[55] The court found that

> the complaint and its exhibits, liberally construed, allege an employer policy or acquiescence in a practice of compelling female employees to submit to the sexual advances of their male supervisor in violation of Title VII.[56]

Evidently the court viewed a Title VII cause of action as requiring an employer policy or acquiescence in a practice, but additional guidance from the Fourth Circuit is precluded by the opinion's brevity.

Then, in a comprehensive opinion, the District of Columbia Circuit Court of Appeals in Barnes v. Costle[57] reversed a district court dismissal[58] of a complaint in which the plaintiff alleged that, because she rebuffed her director's repeated sexual advances and his intimations that an affair would enhance her career, he abolished her job. The court of appeals found that retention of the plaintiff's job was conditioned upon sexual cooperation with her supervisor, a condition which her supervisor did not apply to male employees.[59] Finding that it was "enough that gender is a factor contributing to the discrimination in a substantial way," the court concluded that her "gender, just as much as her cooperation, was an indispensable factor in the job-retention condition" imposed by her supervisor.[60]

Addressing the issue of the employer's liability for acts of its supervisors, the court observed, "Generally speaking, an employer is chargeable with Title VII violations occasioned by discriminatory practices of supervisory personnel."[61] Citing Miller,[62] the court conceded that

> should a supervisor contravene employer policy without the employer's knowledge and the consequences are rectified when discovered, the employer may be relieved from responsibility under Title VII;[63]

the employer in this case, however, introduced no evidence that a policy against harassment was implemented, or even existed.[64] Addressing the question whether such an employer practice or policy was a necessary element of a cause of action, the court held that a single instance of discrimination could support an individual suit under Title VII.[65]

The most recent case decided upon the grounds of sexual harassment is Tomkins v. Public Service Electric & Gas Co.[66] The Court of Appeals for the Third Circuit reversed a district court holding[67] that there is no cognizable claim of sex discrimination when a female employee's continued employment is conditioned upon her submission to the sexual advances of a male supervisor.[68] The court concentrated on the basic prerequisites of a Title VII claim, "that the acts complained of constituted a condition of employment, and that this condition was imposed by the employer on the basis of sex."[69] The court had no trouble concluding that the first requirement had been satisfied, noting that the fact that sexual advances occurred within the employment context was strong evidence of a job-related condition.[70] The second issue, whether the incident was company policy or a purely personal incident, was found to be a question for the fact finder.[71] The court implied that an employer is not liable for a "purely personal incident,"[72] but found that plaintiff's allegation that her employer either knowingly or constructively acquiesced in the supervisor's conduct was sufficient to withstand a motion to dismiss.[73]

The third essential attribute of the claim, that the discrimination be on the basis of sex, was also satisfied, according to the court. Plaintiff's claim that "her status as a female was the motivating factor in the supervisor's conditioning her continued employment on compliance with his sexual demands"[74] was a sufficient allegation of Title VII sex discrimination, since "[i]t is only necessary to show that gender is a substantial factor in the discrimination."[75]

IV. PRESENT STATE OF THE LAW

The seven cases decided to date almost uniformly accept as basic that Title VII was enacted to prohibit discrimination in employment on the basis of sex and that Title VII is to be liberally interpreted in order to effectuate its purpose.[76] The facts of these cases are not meaningfully distinguishable: the source of the harassment,[77] the kind of harassment,[78] the resulting change in the plaintiff's employment status,[79] and the credence given the plaintiff's claim[80] are all similar. The only possible exception is the presence of an explicit anti-harassment policy in *Miller*.[81] The courts have divergent positions as to three legal issues: whether sexual harassment constitutes discrimination on the basis of sex, whether a plaintiff must show that there is an employer policy or practice of such harassment, and the extent to which a supervisor's actions can be attributed to the employer.

Two of the district courts held that sexual harassment does not constitute discrimination on the basis of sex because gender is incidental to the claim—according to this argument the victim of discrimination is the employee who refuses to furnish sexual favors.[82] These cases were reversed on appeal by courts which explicitly held this kind of conduct to be sex discrimination.[83] The other courts which have considered this issue have reached the same conclusion.[84] Further, each case addressed the legal significance of whether the supervisor's improper conduct reflected an employer policy or practice or was only an isolated incident. Each court, except the court of appeals in *Barnes*[85] and the Eastern District of Michigan in *Munford*,[86] seemed to consider an allegation of an employer policy or practice essential.[87] The *Corne* and *Miller* courts, which disallowed the plaintiff's complaints, found, respectively, that the harassment was merely an isolated incident,[88] and that the employer had an express anti-harassment policy.[89]

Directly related to the necessity of an employer policy is the third issue, an employer's liability for the acts of supervisory employees. Courts disagree as to the extent of an employer's liability for the acts of its supervisors: some courts wish to impose what is virtually strict liability, others wish to impose almost no liability at all.[90]

The law of sexual harassment, then, is inconsistent, ambiguous, and nascent.

V. THE CAUSE OF ACTION FOR SEXUAL HARASSMENT

A. DISCRIMINATION ON THE BASIS OF SEX

In the absence of a consistent line of direct precedent, decisions in sexual harassment cases must rely on analogies to the Title VII cases which have alleged discrimination on the other prohibited grounds—race, religion, national origin, and, particularly, conventional sex discrimination.[91] Those cases outline the following principles for a court which is applying Title VII to a case of sexual harassment. A court must ask whether sexual harassment is a barrier to employment[92] which discriminates on the basis of sex. Disparate treatment[93] of individuals which would not have occurred but for their sex constitutes sufficient unlawful discrimination.[94] If a prohibited factor, such as the employee's gender, partly motivated the employer's decision, the fact that a non-prohibited ground also motivated the decision, for purposes of Title VII, irrelevant.[95] Further, a finding that only some members of one sex were discriminated against,[96] or that there were no similarly situated individuals of the opposite sex[97] does not preclude the possibility that there was unlawful employment discrimination. Finally, courts must be sensitive to the danger that the employer's pretexts might obscure what is in fact prohibited conduct.[98]

Applying these standards directly to sexual harassment, the initial issue is whether a sexual advance can be characterized as discrimination on the basis of sex. When sexual advances are made to only one sex, *discrimination* has occurred,[99] since members of one sex have been disadvantaged and members of the other sex have not. Whether this discrimination is the *kind* prohibited by Title VII can be determined only through an analysis of that law's other elements.

B. ADVERSE EFFECT ON EMPLOYMENT CONDITIONS

Once discrimination on the basis of sex has been demonstrated, the next step toward a Title VII action is to prove a causal relationship between that discrimination and an adverse change in the employee's compensation, terms, conditions, or privileges of employment."[100] Adverse employment effects can be divided into three categories: direct employment actions, constructive discharges, and contamination of the working environment.

Termination of the plaintiff's employment[101] is the most obvious adverse employment action. Reassignment[102] and demotion[103] are other examples of employer actions with clear employment consequences. Discrimination in employment status, of course, may take subtler and less direct forms. Watching an employee more closely,[104] assigning undesirable work,[105] discouraging participation in company job-mobility programs,[106] failing to require co-workers to cooperate where necessary,[107] providing inadequate training,[108] and withholding recommendations for promotion[109] have all been termed adverse employment actions in violation of Title VII. In other words, acts of omission and indirection are as cognizable as firings, demotions, and transfers, though the court's task

becomes more difficult as the employer's subtlety increases.

The second category of adverse employment effects involves cases in which the employer makes an employee's working conditions so intolerable that the employee is forced to resign. This kind of resignation is judicially construed as a constructive discharge[110]—that the plaintiff is the one to sever the employment relationship does not bar a Title VII cause of action.[111] The existence of this category allows victims of sexual harassment whose employers have not altered any clearly cognizable condition of employment to obtain relief. An employee who resigns before instituting a Title VII suit, however, risks losing the job permanently if the subsequent suit fails.[112]

It is not certain whether an employee's legally protected terms, conditions and privileges of employment include the right to a working environment uncontaminated by discrimination.[113] The Equal Employment Opportunity Commission, however, has consistently maintained than an employer must provide an atmosphere free of intimidation, ridicule, and insult.[114] In a few instances courts have approved the principle that an employee's psychological health is protected by Title VII, at least when that health is threatened by racial or ethnic discrimination.[115] However, courts have intimated that they will require clear and substantial proof of claims alleging a discriminatory atmosphere.[116] Support for the application of Title VII to discriminatory working environments may be inferred from the Supreme Court's decision in *Trafficante* v. *Metropolitan Life Insurance*.[117] The Court held that a resident of an apartment complex has standing to sue its management if it excluded minority groups. Otherwise, the Court held, the tenants might be deprived of the benefit of integrated housing and interracial association in violation of the Civil Rights Act of 1964.[118] This implicit recognition of a statutorily

protected right to a nondiscriminatory
housing environment appears analogous
to a right to a nondiscriminatory working environment protected by Title VII.
The propriety of this analogy is evi-
denced by the Court's reliance upon a
Title VII case[119] in *Trafficante*.[120]

Moreover, several circuits have
explicitly held that employees are entitled to a working environment which
does not inhibit interracial association.[121] If an employee has a right to
such a working environment, Title VII
should also be taken to forbid the exclusion of employees of a particular color,
national origin, religion, or gender. The
extent to which discrimination short of
exclusion infringes upon this associa-
tional privilege, however, has not been
defined. For example, it is not clear that
the Supreme Court would extend the
right to a nondiscriminatory housing
environment to include the right to a
housing environment free of racial in-
sults or hasassment. The right presumably would have to be extended that far
if the interracial-association analogy is
to reach sexual harassment. A cause of
action based on contamination of the
working environment would probably
require proof of a persistent and oppres-
sive discriminatory atmosphere;[122] an
isolated incident would be insufficient
to establish such an "atmosphere."

Although the law on the working environment as a condition of employment is still incipient,[123] because of Title
VII's remedial purposes, courts should
read the phrase "terms, conditions or
privileges of employment" broadly to
include the ambience of the workplace.
All employees in the office, not just the
specific targets, are damaged by the discomfort, degradation, and stigma
caused by the discriminatory work environment sexual harassment produces.
Thus, whenever a plaintiff can demonstrate the sexual advances have con-
taminated the working environment, a
claim of sexual harassment should be
cognizable.

C. EMPLOYER PATTERN OR PRACTICE

Title VII provides both for causes of action for aggrieved individuals[124] and for
class action suits.[125] Although plaintiffs
in a class action must show that there
was a pattern or practice of discrimination,[126] individual plaintiffs need not do
so—an isolated incident of impermissible discrimination will support an action.[127] Thus the courts have erred to the
extent that they have required proof of a
pattern or practice of discrimination in
order to establish a condition of
employment in an *individual* suit.[128]

D. THE SOURCE OF HARASSMENT AND THE EMPLOYER'S LIABILITY

An employer's liability for sexual
harassment depends partly on the organizational status of the harasser.[129] Although sexual harassment cases have
involved direct supervisors, two classes
of potential harassers can be distinguished: supervisory and managerial
personnel (*i.e.*, employees responsible
for employment decisions), and non-
supervisory, nonmanagerial personnel.[130]

Although no judicial consensus has
emerged from sexual harassment cases,
Title VII cases involving other types of
discrimination generally hold the employer liable for discriminatory acts of
supervisors and managers.[131] Employers
have been held liable even when they
were unaware of the discrimination,[132]
even when they had anti-discrimination
policies,[133] and even though they had
exemplary anti-discrimination records.[134] Courts have stated only rarely,
and then in dicta, that an employer
under some circumstances might not be
liable for supervisory discrimination.[135]

Nevertheless, several courts confronted with allegations of sexual
harassment by a supervisor have used a
traditional and narrow agency analysis
to gauge the employer's liability.[136]
Such an analysis, this note suggests, is
unnecessary and misleading.[137]

An employer is vicariously liable at

common law for acts of agents only if the agents acted within the scope of their employment or if the employer ratified their acts.[138] Defining "employer" in Section 701 of Title VII to include "any agent of such a person" would mean little if it left unchanged the scope of the employer's liability under common-law vicarious liability concepts.[139] Section 701 may well represent Congress's awareness of the difficulties of proving an agency relationship under the common-law rules, especially when the employer is an institution and not a person. It would be consistent with the broad remedial purpose of Title VII for Congress to have imposed per se liability on the employer for acts of those customarily considered its agents.[140] Since under traditional agency analysis a master is generally not liable for acts of servants outside the scope of their employment,[141] and since "conduct is within the scope of employment only if the servant is actuated to some extent by an intent to serve his master,"[142] it would be the rare Title VII case in which an agency relationship would exist under that analysis.[143] Furthermore, conduct "different *in kind* from that authorized" is outside the scope of employment under traditional agency law.[144] An employer would seldom authorize a supervisor to discriminate in violation of Title VII; more often an employer, if it addresses the subject at all, authorizes a supervisor only to act consistently with Title VII. Similarly, few employers knowingly ratify supervisory discrimination in violation of Title VII. Thus, traditional agency analysis tends to insulate employers from liability in most supervisory discrimination cases,[145] a result Congress surely could not have intended.

But even traditional agency analysis is not confined to the two tests discussed above. Even if the supervisor is acting outside the scope of his employment, the employer may be held liable for his acts if it is negligent in supervising him, if the supervisor is carrying out an employer's nondelegable duty, if an employee has relied on the apparent authority of the supervisor, or if the employer facilitates the supervisor's wrong by making him its agent.[146]

First, an employer should be liable if it negligently allows a supervisor sexually to harass employees.[147] The employer's duty should be to take reasonable steps to insure the supervisor's compliance with these directions.[148] Reasonable steps might include establishing grievance procedures for employees, requiring supervisors to document their reasons for adverse job actions, and having exit interviews for discharged employees conducted by company representatives other than the supervisor.

Second, an employer may be liable if the employee has relied on the apparent authority of the supervisor to act on behalf of the employer or if the supervisor's discriminatory conduct has been facilitated by the existence of the agency relationship.[149] The employer's liability is premised upon placing the supervisor in a position to make employment decisions. Having provided the supervisor with the opportunity to fire or hire, the employer must bear the consequences of discriminatory uses of that authority.[150]

Third, and perhaps most significantly, Title VII should be read as imposing on the employer a nondelegable duty to maintain an establishment free of unlawful employment practices.[151] This reading is supported by judicial interpretations of other federal statutes. Under the Fair Housing Act,[152] for example, courts have imposed a nondelegable duty on owners of real estate to sell it in a nondiscriminatory fashion; the owner is liable for all discriminatory acts of agents and managers.[153] Analogous employment cases include those decided under the Fair Labor Standards Act of 1938,[154] which prohibits child

labor.[155] Courts, confronted with violations by supervisory personnel, found a
societal interest sufficient to justify imposing a nondelegable duty on the employer.[156] The broad remedial and social
objectives of Title VII should command
similar judicial respect.

There is, of course, a second group of
potential harassers—nonsupervisory,
nonmanagerial employees. Apparently
no Title VII claim based upon sexual
harassment by a member of this group
has reached the courts. However, there
is sufficient precedent from other kinds
of Title VII cases to conclude that traditional agency tests of acquiescence and
ratification by the employer or its agent
are the most appropriate ways of determining employer liability for sexual
harassment by nonmanagerial employees.[157] Under the "atmosphere" theory
of liability, where a nonsupervisory employee has sexually harassed a fellow
employee and the employer or its
agents know or should have known[158] of
the harassment but failed to take remedial measures, the employer should be
liable where the other tests of liability
under Title VII are met.[159] Unlike those
cases in which supervisory personnel
are the harassers,[160] however, prompt
investigation and remedial action upon
discovery may in some cases relieve the
employer of Title VII liability.[161] In other
cases prompt remedial action may mitigate the employer's damages.

E. THE AGENT'S LIABILITY UNDER TITLE VII

Although this recourse is rarely used, an
agent of an employer other than the
federal government[162] is directly liable
under Title VII for prohibited acts of
employment discrimination,[163] since
Title VII's definition of "employer" includes "any agent of such a person."[164]
If the individual guilty of discrimination
is in that

fiduciary relation which results from the
manifestation of consent [by the employer]
to [the individual] that the [individual]
shall act on his behalf and subject to his

control, and consent by the [individual] so
to act,

the individual is an agent of the employer.[165]

Most cases which have considered
this issue have only reached the procedural question whether the agent was
a proper defendant.[166] Of the courts
which have ruled on an agent's Title VII
liability, one issued an injunction
against an agent[167] and another assessed
nominal damages, court costs, and the
plaintiff's attorney's fees against the
agent and the employer jointly.[168] Although judicial support is not abundant,
these cases and the language of Title VII
justify an agent's direct liability under
Title VII. Personal liability is especially
appropriate in sexual harassment cases
because of the unusually personal nature of the offense, the possibility that
the offense has harmed the employer as
well as the employee (because the offense easily disrupts the harmony of the
workplace), and because of the difficulty the employer may encounter in
preventing and detecting such offenses.
The threat of personal monetary and injunctive liability for prohibited discrimination could, furthermore, reduce sexual harassment by supervisors more
effectively than suits against the employer. This principle would, however,
be inapplicable to nonsupervisory employees. Only the employer or agent
who knew or should have known of
such activity[169] and failed to remedy it
would be liable.

That an agent may be liable does not,
of course, relieve the employer of liability; the employer would remain jointly
and severally liable for the discriminatory conduct.[170] The liability of the employer assures the successful plaintiff of
adequate monetary relief and of those
kinds of relief, such as reinstatement,
which are beyond the agent's control.[171]

F. POTENTIAL PLAINTIFFS

The most obvious potential plaintiff is
the woman[172] who refuses a sexual advance. Although the seven sexual

harassment cases heard to date involve such plaintiffs, they are not the only potential plaintiffs under Title VII. In every set of circumstances in which an employer receives a sexual advance followed by an employment effect, whether adverse or favorable, some class of employees will be aggrieved and thus be potential Title VII plaintiffs.

A woman confronted by sexual advances but who receives no extraordinary advantage over male employees should be able to pursue a claim of employment discrimination on the ground that she is required to provide sexual favors to maintain parity with male employees. Her claim would be that an additional qualification had been imposed on one sex but not on the other, a situation analogous to one in which blacks but not whites were required to take a test to be eligible for promotion.

Where a sexually cooperative woman not only acquired parity with males but garnered an extraordinary employment advantage, males should be able to maintain an action for being denied the opportunity to make similar progress. Even if the target of the sexual advance were to decline the opportunity, males might still maintain their action, since they would have been denied the extraordinary employment opportunity offered the woman.

Finally, if a court acknowledges that all employees are entitled to a working environment free of sexual harassment,[173] any employee deprived of that benefit would of course have a cause of action. Recognition of this group of plaintiffs would expand substantially the volume of sexual harassment claims brought before the courts.

G. EMPLOYER RESPONSES TO TITLE VII SEXUAL HARASSMENT CLAIMS

Besides disproving the existence of the prerequisites for a sexual harassment cause of action outlined earlier in this note,[174] an employer can avoid liability under Title VII in several ways. First, an employer may not be within the Title VII's jurisdictional standards:[175] very small or temporary businesses may be exempted from coverage. Second, if the employer can show that the employment action of which the employee complains was in no way based on impermissible discrimination or retaliation, the employer will have deprived the employee of an essential element of her cause of action.[176] That is, if the plaintiff was subjected to sexual advances but was terminated for completely independent and valid reasons, discrimination may be found by a court, but the plaintiff will not be entitled to any relief for the legitimate discharge.[177]

Finally, the employer can deny that discrimination on the basis of sex was an element in the sexual advance. This defense would be confined to situations where a bisexual supervisor harasses subordinates of both sexes.[178]

Employer actions subsequent to the discrimination, such as terminating the discriminating supervisor, which fall short of restoring the status quo ante cannot, of course, be grounds for denying the plaintiff relief.[179] Nor will unilateral relief offered to an individual plaintiff defeat a meritorious class action.[180] Furthermore, if an employer discriminatorily denied the plaintiff a promotion, a later promotion of another employee of the same sex[181] or of a better qualified employee of the opposite sex[182] will not defeat a plaintiff's otherwise meritorious claim. The crucial question is whether discrimination occurred; defenses must be based on the employer's treatment of the plaintiff. Subsequent treatment of third parties, however, may be considered by a court in fashioning an appropriate remedy.[183]

H. CONSEQUENCES OF THE SEXUAL HARASSMENT CAUSE OF ACTION

The practical consequences of finding sexual harassment a legitimate basis for a Title VII cause of action are difficult to predict. On the positive side, victims of sexual harassment may be able safely to protest, knowing that Title VII prohibits both sexual harassment and employer retaliation for complaints of such conduct. Supervisors personally liable for sexual harassment or for acquiescence in other employees' sexual advances may be deterred from using their authority in a sexually coercive manner or from tolerating such behavior by their subordinates. The possibility of a Title VII claim may prompt employers to promulgate and strictly enforce policies against sexual harassment and to provide an effective grievance procedure for reporting and investigating complaints of it.

The menace of numerous, frivolous claims is the most often feared consequence of recognizing this cause of action.[184] But that menace, which exists when any type of discrimination is made unlawful, should not preclude meritorious claims and perpetuate barriers to true equal employment. As in any Title VII case, the plaintiff has the burden of establishing a prima facie case. The employer may invoke the defenses discussed above[185] and may attempt to disprove the factual allegations. Further, the traditional judicial protective devices—motions to dismiss, summary judgments, and directed verdicts—may help prevent protracted litigation of clearly frivolous claims. Finally, courts have sought to deter frivolous Title VII suits by assessing plaintiffs guilty of instituting them with defendant's attorney fees.[186] In sum, the solution to the problem of frivolous claims is not to disallow all claims of sexual harassment regardless of their merit, but rather to employ the traditional judicial safeguards.[187]

VI. CONCLUSION

Although all of the seven cases of sexual harassment discussed in this note were based on the same statute, the courts applied different legal principles and rationales. Six of the cases recognized a limited cause of action for sex-

ual harassment. But courts should apply more liberally the strong precedent expressed in other types of Title VII cases in reaching their conclusions. That precedent suggests that sexual advances discriminate on the basis of sex, that a resultant deleterious employment effect constitutes sexual harassment in violation of Title VII, that a pattern of discrimination need not be proved in actions by individuals, and that the employer may be liable for the discriminatory acts of supervisors. Further, judicial recognition that a supervisor may be held personally liable under Title VII, that the employer or supervisor may be held liable for acquiescence in sexual advances by nonsupervisory employees, and that several groups of potential plaintiffs may exist in each instance of sexual harassment, should substantially eliminate sexual cooperation as a condition of employment.

The goal of such a use of Title VII is not to create a sterile, asocial, asexual working environment; it is to prohibit the extortionate use of the employer's power. The fact that the harassment alleged is of a sexual nature is not singled out for disproportionate attention; any demand based on prohibited discrimination and with deleterious employment effects would be equally cognizable. The opportunity to recognize such a cause of action, therefore, should be welcomed by the courts as an opportunity to further Title VII's objective of eliminating invidious and arbitrary barriers to employment.[188]

NOTES

1. Civil Rights Act of 1964, Title VII, Pub. L. No. 88-352, §§ 701-718, 78 Stat. 241 (codified in 42 U.S.C. §§ 2000e to 2000e-17 (1970)).

2. This Note defines a sexual advance as a physical or verbal request for sexual interaction. Sexual harassment is defined as a sexual advance made with an explicit or im-

plicit threat of adverse job consequences for a failure to comply or as one adversely affecting a condition of employment.

Although the precise extent of sexual harassment is unknown, there is some evidence that it occurs significantly often in the employment context. Bralove, "A Cold Shoulder: Career Women Decry Sexual Harassment by Bosses and Clients," *Wall St. J.*, Jan. 29, 1976, at 1, col. 1 (Working Women United's informal survey of 155 working women indicated that 92% believed sexual harassment was a serious problem and 70% had experienced some form of sexual harassment on the job).

3. *Barnes* v. *Train*, 13 Fair Empl. Prac. Cas. 123 (D.D.C. 1974), *revd. sub nom. Barnes* v. *Costle*, 561 F.2d 983 (D.C. Cir. 1977).

4. *Munford* v. *James T. Baines & Co.*, 441 F. Supp. 459 (E.D. Mich. 1977); *Tomkins* v. *Public Serv. Elec. & Gas Co.*, 422 F. Supp. 553 (D.N.J. 1976), *revd.*, 568 F.2d 1044 (3d Cir. 1977); *Garber* v. *Saxon Indus., Inc.*, 14 Empl. Prac. Dec. ¶ 7586 (E.D. Va. 1976), *revd. sub nom. Garber* v. *Saxon Business Prods., Inc.*, 552 F. 2d 1032 (4th Cir. 1977); *Miller* v. *Bank of America*, 418 F. Supp. 233 (N.D. Cal. 1976); *Williams* v. *Saxbe*, 413 F. Supp. 654 (D.D.C. 1976); *Corne* v. *Bausch & Lomb, Inc.*, 390 F. Supp. 161 (D. Ariz. 1975), *vacated on procedural grounds*, 562 F.2d 55 (9th Cir. 1977).

5. *Tomkins* v. *Public Serv. Elec. & Gas Co.*, 568 F.2d 1044 (3d Cir. 1977); *Barnes* v. *Costle*, 561 F.2d 983 (D.C. Cir. 1977); *Garber* v. *Saxon Business Prods., Inc.*, 552 F.2d 1032 (4th Cir. 1977).

6. *E.g.*, Bernstein, "Sexual Harassment on the Job," *Harpers Bazaar*, Aug. 1976, at 12; Lindsey, "Sexual Harassment on the Job and How To Stop It," *Ms.*, Nov. 1977, at 47; Pogrebin, "The Working Woman: Sex Harassment," *Ladies' Home J.*, June 1977, at 24; Safron, "What Men Do to Women on the Job: A Shocking Look at Sexual Harassment," *Redbook*, Nov. 1976, at 149.

7. *E.g.*, Ginsburg & Koreski, "Sexual Advances by an Employee's Supervisor: A Sex-Discrimination Violation of Title VII?," 3 *Employee Rel. L.J.* 83 (1977); Comment, "Employment Discrimination—Sexual Harassment and Title VII—Female Employees' Claim Alleging Verbal and Physical Advances by a Male Supervisor Dismissed as Nonactionable—*Corne* v. *Bausch & Lomb, Inc.*," 51 *N.Y.U.L. Rev.* 148 (1976); 17 *S. Tex. L.J.* 409 (1976).

8. Title VII § 703, 42 U.S.C. § 2000e-2 (1970 & Supp. V 1975).

9. Title VII preempts all other statutory or common-law causes of action against the federal government for employment discrimination. The Supreme Court has commented:

> The balance, completeness, and structural integrity of § 717 are inconsistent with the petitioner's contention that the judicial remedy afforded by § 717(c) was designed merely to supplement other putative judicial relief. His view fails, in our estimation, to accord due weight to the fact that unlike these other supposed remedies, § 717 does not contemplate merely judicial relief. Rather, it provides for a careful blend of administrative and judicial enforcement powers.

Brown v. *General Servs. Admin.*, 425 U.S. 820, 832-33 (1976) (footnote omitted).

10. "Title VII was envisioned as an independent statutory authority meant to provide an aggrieved individual with an additional remedy to redress employment discrimination." H.R. Rep. No. 238, 92d Cong., 1st Sess. 18-19 (1971);

> Despite Title VII's range and its design as a comprehensive solution for the problem of invidious discrimination in employment, the aggrieved individual clearly is not deprived of other remedies he possesses and is not limited to Title VII in his search for relief.

Johnson v. *Railway Express Agency, Inc.*, 421 U.S. 454, 459 (1975).

11. Cf. *Frontiero* v. *Richardson*, 411 U.S. 677 (1973) (statute permitting servicemen but not service women to claim spouse as a "dependent" without regard to actual dependence violates due process clause of fifth amendment); *Reed* v. *Reed*, 404 U.S. 71 (1971) (mandatory statutory preference for men as estate administrators violates equal protection clause of fourteenth amendment).

12. Cf. *Johnson* v. *City of Cincinnati*, 450 F.2d 796, 797 (6th Cir. 1971) (Title VII does not preempt the Civil Rights Act of 1871, 42 U.S.C. §§ 1983, 1985(3) (1970), and an action for discrimination in employment may therefore be brought under that act); *United Packinghouse, Food & Allied Workers Intl. Union* v. *NLRB*, 416 F.2d 1126, 1133 n.11 (D.C. Cir.), *cert. denied*, 396 U.S. 903 (1969) (NLRB has concurrent jurisdiction under the National Labor Relations Act, 29 U.S.C. §§ 151-169 (1976), to deal with some forms of employment discrimination).

13. Title VII § 708, 42 U.S.C. § 2000e-7 (1970 & Supp. V 1975) (Title VII does not

relieve any person from liability under any state law except one requiring employment practices unlawful under Title VII).

14. *Monge v. Beebe Rubber Co.*, 114 N.H. 130, 316 A.2d 549 (1974) (termination by employer in retaliation for rejection of sexual advances constitutes breach of employment contract). *See also* 8 *Creighton L. Rev.* 700 (1975).

15. *Cf. Alexander v. Gardner-Denver Co.*, 415 U.S. 36, 47 (1974) (arbitration is a concurrent, alternative remedy for employment discrimination).

16. *E.g.*, D.C. Code § 22-2304 (1973) (false charges of unchastity).

17. *Cf.* D.C. Code § 22-2305 (1973) (blackmail). The Michigan legislature is considering a bill prohibiting employers from using their power to secure sexual favors from employees. *Detroit Free Press*, May 4, 1978, at 3, col. 2.

18. *Accord*, Whittier & Whittier, "Employment Discrimination: Alternative Remedies to Title VII," 43 *U.M.K.C.L. Rev.* 296, 333 (1975). This Note focuses on individual causes of action under Title VII. While a class action might be maintainable under appropriate circumstances, an individual action will generally be quicker and more effective for individuals in those circumstances.

19. Pub. L. No. 88-352, 78 Stat. 241 (codified in 28 U.S.C. § 1447, 42 U.S.C. §§ 1971, 1975a-1975d, 2000a-2000n-6 (1970)).

20. Civil Rights Act of 1964, Title VII §§ 701-718, 42 U.S.C. §§ 2000e to 2000e-17 (Supp. V 1975).

21. Title VII § 703(a), 42 U.S.C. § 2000e-2(a) (1970).

22. Title VII § 701(b), 42 U.S.C. § 2000e(b) (Supp. V. 1975).

23. It shall be an unlawful employment practice for an employer to discriminate against any of his employees . . . because [such employee] has opposed any practice made an unlawful employment practice by this subchapter, or because he has made a charge . . . under this subchapter.

Title VII § 704, 42 U.S.C. § 2000e-3(a) (Supp. V 1975).

24. All personnel actions affecting employees . . . in executive agencies . . . and in those units of the legislative and judicial branches of the Federal Government having positions in the competitive service . . . shall be made free from any discrimination based on race, color, religion, sex, or national origin.

Title VII, § 717, 42 U.S.C. § 2000e-16(a)

(Supp. V 1975). Though its language differs from that of § 703(a), the Supreme Court has said in construing § 717, "the substantive antidiscrimination law embraced in Title VII was carried over and applied to the Federal Government." *Morton v. Mancari*, 417 U.S. 535, 547 (1974).

25. *See* 110 *Cong. Rec.* 2577 (1964) (remarks of Rep. Smith). *See generally* Wells, "Sex Discrimination and Title VII," 43 *U.M.K.C.L. Rev.* 273, 274-76 (1975).

26. H.R. Rep. No. 238, 92d Cong., 1st Sess. 5, *reprinted in* [1972] *U.S. Code Cong. & Ad. News* 2137, 2141.

27. 110 *Cong. Rec.* 2728, 13,825 (1964).

28. The only exception to this broad proposition is that an employer may hire an individual

on the basis of his religion, sex or national origin in those certain instances where religion, sex or national origin is a bona fide occupational qualification reasonably necessary to the normal operation of that particular business or enterprise.

Title VII § 703(e), 42 U.S.C. § 2000e-2(e) (1970). This exception does not apply to race. *See generally* Sirota, "Sex Discrimination: Title VII and the Bona Fide Occupational Qualification," 55 *Texas L. Rev.* 1025 (1977).

29. The seven cases are: *Munford v. James T. Barnes & Co.*, 441 F. Supp. 459 (D. Colo. 1978); *Tomkins v. Public Serv. Elec. & Gas Co.*, 422 F. Supp. 553 (D.N.J. 1976), *revd.*, 568 F.2d 1044 (3d Cir. 1977); *Garber v. Saxon Indus., Inc.*, 14 Empl. Prac. Dec. ¶ 7586 (E.D. Va. 1976), *revd. sub nom. Garber v. Saxon Business Prods., Inc.*, 552 F.2d 1032 (4th Cir. 1977); *Miller v. Bank of America*, 418 F. Supp. 233 (N.D. Cal. 1976); *Williams v. Saxbe*, 413 F. Supp. 654 (D.D.C. 1976); *Corne v. Bausch & Lomb, Inc.*, 390 F. Supp. 161 (D. Ariz. 1975), *vacated on procedural grounds*, 562 F.2d 55 (9th Cir. 1977); *Barnes v. Train*, 13 Fair Empl. Prac. Cas. 123 (D.D.C. 1974), *revd. sub nom. Barnes v. Costle*, 561 F.2d 978 (D.C. Cir. 1977).

30. *Tomkins v. Public Serv. Elec. & Gas Co.*, 422 F. Supp. 553 (D.N.J. 1976), *revd.*, 568 F.2d 1044 (3d Cir. 1977); *Garber v. Saxon Indus., Inc.*, 14 Empl. Prac. Dec. ¶ 7586 (E.D. Va. 1976), *revd. sub nom. Garber v. Saxon Business Prods., Inc.*, 552 F.2d 1032 (4th Cir. 1977); *Miller v. Bank of America*, 418 F. Supp. 233 (N.D. Cal. 1976); *Corne v. Bausch & Lomb, Inc.*, 390 F. Supp. 161 (D. Ariz. 1975), *vacated on procedural grounds*, 562 F.2d 55 (9th Cir. 1977); *Barnes v. Train*,

13 Fair Empl. Prac. Cas. 123 (D.D.C. 1974), *revd. sub nom. Barnes v. Costle*, 561 F.2d 978 (D.C. Cir. 1977).

31. *Tomkins v. Public Serv. Elec. & Gas Co.*, 422 F. Supp. 553 (D.N.J. 1976), *revd.*, 568 F.2d 1044 (3d Cir. 1977); *Garber v. Saxon Indus., Inc.*, 14 Empl. Prac. Dec. ¶ 7586 (E.D. Va. 1976), *revd. sub nom. Garber v. Saxon Business Prods., Inc.*, 552 F.2d 1032 (4th Cir. 1977); *Barnes v. Train*, 13 Fair Empl. Prac. Cas. 123 (D.D.C. 1974), *revd. sub nom. Barnes v. Costle*, 561 F.2d 978 (D.C. Cir. 1977).

32. 390 F. Supp. 161 (D. Ariz. 1975), *vacated on procedural grounds*, 562 F.2d 55 (9th Cir. 1977).

33. 390 F. Supp. at 163.
34. 390 F. Supp. at 163.
35. 390 F. Supp. at 163.
36. 390 F. Supp. at 164.
37. 413 F. Supp. 654 (D.D.C. 1976).
38. 413 F. Supp. at 657-58.
39. 413 F. Supp. at 659 n.6.
40. 413 F. Supp. at 659 n.6.
41. 413 F. Supp. at 660.
42. 413 F. Supp. at 660-61.
43. 418 F. Supp. 233 (N.D. Cal. 1976).
44. 418 F. Supp. at 234.
45. 418 F. Supp. at 236. The court noted that the plaintiff had failed to file a complaint with the employer's employee relations department, and that the employer had a policy of discouraging and disciplining sexual advances. Since the plaintiff had not given the employer an opportunity to investigate her complaint by means of this internal procedure, there was no showing that the supervisor's actions had the tacit approval of the employer. 418 F. Supp. at 235-36.

46. 418 F. Supp. at 236.
47. 418 F. Supp. at 236.
48. 441 F. Supp. 459 (E.D. Mich. 1977).
49. 441 F. Supp. at 465-66.
50. 441 F. Supp. at 466.
51. 441 F. Supp. at 466.
52. 441 F. Supp. at 466.
53. 14 Empl. Prac. Dec. ¶ 7586 (E.D. Va. 1976), *revd. sub nom. Garber v. Saxon Business Prods., Inc.*, 552 F.2d 1032 (4th Cir. 1977).
54. 14 Empl. Prac. Dec. at ¶ 7586.
55. *Garber v. Saxon Business Prods., Inc.*, 552 F.2d 1032 (4th Cir. 1977).
56. 552 F.2d at 1032.
57. *Barnes v. Costle*, 561 F.2d 983 (D.C. Cir. 1977).
58. *Barnes v. Train*, 13 Fair Empl. Prac. Cas. 123 (D.D.C. 1974), *revd. sub nom.*

Barnes v. Costle, 561 F.2d 983 (D.C. Cir. 1977). The district court reasoned that sexual harassment was not the kind of discriminatory conduct contemplated by Title VII, but was a "controversy underpinned by the subtleties of an inharmonious personal relationship." 13 Fair Empl. Prac. Cas. at 124. The court concluded that the plaintiff was not discriminated against because she refused to comply with her director's sexual demands:

> Regardless of how inexcusable the conduct of plaintiff's supervisor might have been, it does not evidence an arbitrary barrier to continued employment based on plaintiff's sex.

13 Fair Empl. Prac. Cas. at 124.
59. 561 F.2d at 990.
60. 561 F.2d at 990, 992.
61. 561 F.2d at 993.
62. *Miller v. Bank of America*, 418 F. Supp. 233 (N.D. Cal. 1976). *See* text at notes 43-47 *supra*.
63. 561 F.2d at 993.
64. 561 F.2d at 993.
65. 561 F.2d at 993-94. In a lengthy concurring opinion, Judge MacKinnon argued that the case should be reversed and remanded only upon the narrower ground that the employer knew or should have known of the discriminatory conduct of the supervisor. 561 F.2d at 995-1001. MacKinnon first argued that because acts of sexual harassment are outside the supervisor's scope of employment the employer is not liable under the common law of vicarious liability. 561 F.2d at 995-96. Then MacKinnon considered the wording and policies of Title VII and the National Labor Relations Act, which define an employer to include "any agent." 561 F.2d at 997-98. Having found no explicit statement that employers are vicariously liable under Title VII of the Civil Rights Act of 1964, MacKinnon listed three possible rationales for imposing vicarious liability upon the employer: (1) the employer is in a position to know of discriminatory behavior, (2) the employer can take preventive steps, and (3) imposing vicarious liability causes the employer to be especially careful. 561 F.2d at 998-99. MacKinnon concluded that there was sufficient evidence to find that the employer knew or should have known of the supervisor's discriminatory conduct and that the employer was therefore vicariously liable. 561 F.2d at 999-1001.
66. 568 F.2d 1044 (3d Cir. 1977).
67. 422 F. Supp. 553 (D.N.J. 1976), *revd.*, 568 F.2d 1044 (3d Cir. 1977).

68. The United States District Court for New Jersey held that sexual harassment of a female employee by a male supervisor does not constitute sex discrimination under Title VII, but that the summary dismissal of a female employee for filing a grievance alleging sex discrimination was cognizable under Title VII. The plaintiff had alleged that her supervisor made sexual advances toward her and threatened her physically and economically. She complained to the company and sought and obtained a transfer to a less desirable job. Subsequently the plaintiff was fired; she alleged that she was fired because her former supervisor wished to retaliate for her refusal to grant him sexual favors and because the company wished to retaliate for her having filed complaints. 422 F. Supp. at 555.

The court said that Title VII does not provide a federal tort remedy for sexual attacks which "occur in a corporate corridor rather than a back alley." 422 F. Supp. at 556. The court, fearing that "[an] invitation to dinner could become an invitation to a federal lawsuit if a once harmonious relationship turned sour at some later time," concluded that sexual harassment was beyond the intended scope of Title VII. 422 F. Supp. at 557.

The court did find, however, that firing a female employee for filing a complaint of sexual harassment could be discrimination in favor of the retained male supervisor. Regardless of the underlying subject of the complaint, discharge without investigation of a person who complained of illegal discrimination violates Title VII. The court therefore denied the employer's motion to dismiss this part of the plaintiff's claim. 422 F. Supp. at 557.

69. 568 F.2d at 1046.
70. 568 F.2d at 1046-47.
71. 568 F.2d at 1047 n.3.
72. 568 F.2d at 1047 n.3.
73. 568 F.2d at 1046-47.
74. 568 F.2d at 1047.
75. 568 F.2d at 1047 n.4.
76. *Corne* was the major exception to the view that Title VII should be liberally construed. *See* text at notes 32-36 *supra*.
77. In each case the harasser was the plaintiff's immediate supervisor.
78. In each case there was an allegation of an explicit request by the immediate supervisor that the plaintiff engage in sexual relations with him. There were also allegations of sexual remarks, reprimands, verbal abuse and physical force. Despite variations in the combination, repetition, and sequence of these kinds of harassment, each court based its decision on the demand for sexual relations.

The opinions describe the facts of the cases only briefly. The EEOC Charge of Discrimination form in the *Garber* case provides a detailed example of a typical allegation:

When I started in July, Mr. Johnson had nothing but praise for my skills, stating they were ten times superior to those of my predecessors. The *only* reason I was given for my termination was my skills were poor, and that I had refused to take a refresher course in shorthand. I was reviewed on October 25, 1974, and told then to take the course. I called the community college and recreation department and was informed in both instances that the courses would not start again until January. I relayed this to Mr. Johnson and he said fine.

On January 2, when I was informed of my termination, I went to an employment agency and my skills were tested. With unfamiliar equipment and rather tense circumstances I passed an 80WPM dictation exam and typed 84WPM with 2 errors!

I feel the *real* reason I was fired was because I refused to engage in an affair with Mr. Johnson. When I first joined the company I found him to be interesting to talk to. I also felt sorry for him because he was so emotionally disturbed about the total lack of organization in the office and his 4th marriage was in the process of falling apart.

He started coming over to my apartment at all hours of the night. I realize that letting him in was my own mistake, but I had no idea of his intentions. I had heard a lot of office gossip about the affair between him and the ex-secretary but didn't pay any attention to it until sometime later when she reappeared and they had all their afternoon outings and private calls.

A short time later he really started hassling and frightening me to where I had to get my neighbors to come over whenever they saw his car. Too many innocent people, including other employees, had become involved and I finally got up the guts to tell him to stop coming over that I wasn't interested in him. He still persisted.

On December 12, Mr. Johnson said I owed him a dinner and he wanted to talk to me. I agreed to buy him dinner in the hopes we could establish a friendly, but professional relationship. It ended up being more of the same until we were joined by two men from our corporate offices. I decided I had best wait until another time and when he took me home he really shocked me by telling me he was going to spend the night with me! I ordered him to leave and when he did he slammed the door so hard that it cracked and once again my neighbors were alarmed.

He didn't bother me anymore at home and I thought things would be okay then. When he terminated me he said he had made the decision the middle of December but out of the "goodness of his heart" had decided to postpone telling me until January.

79. Each plaintiff's employment status worsened significantly after the alleged harassment. The plaintiffs in *Munford* v. *James T. Barnes & Co.*, 441 F. Supp. 459 (E.D. Mich. 1977); *Williams* v. *Saxbe*, 413 F. Supp. 654 (D.D.C. 1976); *Garber* v. *Saxon Indus., Inc.*, 14 Empl. Prac. Dec. ¶ 7586 (E.D. Va. 1976), *revd. sub nom. Garber* v. *Saxon Business Prods., Inc.*, 552 F.2d 1032 (4th Cir. 1977); and *Miller* v. *Bank of America*, 418 F. Supp. 233 (N.D. Cal. 1976); were fired, allegedly in retaliation for refusing the supervisor's sexual demands. The plaintiffs in *Corne* v. *Bausch & Lomb, Inc.*, 390 F. Supp. 161 (D. Ariz. 1975), *vacated on procedural grounds*, 562 F.2d 55 (9th Cir. 1977), resigned and alleged a constructive discharge. 390 F. Supp. at 162. Termination for filing a complaint of sexual harassment was alleged in *Tomkins* v. *Public Serv. Elec. & Gas. Co.*, 422 F. Supp. 553 (D.N.J. 1976), *revd.*, 568 F.2d 1044 (3d Cir. 1977), while failure to submit to sexual advances allegedly led to the abolition of the plaintiff's job and an unfavorable reassignment in *Barnes*. Except for the constructive discharge in *Corne*, the losses were the direct result of an allegedly retaliatory decision by the plaintiff's immediate supervisors.

80. Since all these cases came upon the defendants' motions to dismiss or on motions for summary judgment, the courts were required to consider all the plaintiffs' factual allegations as true.

81. 418 F. Supp. at 234. The legal significance attached to this fact by the court may have been overstated. *See* text at notes 138-46 *infra*.

82. *Barnes* v. *Train*, 13 Fair Empl. Prac. Cas. 123, 124 (D.D.C. 1974), *revd. sub nom. Barnes* v. *Costle*, 561 F.2d 983 (D.C. Cir. 1977); *Tomkins* v. *Public Serv. Elec. & Gas Co.*, 422 F. Supp. 553, 556 (D.N.J. 1976), *revd.*, 568 F.2d 1044 (3d Cir. 1977).

83. *Barnes* v. *Costle*, 561 F.2d 983, 988-90 (D.C. Cir. 1977); *Tomkins* v. *Public*

Serv. Elec. & Gas Co., 568 F.2d 1044, 1046-47 (3d Cir. 1977).

84. *Munford* v. *James T. Barnes & Co.*, 441 F. Supp. 459 (E.D. Mich. 1977); *Williams* v. *Saxbe*, 413 F. Supp. 654, 658 (D.D.C. 1976). In *Garber*, the court apparently assumed that harassment is a form of sex discrimination since it held that the plaintiff had stated a cause of action under Title VII. *Garber* v. *Saxon Business Prods., Inc.*, 552 F.2d 1032 (4th Cir. 1977). The courts in *Corne* and *Miller* granted the defendants' motions on other grounds and thus did not confront this issue.

85. *Barnes* v. *Costle*, 561 F.2d 983, 993-94 (D.C. Cir. 1977), allowed an action to be maintained on the basis of a single incident.

86. *Munford* v. *James T. Barnes & Co.*, 441 F. Supp. 459 (E.D. Mich. 1977). The court did not discuss this issue but allowed the cause of action.

87. In *Corne* and *Williams* the courts held there would be no cause of action if the complained of activity was merely an isolated incident and was not indicative of an employer policy. *Corne* v. *Bausch & Lomb, Inc.*, 390 F. Supp. 161, 163 (D. Ariz. 1975), *vacated on procedural grounds*, 562 F.2d 55 (9th Cir. 1977); *Williams* v. *Saxbe*, 413 F. Supp. 654, 660 (D.D.C. 1976). The *Miller* court, which in addition took note of an explicit employer policy forbidding sexual harassment concurred in this view. *Miller* v. *Bank of America*, 418 F. Supp. 233, 236 (N.D. Cal. 1976). In *Tomkins*, the court implied that a finding of an employer policy is necessary. *Tomkins* v. *Public Serv. Elec. & Gas Co.*, 568 F.2d 1044, 1047 n.3 (3d Cir. 1977). In *Garber*, the court without discussion held that a cause of action exists when the complaint alleges a policy or practice. *Garber* v. *Saxon Business Prods., Inc.*, 552 F.2d 1032 (4th Cir. 1977).

88. *Corne* v. *Bausch & Lomb, Inc.*, 390 F. Supp. 161 (D. Ariz. 1975), *vacated on procedural grounds*, 562 F.2d 55 (9th Cir. 1977).

89. *Miller* v. *Bank of America*, 418 F. Supp. 233 (N.D. Cal. 1976).

90. At one extreme, the *Corne* court held that an employer is not liable for acts unrelated to the supervisor's job. *Corne* v. *Bausch & Lomb, Inc.*, 390 F. Supp. 161, 163 (D. Ariz. 1975), *vacated on procedural grounds*, 562 F.2d 55 (9th Cir. 1977). At the other extreme *Williams*, as a matter of law, imputed the policy of the supervisor to the employer.

Williams v. *Saxbe*, 413 F. Supp. 654, 660 (D.D.C. 1976).

91. Although EEOC decisions will be cited occasionally, this Note relies primarily upon judicial precedent because of the unresolved issue of the proper weight to be accorded to agency rulings. *Compare* the majority opinions in *General Elec. Co.* v. *Gilbert*, 429 U.S. 125, 141 (1976):

This does not mean that EEOC guidelines are not entitled to consideration in determining legislative intent. But it does mean that courts properly may accord less weight to such guidelines than to administrative regulations which Congress has declared shall have the force of law, or to regulations which under the enabling statute may themselves supply the basis for imposition of liability.

(citations omitted), *with* Justice Brennan's dissent:

[P]rior Title VII decisions have consistently acknowledged the unique persuasiveness of EEOC interpretations in this area. These prior decisions, rather than providing merely that Commission guidelines are "entitled to consideration," as the Court allows, *ante*, at 141, hold that the EEOC's interpretations should receive "great deference."

429 U.S. at 155-56 (citations omitted).

92. The Supreme Court defined the ambit of Title VII in *Griggs* v. *Duke Power Co.*, 401 U.S. 424, 431 (1971):

Discriminatory preference for any group, minority or majority, is precisely and only what Congress has proscribed. What is required by Congress is the removal of artificial, arbitrary, and unnecessary barriers to employment when the barriers operate invidiously to discriminate on the basis of racial or other impermissible classification.

The court recently reiterated that the policy of Title VII is to "prohibit all practices in whatever form which create inequality in employment opportunity" and that this policy should have "highest priority." *Franks* v. *Bowman Transp. Co.*, 424 U.S. 747, 763 (1976).

93. Discrimination may take two forms:

"Disparate treatment" such as alleged in the present case is the most easily understood type of discrimination. The employer simply treats some people less favorably than others because of their race, color, religion, sex, or national origin. Proof of discriminatory motive is critical, although it can in some situations be inferred from the mere fact of differences in treatment. Undoubtedly disparate treatment was the most obvious evil Congress had in mind when it enacted Title VII.

Claims of disparate treatment may be distinguished from claims that stress "disparate impact." The latter involve employment practices that are facially neutral in their treatment of different groups but that in fact fall more harshly on one group than another and cannot be justified by business necessity. Proof of discriminatory motive, we have held, is not required under a disparate impact theory. Either theory may, of course, be applied to a particular set of facts.

International Bhd. of Teamsters v. *United States*, 431 U.S. 324, 335 n.15 (1977) (citations omitted). Claims of sexual harassment fall within the disparate treatment category; the allegation is that the employer treats the plaintiff less favorably than others because of the plaintiff's sex. *See Krzyzewski* v. *Metropolitan Govt. of Nashville*, 14 Empl. Prac. Dec. ¶ 7726, at 5576 (M.D. Tenn. 1976)

([W]hen two employees (of different sexes) with work records of comparable quality are given disparate punishment for engaging in the same conduct, the defendant is guilty of conduct proscribed by Title VII, absent some real and substantial justification for the differing treatment).

94. *McDonald* v. *Santa Fe Trail Transp. Co.*, 427 U.S. 273, 282 n.10 (1976) ("'[n]o more is required to be shown than that race was a 'but for' cause").

95. This is known as "sex-plus" discrimination. For example, an employer may legally refuse to hire married individuals or parents with pre-school children. An employer may not, however, add an illegitimate condition, such as the sex of the employee. Thus, an employer may not refuse to hire married women or women with pre-school-age children. *E.g., Phillips* v. *Martin Marietta*, 400 U.S. 542 (1971); *Sprogis* v. *United Airlines, Inc.*, 444 F.2d 1194 (7th Cir.), *cert. denied*, 404 U.S. 991 (1971). *Contra, Willingham* v. *Macon Tel. Publishing Co.*, 507 F.2d 1084 (5th Cir. 1975) (discrimination against men with long hair not cognizable under Title VII since the interest in the length of one's hair is de minimis).

96. While many Title VII suits allege discrimination against an entire minority class, suits may allege discrimination against only a portion of it. *See* Equal Employment Opportunity Commission Guidelines on Discrimination Because of Sex, 29 C.F.R. § 1604.4(a) (1976).

97. *Sprogis* v. *United Airlines, Inc.*, 444 F.2d 1194, 1198 (7th Cir.), *cert. denied*, 404 U.S. 991 (1971)

([n]or is the fact of discrimination negated by [the defendant's] claim that the female employees occupy a unique position so that there is no distinction between members of opposite sexes within the job category).

The decision in *General Elec. Co. v. Gilbert*, 429 U.S. 125 (1976), holding that pregnancy need not be covered in an employer's disability plan, is distinguished on the grounds that pregnancy is both "confined to women" and "significantly different from the typical covered disease or disability." 429 U.S. at 136. Sexual harassment, on the other hand, is not necessarily confined to one gender.

98. *McDonald Douglas Corp. v. Green*, 411 U.S. 792, 801-04 (1973)

(Title VII tolerates no racial discrimination, subtle, or otherwise. . . . [N]either does it permit petitioner to use respondent's conduct as a pretext for the sort of discrimination prohibited by § 703(a)(1)).

99. Sexual harassment is discrimination on the basis of sex whether the advances are heterosexual or homosexual, provided the advances are directed at only one sex. If sexual advances of the same magnitude are directed at both sexes by a bisexual supervisor, there is no discrimination. *Cf. Bradford v. Sloan Paper Co.*, 383 F. Supp. 1157, 1161 (N.D. Ala. 1974) (no Title VII violation where supervisor was equally offensive to members of both races). *Accord, Williams v. Saxbe*, 413 F. Supp. 654, 659 n.6 (D.C. Cir. 1976); *Barnes v. Costle*, 561 F.2d at 978, 990 n.51 (D.C. Cir. 1977).

No discrimination on the basis of sex occurs if male and female homosexuals are treated similarly. EEOC Decisions 76-67, 76-75 (1976). *See generally*, Siniscalco, "Homosexual Discrimination in Employment," 16 *Santa Clara L. Rev.* 495 (1976). The crucial inquiry, regardless of the sexual orientation of the supervisor and the employee, is whether the advance is directed at members of only one sex. If so, discrimination on the basis of sex has occurred sinch such behavior is "conduct which, had the victim been a member of the opposite sex, would not have otherwise occurred." *Voyles v. Ralph K. Davies Medical Center*, 403 F. Supp. 456 (N.D. Cal. 1975).

100. Title VII § 703(a)(1), 42 U.S.C. § 2000e-2(a)(1) (1970 & Supp. V 1975).

101. This occurred in five of the cases discussed above. *See* note 79 *supra*.

102. *Barnes v. Costle*, 561 F.2d 983, 985 n.7 (D.C. Cir. 1977).

103. Dec. No. 71-2725, [1973] *EEOC Decisions* (CCH) ¶ 6290 (1971).

104. *Harrington v. Vandalia-Butler Bd. of Educ.*, 418 F. Supp. 603 (S.D. Ohio 1976).

105. *Slack v. Havens*, 7 Fair Empl. Prac. Cas. 885 (S.D. Cal. 1973).

106. *Reyes v. Mathews*, 13 Empl. Prac. Dec. ¶ 6066 (D.D.C. 1976).

107. Dec. 71-2725, [1973] *EEOC Decisions* (CCH) ¶ 6290 (1971).

108. Dec. 72-0777, [1973] *EEOC Decisions* (CCH) ¶ 6331 (1971).

109. *Baxter v. Savannah Sugar Ref. Corp.*, 495 F.2d 437 (5th Cir.), *cert. denied*, 419 U.S. 1033 (1974); *Gillen v. Federal Paper Bd. Co.*, 479 F.2d 97 (2d Cir. 1973); *Rowe v. General Motors Corp.*, 457 F.2d 348 (5th Cir. 1972).

110. The concept of constructive discharge evolved in the field of labor relations, where it was applied to employer actions designed to discourage union activity. *See J. P. Stevens & Co. v. NLRB*, 461 F.2d 490, 494 (4th Cir. 1972):

Where an employer deliberately makes an employee's working conditions intolerable and thereby forces him to quit his job because of union activities or union membership, the employer has constructively discharged the employee in violation of § 8(a)(3) of the Act.

Accord, NLRB v. Holly Bra of Cal., Inc., 405 F.2d 870, 872 (9th Cir. 1969).

111. *Young v. Southwestern Sav. & Loan Assn.*, 509 F.2d 140 (5th Cir. 1975) (constructive discharge cognizable). The constructive discharge approach was successfully employed in *Corne* to bring the issue of sexual harassment before a court. Although that court disallowed the claim on other grounds, the court implicitly accepted the constructive discharge as sufficient proof of an adverse employment effect. *Corne v. Bausch & Lomb, Inc.*, 390 F. Supp. 161, 162 (D. Ariz. 1975), *vacated on procedural grounds*, 562 F.2d 55 (9th Cir. 1977).

112. *Brown v. President, Natl. Maritime Union*, 14 Empl. Prac. Dec. ¶ 4546 (S.D.N.Y. 1977) (failure to establish discriminatory conduct renders voluntary resignation nonactionable).

113. *See* Note, "Work Environment Injury Under Title VII," 82 *Yale L.J.* 1695 (1973). *See, e.g.*, cases cited in note 116 *infra*.

114. Dec. No. 74-05, 6 Fair Empl. Prac. Cas. 834 (1973); Dec. No. 72-1561, [1973] *EEOC Decisions* (CCH) ¶ 6354 (1972); Dec. No. 71-2598, [1973] *EEOC Decisions* (CCH)

¶ 6284 (1971). For a detailed analysis of the EEOC's interpretation of the working environment as a condition of employment, see 51 *N.Y.U.L. Rev.* 148, 153-59 (1976).

115. *Rogers* v. *EEOC*, 454 F.2d 234, 238 (5th Cir. 1971), *cert. denied*, 406 U.S. 957 (1972):

> Therefore, it is my belief that employees' psychological as well as economic fringes are statutorily entitled to protection from employer abuse, and that the phrase "terms, conditions, or privileges of employment," in Section 703 is an expansive concept which sweeps within its protective ambit the practice of creating a working environment heavily charged with ethnic or racial discrimination.

Accord, Gray v. *Greyhound Lines, East*, 545 F.2d 169 (D.C. Cir. 1976); *EEOC* v. *International Longshoremen's Assn.*, 511 F.2d 273 (5th Cir.), *cert. denied*, 423 U.S. 994 (1975).

116. *Rogers* v. *EEOC*, 454 F.2d 234, 238 (5th Cir. 1971), *cert. denied*, 406 U.S. 957 (1972):

> I do not wish to be interpreted as holding that an employer's mere utterance of an ethnic or racial epithet which engenders offensive feelings in an employee falls within the proscription of Section 703. But by the same token I am simply not willing to hold that a discriminatory atmosphere could under no set of circumstances ever constitute an unlawful employment practice. One can readily envision working environments so heavily polluted with discrimination as to destroy completely the emotional and psychological stability of minority group workers, and I think Section 703 of Title VII was aimed at the eradication of such noxious practices.

Cf., Dickerson v. *United States Steel Corp.*, 439 F. Supp. 55 (E.D. Pa. 1977) (denying cause of action for racially discriminatory atmosphere):

> As a class claim, [racially discriminatory atmosphere] is virtually incapable of proof in all but the most blatant of situations. Such a nebulous concept— that of 'atmosphere'— is not susceptible to any accepted methods of proof in a court of law.

439 F. Supp. at 74.

117. 409 U.S. 205 (1972).

118. 42 U.S.C. § 3604(a) (1970).

119. *Hackett* v. *McGuire Bros.*, 445 F.2d 442 (3d Cir. 1971).

120. 409 U.S. at 209. For an extensive discussion of the application of *Trafficante* to Title VII, see *EEOC* v. *Bailey Co.*, 563 F.2d 439, 452-54 (6th Cir. 1977).

121. *E.g., Waters* v. *Heublein, Inc.*, 547 F.2d 466 (9th Cir. 1976), *cert. denied*, 431

U.S. 966 (1977); *EEOC* v. *Bailey Co.*, 563 F.2d 439 (6th Cir. 1977). *See also* Note, *supra* note 113, at 1695 (1973).

122. *See* note 116 *supra*.

123. One recent case suggests Title VII applies to the "entire scope of the working environment," *Lucido* v. *Cravath, Swaine & Moore*, 425 F. Supp. 123, 126 (S.D.N.Y. 1977), but another criticizes the concept of atmosphere as "nebulous" and "not susceptible to any accepted methods of proof in a court of law," *Dickerson* v. *United States Steel Corp.*, 439 F. Supp. 55 (E.D. Pa. 1977).

124. Title VII §§ 703, 717, 42 U.S.C. §§ 2000e-2, 2000e-16 (1970 & Supp. V 1975).

125. Title VII § 706. The plaintiff may bring and pursue both an individual and a class action suit simultaneously, and dismissal of the individual suit will not bar the plaintiff from pursuing the class action suit. *Moss* v. *Lane Co.*, 471 F.2d 853 (4th Cir. 1973); *Roberts* v. *Union Co.*, 487 F.2d 387 (6th Cir. 1973); *Capaci* v. *Katz & Besthoff, Inc.*, 72 F.R.D. 71 (E.D. La. 1976).

126. *International Bhd. of Teamsters* v. *United States*, 431 U.S. 324, 336 (1977); *Dickerson* v. *United States Steel Corp.*, 439 F. Supp. 55, 65 (E.D. Pa. 1977); *Croker* v. *Boeing Co.* (Vertol Div.), 437 F. Supp. 1138, 1191 (E.D. Pa. 1977).

127. *McDonald* v. *Santa Fe Trail Transp. Co.*, 427 U.S. 273, 281-82 n.8 (1976). Senator Humphrey distinguished "pattern or practice" from "isolated acts" as follows:

> [A] pattern or practice would be present only when the denial of rights consists of something more than an isolated, sporadic incident, but is repeated, routine, or of a generalized nature. There would be a pattern or practice if, for example, a number of companies or persons in the same industry or line of business discriminated, if a chain of motels or restaurants practices racial discrimination throughout all or a significant part of its system, or if a company repeatedly and regularly engaged in acts prohibited by the statute.

110 *Cong. Rec.* 14270 (1964).

128. *See* discussion of cases at note 87 *supra*.

129. 42 *Mo. L. Rev.* 613, 614 (1977).

130. A third possibility is that the harasser owns the business. A sole proprietor who harasses an employee is liable under the wording of Title VII. § 703(a)(1), 42 U.S.C. § 2000e-2(a)(1) (1970 & Supp. V 1975). Similarly, discriminatory treatment resulting from the collective action of the individuals composing a partnership will expose the entity to

Title VII liability. *Lucido* v. *Cravath, Swaine & Moore,* 425 F. Supp. 123 (S.D.N.Y. 1977) (partnership may be held liable for prohibited discrimination in selection of partners); Note, "Applicability of Federal Antidiscrimination Leglslation to the Selection of a Law Partner," 76 *Mich. L. Rev.* 282 (1977).

131. *See e.g., Flowers* v. *Crouch-Walker Corp.,* 552 F.2d 1277, 1282 (7th Cir. 1977) (employer liable as a principal for violations of Title VII by supervisor); *Young* v. *Southwestern Sav. & Loan Assn.,* 509 F.2d 140, 144 n.7 (5th Cir. 1975) (employer liable for supervisor's acts where consistent with supervisor's apparent authority); *Anderson* v. *Methodist Evangelical Hosp., Inc.,* 464 F.2d 723, 723 (6th Cir. 1972) (employer liable for acts of lower level management); *Rowe* v. *General Motors Corp.,* 457 F.2d 348 (5th Cir. 1972) (corporation liable for discriminatory promotion recommendations of its foremen).

132. *Rowe* v. *General Motors Corp.,* 457 F.2d 348, 359-60 (5th Cir. 1972).

133. *Macey* v. *World Airways, Inc.,* 13 *Empl. Prac. Dec.* ¶ 11,581 (N.D. Cal. 1977).

134. *Anderson* v. *Methodist Evangelical Hosp., Inc.,* 464 F.2d 723, 725 (6th Cir. 1972).

135. *Croker* v. *Boeing Co.* (Vertol Div.), 437 F. Supp. 1138, 1191 (E.D. Pa. 1977); *United States* v. *United States Steel Corp.,* 371 F. Supp. 1045 (N.D. Ala. 1973), *cert. denied,* 429 U.S. 817 (1977).

136. *Corne* v. *Bausch & Lomb, Inc.,* 390 F. Supp. 161, 163 (D. Ariz. 1975), *vacated on procedural grounds,* 562 F.2d 55 (9th Cir. 1977); *Munford* v. *James T. Barnes & Co.,* 441 F. Supp. 459, 466 (E.D. Mich. 1977); *Barnes* v. *Costle,* 561 F.2d 983, 995 (D.C. Cir. 1977) (MacKinnon, J., concurring).

137. Courts have also disagreed as to the applicability of the doctrine of respondeat superior to other civil rights statutes. *Compare Hesselgesser* v. *Reilly,* 440 F.2d 901 (9th Cir. 1971), and *Hill* v. *Toll,* 320 F. Supp. 185 (E.D. Pa. 1970), *with Jennings* v. *Davis,* 476 F.2d 1271 (8th Cir. 1973), and *Salazar* v. *Dowd,* 256 F. Supp. 220 (D. Colo. 1966). For implicit support of a traditional agency analysis in the sexual harassment area, *see* 17 *S. Tex. L.J.* 409, 412, 414 (1976).

138. Note, "Responsibility of Employers for the Actions of Their Employees: The Negligent Hiring Theory of Liability," 53 *Chi.-Kent L. Rev.* 717 (1977); 20 *Okla. L. Rev.* 946 (1976).

139. The agent may of course be personally liable. *See* text at notes 162-71 *infra.* This, however, does not resolve the issue of an employer's liability.

140. This more expansive view of employer liability was taken by the court in *Williams* v. *Saxbe,* 413 F. Supp. 654, 660 (D.D.C. 1976).

141. Restatement (Second) of Agency § 219(2) (1958).

142. Restatement (Second) of Agency § 235, Comment a (1958).

143. Although the court in *Corne* did not refer to agency theory, it implicitly relied on this point when it noted that the supervisor's conduct did not benefit the employer. *Corne* v. *Bausch & Lomb, Inc.,* 390 F. Supp. 161, 163 (D. Ariz. 1975), *vacated on procedural grounds,* 562 F.2d 55 (9th Cir. 1977). The concurring opinion in *Barnes* explicitly relied on it. *Barnes* v. *Costle,* 561 F.2d 983, 995 (D.C. Cir. 1977).

144. Restatement (Second) of Agency § 228(2) (1958).

145. *See Barnes* v. *Costle,* 561 F.2d 983, 995-1001 (D.C. Cir. 1977) (concurring opinion). An employer may be liable under agency theory if the employer had "constructive knowledge" of (*Tomkins* v. *Public Serv. Elec. & Gas Co.,* 568 F.2d 1044, 1048 (3d Cir. 1977)) or gave "tacit approval" to (*Miller* v. *Bank of America,* 418 F. Supp. 233, 235 (N.D. Cal. 1976)) the agent's act.

146. Restatement (Second) of Agency § 219(2)(b), (c) & (d) (1958).

147. Restatement (Second) of Agency § 213 (1958).

148. For a view which recognizes an employer's prima facie liability but which imposes less rigorous steps to ensure supervisors' compliance, *see Industrial Linens Supply Co.* v. *Missouri Commn. on Human Rights,* 539 S.W.2d 641, 644 (Mo. Ct. App. 1976) (decided under state legislation similar to Title VII, Mo. Rev. Stat. §§ 296.010-296.070 (1969)):

It is unnecessary for the purpose of this opinion to decide whether either the doctrine of apparent agency or the doctrine of respondeat superior should be applied in full rigor in proceedings to enforce this type of governmental regulation. For present purposes it suffices to say that an employer is prima facie liable for the acts of its employee done in the course of his duties, and the employer to escape that liability must at least undertake the burden of showing that the employee's acts of discrimination were contrary to express instructions not to discriminate.

149. Restatement (Second) of Agency § 265 (1958):

§ 265. General Rule

(1) A master or other principal is subject to liability for torts which result from reliance upon, or belief in, statements or other conduct within an agent's apparent authority.

(2) Unless there has been reliance, the principal is not liable in tort for conduct of a servant or other agent merely because it is within his apparent authority or apparent scope of employment.

150. *Tidwell* v. *American Oil Co.*, 332 F. Supp. 424 (D. Utah 1971) (employee discriminatorily discharged on basis of race by regional accounting manager).

When American Oil gave its Regional Accounting Manager authority to fire employees, it also accepted responsibility to remedy any harm caused by his unlawful exercise of that authority. The modern corporate entity consists of the individuals who manage it, and little, if any progress in eradicating discrimination in employment will be made if the corporate employer is able to hide behind the shield of individual employee action.

332 F. Supp. at 436. Judge MacKinnon, in his concurring opinion in *Barnes* v. *Costle*, 561 F.2d 978, 995 (D.C. Cir. 1977), takes the opposite view, suggesting that this exception to the scope of employment rule is inapplicable to these circumstances. He does, however, agree that "the supervisor has been provided with an opportunity by the agency." 561 F.2d at 996.

151. Restatement (Second) of Agency § 214 (1958).

§ 214. Failure of Principal To Perform Non-delegable Duty

A master or other principal who is under a duty to provide protection for or to have care used to protect others or their property and who confides the performance of such duty to a servant or other person is subject to liability to such others for harm caused to them by the failure of such agent to perform the duty.

Judge MacKinnon, however, dismissed this consideration without any discussion. *Barnes* v. *Costle*, 561 F.2d 983, 995 (D.C. Cir. 1977).

152. Civil Rights Act of 1968, Title VIII, §§ 801-12, 42 U.S.C. §§ 3601-12 (1977). Under § 804, it is "unlawful [t]o refuse to sell . . . a dwelling to any person because of race, color, religion, sex, or national origin."

153. *Harrison* v. *Otto G. Heinzeroth Mortgage Co.*, 430 F. Supp. 893, 896-97 (N.D. Ohio 1977):

Thus the Court has no difficulty in finding the defendant [employee] liable to the plaintiff. Under the law, such a finding impels the same judgment against the defendant Company and . . . its president, for it is clear that their duty not to discriminate is a non-delegable one, . . . and that in this area a corporation and its officers are responsible for the acts of a subordinate employee, even though these acts were neither directed nor authorized. . . . This ruling troubles the Court to some extent, for it seems harsh to punish innocent and well-intentioned employers for the disobedient wrongful acts of their employees. However, great evils require strong remedies, and the old rules of the law require that when one of two innocent people must suffer, the one whose acts permitted the wrong to occur is the one to bear the burden of it.

United States v. *Youritan Constr. Co.*, 370 F. Supp. 643, 649 (N.D. Cal. 1973), *modified on other grounds*, 509 F.2d 623 (9th Cir. 1975):

The discriminatory conduct of an apartment manager or rental agent is, as a general rule, attributable to the owner and property manager of the apartment complex, both under the doctrine of *respondeat superior* and because the duty to obey the law is non-delegable.

Accord, Williamson v. *Hampton Management Co.*, 339 F. Supp. 1146, 1149 (N.D. Ill. 1972); *Marr* v. *Rife*, 503 F.2d 735, 742 (6th Cir. 1974).

154. Fair Labor Standards Act of 1938, ch. 676, 52 Stat. 1060 (codified in 29 U.S.C. §§ 201-19 (1976)).

155. 29 U.S.C. §§ 203(*1*), 212 (1976).

156. *Lenroot* v. *Interstate Bakeries Corp.*, 146 F.2d 325, 328 (8th Cir. 1945):

[T]he Act contains no suggestion that the mere declaration by corporate officers of a policy of obedience to the law, or the absence of a grant of authority by them to the hiring foremen to disobey it, leaves the court with no duty of enforcement. On the contrary, such corporations must be held strictly accountable for the child labor violations of subordinates. Their duty does not end with mere directive communication to such subordinates. . . . [T]he mandate of the statute is directed to the employer and "he may not escape it by delegating it to others." The "duty rests on the employer to inquire into the conditions prevailing in his business. He does not rid himself of that duty because the extent of the business may preclude his personal supervision, and compel reliance on subordinates. He must then stand or fall with those whom he selects to act for him. . . . [T]he duty must be held personal, or we nullify the statute. . . ."

(Footnotes omitted.) *Accord, Shultz v. Salinas*, 416 F.2d 412, 414 (5th Cir. 1969); *Goldberg v. Kickapoo Prairie Broadcasting Co.*, 288 F.2d 778, 781 (8th Cir. 1961).

157. See, e.g., *Washington v. Safeway Corp.*, 467 F.2d 945 (10th Cir. 1972); *Croker v. Boeing Co.*, 437 F. Supp. 1138 (E.D. Pa. 1977); *Dickerson v. United States Steel Corp.*, 439 F. Supp. 55 (E.D. Pa. 1977); *Howard v. National Cash Register Co.*, 388 F. Supp. 603 (S.D. Ohio 1975).

158. The "reason to know" provision has been added here to clarify the duty of a reasonably prudent employer or agent. Its presence makes unnecessary the difficult task of proving actual knowledge and precludes an employer from ignoring discrimination in order to avoid liability for it.

159. [A]cts of fellow employees are not usually bases of claims against the employer. "Liability can only be premised on the employer's failure to take reasonable steps to prevent racial harassment of which its upper level management is aware.

Dickerson v. United States Steel Corp., 439 F. Supp. 55, 75 (E.D. Pa. 1977) (quoting *Croker v. Boeing Co.* (Vertol Div.), 437 F. Supp. 1138, 1192 (E.D. Pa. 1977)).

160. Prompt remedial action by the employer following its discovery of supervisory discrimination may, of course, effectively resolve and settle Title VII discrimination claims, and while such action cannot relieve the employer of legal liability under agency theory, it should sometimes mitigate the employer's damages. This approach encourages employers to investigate and reconcile discrimination claims.

161. *Marlowe v. Fisher Body Div. of Gen. Motors*, 11 Fair Empl. Prac. Cas. 1357, 1358 (E.D. Mich. 1975).

162. *Keeler v. Hills*, 408 F. Supp. 386, 387 (N.D. Ga. 1975):

[U]nder the 1972 Amendments to Title VII, 42 U.S.C. § 2000e-16(c), these federal defendants may only be sued in their official capacity, not individually. . . . This is because § 2000e-16(c) requires that a suit by a federal employee alleging racial discrimination be maintained against the head of the department which employs the plaintiff employee.

163. *Tillman v. City of Boaz*, 548 F.2d 592 (5th Cir. 1977); *Curran v. Portland Superintending School Comm.*, 435 F. Supp. 1063 (D. Me. 1977); *Compston v. Borden, Inc.*, 424 F. Supp. 157 (S.D. Ohio 1976); *Harbert*

v. Rapp, 419 F. Supp. 6 (W.D. Okla. 1976); *Padilla v. Stringer*, 395 F. Supp. 495 (D.N.M. 1974).

164. Title VII, § 701(b), 42 U.S.C. § 2000e(b) (1970 & Supp. V 1975).

165. Restatement (Second) of Agency § 1(3) (1958).

166. See, e.g., *Tillman v. City of Boaz*, 548 F.2d 592 (5th Cir. 1977); *Curran v. Portland Superintending School Comm.*, 435 F. Supp. 1063 (D. Me. 1977); *Munford v. James T. Barnes & Co.*, 441 F. Supp. 459 (E.D. Mich. 1977); *Harbert v. Rapp*, 419 F. Supp. 6 (W.D. Okla. 1976); *Doski v. M. Goldseker Co.*, 9 Empl. Prac. Dec. ¶ 10,135 (D. Md. 1975).

167. *Padilla v. Stringer*, 395 F. Supp. 495 (D.N.M. 1974).

168. *Compston v. Borden, Inc.*, 424 F. Supp. 157 (S.D. Ohio 1976).

169. The employer's liability is discussed in text at notes 129-61 *supra*.

170. Restatement (Second) of Agency § 217A, Comment on Clause (a) (1958): "A principal is jointly and severally liable with the agent for whose tortious conduct he is responsible. . . ."

171. See *Tillman v. City of Boaz*, 548 F.2d 592 (5th Cir. 1977) (order dismissing claim against city for lack of jurisdiction under Title VII reversed).

[T]he charge was made against both the Mayor [who terminated plaintiff], acting as a city official, and the City. Further, the reinstatement requested by [plaintiff] could only be granted by the City as her employer.

548 F.2d at 594.

An analogy may be drawn to cases in which unions are joined as defendants in suits against employers in order to allow the plaintiff complete relief and to protect the unions' own interests. See *Grogg v. General Motors Corp.*, 72 F.R.D. 523 (S.D.N.Y. 1976); *Evans v. Shermon Park Hotel*, 503 F.2d 177 (D.C. Cir. 1974). See Fed. R. Civ. P. 19(a)(1).

172. For purposes of clarity in this section, "woman" is used in place of "the aggrieved." Corresponding references to the sex opposite that of the aggrieved are phrased in the male gender. These labels are employed only for clarity; the analysis is equally applicable if the labels are interchanged, or if both individuals are of the same sex.

173. See text at notes 117-23 *supra* for the suggestion that the right to an interracial en-

vironment might include a right under Title VII to a work environment free of illegal discrimination.

174. *See* text at notes 99-109 *supra*.

175. Title VII sets down jurisdictional standards by defining an employer in § 701(b) as

a person engaged in an industry affecting commerce who has fifteen or more employees for each working day in each of twenty or more calendar weeks in the current or preceding calendar year.

42 U.S.C. § 2000e(b) (1970 & Supp. V 1975).

176. *See Lewis* v. *General Motors Corp.*, 557 F.2d 1255 (8th Cir. 1977); *McDonnell Douglas Corp.* v. *Green*, 411 U.S. 792 (1973).

177. *Cf. Compston* v. *Borden, Inc.*, 424 F. Supp. 157 (S.D. Ohio 1976) (court awarded nominal damages because supervisor demeaned employee's religion, but it awarded no reinstatement or back pay, since discharge was not motivated by discrimination against the religion).

178. *Barnes* v. *Costle*, 561 F.2d 983, 990 (D.C. Cir. 1977); *Williams* v. *Saxbe*, 413 F. Supp. 654, 659 n.6 (D.D.C. 1976). An analogy can be drawn to those cases in which employees of both sexes or races were subjected to other kinds of offensive conduct. *See, e.g., Gilliam* v. *City of Omaha*, 388 F. Supp. 842, 854 (D. Neb. 1975), *affd.*, 524 F.2d 1013 (8th Cir. 1975) (all employees, regardless of race or sex, were subjected to abusive treatment); *Bradford* v. *Sloan Paper Co.*, 383 F. Supp. 1157, 1161 (N.D. Ala. 1974).

179. *Reyes* v. *Mathews*, 13 Empl. Prac. Dec. ¶ 11,323 (D.D.C. 1976).

180. *Senter* v. *General Motors Corp.*, 532 F.2d 511 (6th Cir.), *cert. denied*, 429 U.S. 870 (1976).

181. *Skelton* v. *Balzano*, 424 F. Supp. 1231 (D.D.C. 1976).

182. *Gillin* v. *Federal Paper Board Co.*, 479 F.2d 97 (2d Cir. 1973).

183. One other employer defense deserves attention. There is some support for the proposition that if "sex plus" discrimination only insignificantly affects employment opportunities, then the employer will not be found in violation of Title VII. *See Dodge* v. *Giant Food, Inc.*, 488 F.2d 1333 (D.C. Cir. 1973) (grooming standards which differed on the basis of sex not violative of Title VII). *See* B. Schlei & P. Grossman, *Employment Discrimination Law* 117 (1976). This principle has been limited to cases in which courts

have found no distinct employment disadvantages for either sex and in which the individual right infringed upon is not fundamental. *Dodge* v. *Giant Food, Inc.*, 488 F.2d at 1337. Therefore, this defense would probably not be available to an employer in a sexual harassment case—such discrimination does not produce obvious and significant disadvantages for one sex. *See Sprogis* v. *United Airlines, Inc.*, 444 F.2d 1194 (7th Cir.), *cert. denied*, 404 U.S. 991 (1971).

184. *Miller* v. *Bank of America*, 418 F. Supp. at 236 ("flirtations of the smallest order would give rise to liability"); *Corne* v. *Bausch & Lomb, Inc.*, 390 F. Supp. at 164 (employer would be required to hire "employees who were asexual").

185. *See* text at notes 174-83 *supra*.

186. *Carrion* v. *Yeshiva Univ.*, 535 F.2d 722 (2d Cir. 1976); *United States Steel Corp.* v. *United States*, 519 F.2d 359 (3d Cir. 1975); *Copeland* v. *Martinez*, 435 F. Supp. 1178 (D.D.C. 1977). *See* Title VII, § 706(k), 42 U.S.C. § 2000e-5(k)(1970 & Supp. V 1975).

187. *Accord, Barnes* v. *Costle*, 561 F.2d at 994 n.81; *Tomkins* v. *Public Serv. Elec. & Gas Co.*, 422 F. Supp. at 556; 51 *N.Y.U.L. Rev.* 148, 162-66 (1976). Similarly, traditional judicial relief—actual damages and injunctive orders—is available under Title VII. The courts also enjoy some flexibility in awarding Title VII relief. They may safeguard against renewed discrimination, *Ostapowicz* v. *Johnson Bronze Co.*, 369 F. Supp. 522 (W.D. Pa. 1973), *modified on other grounds*, 541 F.2d 394 (3d Cir. 1976), *cert. denied*, 429 U.S. 1041 (1977), and use creative kinds of remedies, *e.g.*, requiring supervisors to be trained in the law and application of Title VII. *Johnson* v. *Ryder Truck Lines, Inc.*, 555 F.2d 1181 (4th Cir. 1977). Courts can thus provide adequate relief for any Title VII plaintiff, including victims of sexual harassment. Comment, 51 *N.Y.U.L. Rev.* at 166 (1976). *See generally* Comment, "Affirmative Relief Under Title VII of the Civil Rights Act of 1964," 29 *Baylor L. Rev.* 373 (1977); Comment, "Title VII: Making Discrimination Victims Whole," 13 *Willamette L.J.* 109 (1976).

188. Three sexual harassment cases have arisen in the federal courts since the completion of this Note. In *Neeley* v. *American Fidelity Assurance Co.*, 17 Fair Empl. Prac. Cas. 482 (W.D. Okla. 1978), a vice-president had told a female employee dirty jokes and

placed his hands on her shoulders while explaining work duties. The court held there had been no violation of Title VII since the defendant had a strictly enforced policy against sexual harassment, the employer did not know of the vice-president's behavior, and continued benefits or employment were not conditioned on the plaintiff's acquiescence. In both *Rinkel* v. *Associated Pipeline Contractors*, 17 Fair Empl. Prac. Cas. 224 (D. Alas. 1978), and *Stringer* v. *Commonwealth of Pa. Dept. of Community Affairs, Bureau of Human Resources*, 446 F. Supp. 704 (M.D. Pa. 1978), causes of action for sexual harassment were recognized, for a failure to hire and for a discharge, respectively, in reliance on *Tomkins* v. *Public Serv. Elec. & Gas Co.*, 568 F.2d 1044 3d Cir. 1977).

16. Sexual Harassment: Finding a Cause of Action Under Title VII*

WILLIAM C. SEYMOUR

A female employee rejects an invitation to dinner from her supervisor. She returns to work the following day to discover that her pay has been cut, a retaliatory action taken by the supervisor. Another female worker is repeatedly the victim of sexual overtures and unwanted physical contact by her boss. This pressure becomes sufficient for her to resign in order to avoid further embarrassment.

The above situations are illustrative of a problem which is rapidly emerging in the American business community: sexual harassment. While there is no precise definition of the term, sexual harassment involves the problem of individuals who use their power and position in an organization to extort sexual gratification from their subordinates.

The discussion in this paper is divided into four parts. The introductory section briefly presents some of the studies which indicate the degree of sexual harassment which, in fact, exists in business. Section two provides a comparison between an aggrieved employee's available remedies under state tort law and the employee's potential remedy under Title VII of the 1964 Civil Rights Act, the principal federal employment discrimination remedy.

The third part of this presentation focuses upon the question of whether Title VII's prohibition against "sex discrimination" includes a prohibition against "sexual harassment." While there are a number of courts which permit a plaintiff to make a claim under Title VII for sexual harassment, there are other courts (most notably the Arizona District Court) which find that sexual harassment is not sex discrimination, and therefore cannot be controlled by use of Title VII.

Section four explores the principal evolving theory in the federal court system which permits the plaintiff to include the corporate employer in her Title VII claim (as opposed to the plaintiff suing the supervisor alone). This trend is highly significant, because it refutes the approach taken by both state tort law and by the Arizona District Court, in which a supervisor's act of harassment would normally *not* implicate the corporate employer, unless the employer authorized or condoned the supervisor's conduct.

What is the incidence of sexual harassment today? A study made by the United Nations Ad Hoc Group on Equal Rights for Women in 1975 received responses from 875 women and men employed by the UN in New York. The responses indicated that a startling 50 percent of the women and 31 percent of the men had either personally experienced, or had witnessed, some form of sexual harassment by individuals in positions of authority. The report by the Ad Hoc group indicated that:

[t]he single most specific situation in which such unprofessional conduct was

*Source: From Labor Law Journal (March 1979), pp. 139-55. Copyright © 1979 by William C. Seymour. Reprinted by permission.

reported was in the matter of promotion (62 percent of all women who named cases); followed by recruitment (13 percent); obtaining a permanent contract (11 percent); and transfer and going on missions (7 percent each).[1]

The problem of sexual harassment was also extensively researched in 1976, by *Redbook* magazine.

Nine thousand women responded to the magazine's questionnaire; the majority were in their 20's and early 30's and earned between $5,000 and $10,000 per year in white-collar jobs. Nine out of ten respondents said they had experienced unwanted sexual attention at work, ranging from leers and remarks to overt requests for sexual favors with the implied threat of retaliation.[2]

To say that the position of a victim of harassment is difficult greatly understates the extent of her problem. Although she has been harassed, an employee may well be reluctant to bring a complaint against her supervisor to a higher level of management. Many employees fear that their complaint will be shrugged off by higher management, leaving them in the still less desirable position of returning to work under the same supervisor, who is aware that the employee attempted to report him. Many other employees may be deterred simply because the supervisor's acts of harassment may be taken as implied acquiescence by higher management; an employee may well assume that a truly interested management would not allow such acts of harassment to continue.

An injured employee also faces economic ramifications from acts of harassment. Should she resign in the face of pressure, it is unlikely that the employee will be eligible for unemployment compensation. Further, there remains the potential problem of negative ratings from the employee's former employer (which may have been the product of a rejected supervisor), which may act to injure the individual's future employment prospects.[3]

Should an aggrieved employee seek a remedy in the legal arena, her choices fall into two broad categories: state tort law, and specific antidiscrimination statutes. A brief overview of the legal tools available to a plaintiff will demonstrate the reason why plaintiffs may prefer to bring cases under Title VII rather than under state law.

STATE TORT LAW AND TITLE VII

In the absence of any specific state antidiscrimination law, a plaintiff who has been harassed will probably have to rely upon the state's law of intentional torts. The plaintiff may argue that the supervisor has committed an assault and battery against her when the supervisor forces his attentions upon the plaintiff. Assault involves fear of imminent physical injury, while battery requires an "unpermitted contact," ranging from severe injury to a physical contact, such as squeezing an arm.

The limitation in using these intentional torts as a basis of recovery lies in the general unwillingness of the court system to hold anyone liable for the misconduct other than the supervisor himself. The law, as a rule, will not impute an intentional tort to an employer, unless the employer has specifically authorized the employee to perform the act. Since the likelihood that a corporate employer has explicitly authorized acts of sexual harassment is small, the plaintiff will probably be limited to recovering from the supervisor alone.[4]

The drawback of this position from the plaintiff's point of view is that the corporate employer rather than the supervisor is the defendant with the most financial resources. If the supervisor is a low level employee, he may well turn out to be judgmentproof; and in the absence of suing the corporate employer, the plaintiff will be left with an unenforced judgment.

The other intentional tort which a plaintiff might utilize is "intentional infliction of emotional distress." The plaintiff suing under this theory again encounters the problem of court reluctance to impute the supervisor's actions to the corporate employer. This reluctance is often due to the court's fear that a flood of questionably valid lawsuits may be filed by plaintiffs who seek to "cash in" on the claim of emotional injury.

This fear leads some states to require that the "distress" be accompanied by an intention on the part of the defendant to cause physical harm (making the action a variant of assault). A few courts actually require a showing of physical contact before granting a recovery for emotional injury (an analogy to battery). Finally, many courts refuse to award a recovery unless the plaintiff can prove that her injury has resulted in a *physiological* symptom. For example, a plaintiff may be required to prove that the defendant's actions resulted in the plaintiff getting migraine headaches, an ulcer, or a nervous tic. The remaining courts are more willing to accept the premise that sufficiently egregious conduct by a defendant can generate emotional distress, and will accept this claim on the strength of the plaintiff's assertion that purely emotional injury resulted.[5]

Title VII, in contrast, has been construed by a number of courts and by the Equal Employment Opportunity Commission as protecting not only the employee's financial status from discriminatory conduct but also the employee's emotional well being while on the job. The Fifth Circuit Court of Appeals in a 1971 racial discrimination case stated:

> Therefore, it is my belief that the employee's psychological as well as economic fringes are statutorily entitled to protection from employer abuse, and that the phrase "terms, conditions, or privileges of employment" in section 703 is an expansive concept which sweeps within its protective ambit the practice of creating a work environment heavily charged with ethnic or racial discrimination.[6]

A second broad disincentive to a plaintiff suing under state law is the problem of retaliation by the employer as a response to an employee's decision to bring suit. Absent legislation specifically limiting the employer's right to dismiss an employee, this potential action by the employer may be viewed as a sufficiently strong deterrent to prevent a plaintiff from ever filing a suit.

Title VII explicitly provides protection for the plaintiff. Section 704 states:

> It shall be an unlawful employment practice for an employer to discriminate against any of his employees . . . because [the employee] has opposed any practice made an unlawful employment practice by this title, or because [the employee] has made a charge, testified, assisted, or participated in any manner in an investigation, proceeding, or hearing under this title.[7]

A plaintiff will also be concerned about the amount of time which must pass before a court schedules her claim to be heard. In both the state and federal court system, this delay in civil matters can run into years. In an effort to alleviate this problem, Title VII states that when an action under the Act is filed in district court, a judge is to be immediately designated to hear the case at the earliest possible time.[8]

The cost of an attorney, as well as the problem of finding a lawyer with the necessary expertise in the field, may act to deter a plaintiff who is considering recourse to the legal system. In a state suit, the plaintiff will have to engage an attorney if her case is to be processed, or else she must proceed in a pro se action and represent herself. Payment of the attorney will have the result of reducing a plaintiff's award. For example, if a case is handled under a contingent fee arrangement, one third to one half of the recovery may go to the plaintiff's attorney as payment.

Title VII responds to these difficulties in two ways. The 1972 amendments to the 1964 Act gave the Equal Opportunity Commission the power to conduct suits in the agency's name on behalf of injured plaintiffs. This policy benefits an injured plaintiff both in the saving of financial resources, and also by the expertise which the EEOC can bring to bear on the problem.[9] The Act also alleviates some of the plaintiff's financial burden by permitting the court to award payment of reasonable attorney's fees as an independent part of the plaintiff's recovery.[10]

In considering the advantages which the state system offers over those of Title VII, two features stand out. Title VII has been construed by the 6th Circuit to permit only the award of actual or compensatory damages to a plaintiff. Actual damages reflect the real injury suffered by the plaintiff, and include injuries resulting from loss of income, the cost of medical expenses, and mental or emotional distress. However, the Act has been construed to prevent the award of punitive damages, which reflect the court's decision to punish the defendant for exceptional carelessness or for a defendant's willful injury of another.[11] These damages are not based upon proof of injury actually suffered by a plaintiff. Rather, the plaintiff in such a circumstance is a windfall beneficiary.

State tort law, in contrast, permits punitive damages to be awarded in the case of intentional torts.[12] The plaintiff must therefore evaluate the likelihood of receiving the bonus of a punitive damages award when considering the question of which law to use as the basis of her action.

A second advantage of using state law to litigate a claim is the difference between the Title VII and state tort statute of limitations. A statute of limitations is a legislatively created "time limit" within which a legal claim must be filed. If the claim is filed after the limitations period, a court will refuse to consider the claim. Title VII has a six month time limit within which a claim of discrimination must be reported.[13] State tort law usually contains a longer limitation period, usually two years from time of injury.[14] Thus, a plaintiff who has waited too long before bringing a Title VII action may be forced to fall back on state tort law as the only method of obtaining relief.

CASES DENYING RECOVERY

Two federal courts have rejected a plaintiff's claim that sexual harassment is sex discrimination prohibited by Title VII. In the case of *Tomkins* v. *Public Service Electric and Gas Co.* (*Tomkins I*, 1976),[15] the plaintiff was approached by her supervisor while the two were discussing possible job advancement for the plaintiff. After the plaintiff rejected the supervisor's sexual suggestion (which were accompanied by efforts to restrain the plaintiff by force), the supervisor engaged in harassment taking the form of disciplinary layoffs and threats of demotion. The plaintiff was finally terminated by the corporation fifteen months after the original incident with the supervisor.

Tomkins I first poses an interesting, yet specious, argument concerning the scope of Title VII. Rather than viewing harassment as being discrimination against an individual because of her sex, the court views it as merely being discrimination because of an individual's refusal to engage in sexual activity. The court's basic point is that discrimination due to *sexual* activities is not sex discrimination under the statute.

> Title VII was enacted in order to remove those artificial barriers to employment which are based upon unjust and long encrusted prejudice. Its aim is to make careers open to talents irrespective of race or sex. It is not intended to provide a federal tort remedy for what amounts to physical attack motivated by sexual desire on the part of a supervisor and which happened to occur in a corporate corridor rather than in a back alley.[16]

The court's concern over sexual harassment cases reaching the federal system appears to be based upon the fear that a large number of lawsuits could result from situations where a female plaintiff claims that a supervisor's decision not to promote or hire

her is retaliation for spurned sexual advances. The court is undoubtedly concerned about the overcrowded dockets which exist in many of the federal courts. Additionally, in rejecting the EEOC's contention that the volume of cases would not increase substantially, the court may also have been concerned with the EEOC's current unenviable track record of an estimated 130,000 backlogged cases.[17]

The court's argument, however, ignores the plain fact that the supervisory conduct was directed *only* at females. The Court of Appeals for the District of Columbia stated:

> But for her womanhood, from all that appears, her participation in sexual activity would never have been solicited . . . [She] became the target of her superior's sexual demands as the price for holding the job.[18]

The key to a Title VII action is conduct which acts principally against employees protected under the Act, resulting in a disproportionate percentage of this group being adversely treated. The act does not limit the type of barrier which might be erected against one of these groups. The basic provision of Title VII articulates a comprehensive, broad prohibition against *all* discrimination, regardless of form.

> It shall be an unlawful employment practice for an employer to fail or refuse to hire or to discharge any individual or otherwise to discriminate against any individual with respect to his compensation, terms, conditions, or privileges of employment, because of such individual's race, color, religion, sex, or national origin.[19]

If the conduct being examined is, in fact, sex discrimination, then whether or not the courts will have to accommodate additional cases is irrelevant to the plain fact that an aggrieved plaintiff has the right to bring her case into the judicial system. Other courts have considered the danger of a multitude of lawsuits, and have regarded this hazard as minimal. The position has been supported by the Third Circuit in *Tomkins II* (the decision which reversed the *Tom-*

kins I case) and by the U.S. District Court in the District of Columbia in *Williams* v. *Saxbe*.[20]

Further, the court has not given adequate consideration to the fact that, while a plaintiff may be able to bring a totally spurious claim into the federal court system, that claim will not survive a motion to dismiss nor a directed verdict if the plaintiff fails to support her claim. A plaintiff in a Title VII action is required to establish a prima facie claim of discrimination.

The individual plaintiff must prove that she is within a class of individuals protected by Title VII (here, that she is a member of the female sex). Next, she must demonstrate that she was qualified for the particular job or promotion, that she was denied the opportunity, and that the employer afterward continued to search for a candidate for the position.[21] The potential flood of lawsuits, while they might initially occur, would probably not continue if the courts demonstrated an unwillingness to permit cases to remain in the system which could not establish a prima facie case of discrimination.

The leading case denying recovery to a harassed plaintiff under Title VII is *Corne* v. *Bausch and Lomb*.[22] In a fact pattern similar to *Tomkins I*, two women plaintiffs rejected the sexual advances of their supervisor. The harassment continued to the point that the plaintiffs resigned rather than continue to be subjected to abuse. The *Corne* court rejected the plaintiff's Title VII claim.

The court in *Corne* took the position that harassment committed by the supervisor was the act of the supervisor only, and bore *no* relationship to the employer corporation. Because the supervisor's conduct was not the result of a company policy, the court concluded that the corporation would in fact be harmed rather than benefited when such conduct took place. Since under this theory the corporation would not have anything to gain from the supervisor's misconduct, the corporation should not be held liable for discrimination under Title VII.

The court stated:

In the present case, Mr. Price's conduct appears to be nothing more than a personal proclivity, peculiarity, or mannerism. By his alleged sexual advance, Mr. Price was satisfying a personal urge. . . . Nothing in the complaint alleges, nor can it be construed, that the conduct complained of was company directed policy which deprived women of employment opportunities. A reasonably intelligent reading of the statute demonstrates it can only mean that an unlawful employment practice must be discrimination on the part of the employer, Bausch and Lomb. Further, there is nothing in the act which could reasonably be construed to have it apply to "verbal and physical sexual advances" by another employee, even though he be in a supervisory capacity where such complained of acts or conduct had no relationship to the nature of the employment.

The *Corne* court notes that there is little in the Act, or in the history surrounding Title VII, to explain or develop the concept of "sex discrimination."

It may be observed further that Title VII itself is ambiguous regarding the relationship between the supervisor and his employer for the purpose of imposing liability against the employer. The statute defines "employer" as "a person engaged in an industry affecting commerce . . . and any agent of such a person. . . ."[23] Beyond this rather unhelpful definition, the statute and the legislative history offer little in the way of concrete assistance. The *Corne* court thus falls back upon the concepts of agency and respondeat superior (master and servant) liability, as developed in the state and common law.

The concept of respondeat superior (or, "let the master answer") has developed into an extensive body of legal concepts designed to allow a person injured by a subordinate of a corporation to hold the corporation or employer liable for the subordinate's actions. This legal doctrine permits inclusion of the

corporation as a defendant on the theory that the corporation was the "master" of its employees.[24]

There are, however, two obstacles to the application of respondeat superior in a Title VII case. It is first necessary to prove that the subordinate is, in fact, a "servant" rather than simply an agent of the corporation. An agent is an employee whose duty is to perform a limited range of acts for the employer. The employer takes no responsibility beyond the agent's performance of his limited duty.

The term "servant" requires that there be an employment relationship in which the employer has the authority to control the physical details of the servant's work.[25] This requirement would seem to pose little problem to a Title VII plaintiff, since the supervisor in the harassment situation is not a limited agent, and would appear to fit the category of servant.

The more difficult hurdle to the plaintiff in a harassment case lies in the observation that courts generally will *not* hold a master responsible for a willful or intentional tort committed by the master's servant. Typically, only acts involving employee carelessness, forgetfulness, or error in judgment (negligence) form the basis for employer liability. The rationale behind this reluctance stems from the factors which a court normally uses in considering whether a servant's actions are within the "scope of his employment" with the master.

While there is no single test to determine the "scope of employment" question, some of the factors which a court would normally include in its assessment consist of the following. Is the type of conduct which the servant has undertaken an act normally performed by this category of worker? Is the act being performed at the usual time and place for such activity? Is the activity performed for the benefit of the master?[26]

In essence, a court is concerned with whether or not the action of the servant has been authorized by the master or is the type of activity which the master would have reason to know his servant is likely to perform. This is the argument upon which *Corne* is based.

In the case of sexual harassment, a plaintiff would have to argue: that there is an explicit or tacit company policy which condones the taking of sexual liberties among its employees; that the employer has reason to know that one of his employees has or may commit an act of sexual harassment; and that the employer has done nothing to prevent the occurrence. While not frequent, the situation where management condones employer abuses does occasionally occur in the employment context.

In *Slack* v. *Havens*,[27] a California district court found an employer liable for a supervisor's racial slurs against a group of employees who were assigned duties as custodial cleaners. The slurs were statements to the effect that "blacks should keep in their places." The court based its conclusion in part upon the finding that:

> Finally, by backing up [the supervisor's] ultimatum the top level management of Industries ratified his discriminatory conduct and must be held liable for the consequences thereof.

FURTHER TRENDS

Significantly, however, there appears to be an increasing willingness on the part of both the EEOC and of the federal courts to find an employer liable *without* an additional finding of employer acquiescence, ratification, or unreasonable lack of awareness of the employee's acts. Note that this approach was proposed by the plaintiff in the *Tomkins I and II* series of cases as a basis for recovery, although the appellate court did not reach the argument since the plaintiff had already established a violation of Title VII on other grounds.[28]

An employer, for example, has been held liable by the EEOC for its supervisor's act of addressing a black employee as "boy" while not addressing white employees in the same fashion.[29] The EEOC has also found liability for supervisors' acts of calling black employees "Sambo" or "nigger."[30] Instances in which an employee's religious preferences have been criticized may render an employer liable under Title VII.[31] Employers have also been liable for the derogatory statements made by other employees to employees with Hispanic surnames.[32]

The court majority opinion in *Barnes* v. *Costle* took the position that "[g]enerally speaking, an employer is chargeable with Title VII violations occasioned by discriminatory practices of supervisory personnel." However, the majority softened the impact of its position by permitting an employer a defense if the employer promptly remedied the discriminatory conduct once it was made aware of the supervisor's actions.

Four years later, the District of Columbia District Court again considered this theory of liability in its refusal to dismiss a sexual harassment case brought against the Department of Justice in the case of *Williams* v. *Saxbe*. The court concluded that the plaintiff's allegations to the effect that the supervisor imposed sexual gratification as a condition of employment were sufficient to raise a question under Title VII. If the conduct was an employment policy of the *supervisor*, the court concluded, then that conduct would also be considered a policy of the *Department*.

One of the most extreme examples of a judicial decision holding a corporate employer liable for actions of a subordinate is found in *Anderson* v. *Methodist Evangelical Hospital, Inc.*[33] The Sixth Circuit Court of Appeals affirmed a verdict against the defendant hospital based on the evidence that a low level managerial supervisor discharged the plaintiff because of her race. The court accepted the findings of the district court that the corporation and the upper management had in fact maintained an excellent record in the area of race relations.

The district court went on to note that there was no finding of intention or desire to discriminate on the part of upper management. Despite these findings, both the district court and the court of appeals held against the hospital, on the theory that:

> where a discharge by a person in authority at a lower level of management is racially motivated, Title VII provides the aggrieved employee with a remedy.

Although state tort law refuses to extend liability for a supervisor's intentional torts to the corporate employer, there appear to be two major rationalizations which are useful to explain EEOC's and district courts' departures from expected court practice. The first approach involves consideration not only of the supervisor's act of sexual harassment but also focuses upon the supervisor's act of retaliation in disciplining or firing the employee. While the supervisor's *harassment* may be outside the scope of his employment, as soon as the supervisor exercises his power to fire, demote, or *discipline* the employee in retaliation for spurned advances, this conduct must of necessity be considered within the scope of the supervisor's employment if the dismissal is not challenged by the employer.

It would be literally impossible for the supervisor to exercise his power of firing or disciplining an employee without the authorization of the employer which empowers the supervisor to act. This authorization cannot be conditioned to enable the employer to disavow responsibility for a misuse of the clearly delegated power which a supervisor may hold.

This was unequivocably stated by the U.S. District Court in Utah.

> The EEOC, in its "Post-Trial Memorandum of Law" correctly states: "When American Oil gave its Regional Accounting Manager authority to fire employees, it also accepted responsibility to remedy any harm caused by his unlawful exercise of that authority. The modern corporate entity consists of the individuals who manage it, and little, if any, progress in eradicating discrimination will be made if the corporate employer is able to hide behind the shield of individual employee action."[34]

The second approach is by the use of a variant of the concept of "apparent authority." Apparent authority occurs where a master represents its servant as having a particular authority or power. If a third party relies upon these representations to his or her detriment, the courts will hold both the agent and the principal liable for the injuries which the plaintiff has sustained.[35] In a harassment case, should a corporation represent a supervisor as having the power to compel sexual favors, this would clearly fall under the apparent authority concept and the corporation would be held liable.

However, this type of blatant support from upper management is probably quite rare. A more likely scenario could occur where a supervisor himself claimed that he had plenary authority, and the employee relied upon the supervisor's representation, without the upper management having made any statements at all. In a concurring opinion to *Barnes*, one federal appellate judge considered this situation and concluded that no employee would seriously believe that a supervisor's demand for sexual gratification was truly founded in corporate policies or was based upon consent of the supervisor's employer.

But is it appropriate to offhandedly dismiss the theory that a corporation should be held liable for the misrepresentations of its supervisors? There exists at least one appellate court which thinks otherwise. In a significant footnote in the case of *Young v. Southwestern Savings & Loan Association*,[36] the Fifth Circuit established liability against the corporation based upon the evident authority of the supervisor, even though the supervisor lacked any actual authority to carry out the threats he made against the plaintiff. The case was a Title VII suit brought on the grounds of religious discrimination. The plaintiff was told by her supervisor that attending meetings which involved prayer sessions was mandatory, despite the plaintiff's objection that she was an atheist and did not wish to attend the prayer session. The plaintiff resigned.

In explaining its decision for the plaintiff against the corporation the court stated:

> Southwestern argues that Mrs. Young could not have been discharged because Bostain [the supervisor] had no authority to fire any of the employees at the Bellaire branch. While it is certain that Southwestern is correct with respect to the extent of Bostain's actual authority, it is also certain that Mrs. Young had no reason to know of this limitation, and in fact had every reason to assume the contrary, in view of Bostain's firm language of September 15, and of plaintiff's knowledge that her original application for employment had been submitted to Bostain for his approval. Under these circumstances, Southwestern cannot disclaim responsibility for Bostain's apparently authorized actions.

The *Southwestern Savings* court has evidently taken the approach of the *Tidewell* court of analyzing the problem *not* simply in terms of the act of harassment, but of examining the supervisor's act of using or abusing the power *delegated* to him by the corporate employer. By focusing upon the abuse of the supervisor's delegated power, the *Southwestern Savings* decision receives strong support from the Restatement (Second) of Agency, Section 161:

> A general agent for a disclosed or partially disclosed principal subjects his principal to liability for acts done on his account which usually accompany or are incidental to transactions which the agent is authorized to conduct if, although they are forbidden by the principal, the other party reasonably believes that the agent is authorized to do them and has no notice that he is not so authorized.

THE *MILLER* AND *ALEXANDER* CASES

The most recent decisions dealing with sexual harassment have focused upon the question of whether or not the employer had knowledge of the supervisor's misconduct, followed by an assessment of whether the employer acted to remedy the situation. One of the leading cases in this area is *Miller* v. *Bank of America.*[37] A female employee rejected her supervisor's sexual advances and as a result lost the promotion she had been promised. In addition, she was eventually fired by the supervisor. The basis of the plaintiff's claim, rather than a respondeat superior argument, was that the employer (the corporation) had either explicitly or tacitly approved of the harassment.

The court, in *rejecting* the plaintiff's claim under Title VII, focused upon the corporation's policies in dealing with instances of sexual harassment:

> It is undisputed that [the] Bank has a policy of discouraging sexual advances of the sort here alleged and of affirmatively disciplining employees found guilty of such conduct.

The court also noted that part of the bank's personnel department consisted of an employer relations department whose purpose was the investigation of employee complaints, including those of sexual harassment.

The court's finding against the plaintiff stemmed largely from its conclusion that, since the plaintiff had never contacted the employer relations department and had not allowed a complaint to be processed by the department, there was no way for the employer to have known about the supervisor's misconduct. Therefore, the employer could not be said to have consented to the supervisor's action at all.

The *Miller* court in essence imposes upon the plaintiff the requirement that she first process a complaint with a personnel department if she wishes the court to give any serious consideration to her Title VII claim under *any* theory of employer responsibility.

> Where, as here, however, there exists a company-wide policy expressly condemning the alleged misconduct and there exist responsive internal mechanisms established to process employee complaints of the instant sort, a failure on the part of the employee allegedly aggrieved by the condemned practice to avail him or herself of internal avenues of redress renders tenuous a finding of employer culpability. The Court is not to be understood as holding that exhaustion of company remedies is a prerequisite to suit under Title VII. Rather, failure of exhaustion goes more to whether the employer is liable at all.

This position, while desirable from the corporation's standpoint, cannot help but be unfavorably compared to the 1974 Supreme Court decision in *Alexander* v. *Gardner-Denver*.[38] Alexander, a black employee, was discharged by his employer for having produced defective machine parts. Alexander brought a grievance proceeding pursuant to the procedures set forth in the collective bargaining agreement between the employer and his representative union. The grievance subsequently included a claim that Alexander had been discharged because of his race. The grievance eventually resulted in an arbitration award for the corporation. Alexander immediately thereafter filed a Title VII charge, and the corporation moved to dismiss the complaint on the grounds that Alexander, in using the grievance procedure machinery to resolve his dispute, had forgone his opportunity to later bring an action under Title VII.

The Supreme Court, in *Alexander*, drew two conclusions relevant to the *Miller* decision. The first dealt with the rights of a plaintiff to bring a Title VII action where there already exists a mechanism to resolve a grievance. The second conclusion set out standards which should govern the weight a court gives to a prior arbitration decision.

The Supreme Court, in *Alexander*, es-tablished a minimum set of standards applicable when an employee is attempting to choose between a judicial remedy under Title VII and a remedy undertaken through his representative union in the form of a grievance and arbitration. *Miller*, in an analogous situation, dealt with an employee choice between a judicial remedy and an employer-sponsored and controlled resolution process. Is the analogy sufficiently close to require that *Miller* be considered in light of *Alexander*?

The position of the employee in an *Alexander*-type situation would appear to be preferable to his or her position under a *Miller*-type employer program. In a union-sponsored grievance procedure, there is at least the sense of being represented by the employee's own National Labor Relations Board certified union representative. Further, in the event that the union fails to adequately process the employee's grievance, the employee may bring an action against the union on the grounds that the union failed to meet its duty to fairly represent its members under the Taft-Hartley Act.[39]

On the other hand, when there is available to the employee only the remedy of an employer-sponsored investigatory procedure, there may be a less satisfactory handling of the issues for many reasons. First, the employee may simply be reluctant to challenge a supervisor through the mechanism of an employer program, for fear of a negative impact upon her career with the company. This problem would seem to be particularly prevalent in the situation where, as in *Southwestern Savings*, the supervisor has indicated that he is authorized to discipline the employee. If the employee is under the impression that the employer approves of the supervisor's behavior, there is little likelihood that the employer investigation program will be used.

Even where there is not a supervisor created disincentive to the employee, there may be other reasons why the employee may not wish to utilize an employer investigatory procedure. An individual employee may be intimidated by the very prospect of initiating an investigation within the company, regardless of how fair minded the employer may be. This would be particularly likely where there is not an adequate guarantee of anonymity provided to the employee who initiates such a procedure. Even if legitimately brought, such employee action could easily result in his or her being labelled as a "trouble-maker". This possibility would be even greater where the investigation resulted in a finding of supervisor innocence.[40]

Finally, an employee may easily be intimidated by the procedural steps which must be taken to bring an effective complaint. Perhaps the investigatory process requires a written complaint. Perhaps the complaining employee will have the opportunity to ask his or her own questions of the supervisor who has been charged with misconduct. These steps may seem insurmountable to many employees unfamiliar with the corporate bureaucracy. Where a union exists, much of the employee's fear over not knowing what to do can be alleviated with the assistance of a union representative, who will probably assist the employee throughout the grievance process. In the absence of a person or group with the expertise to understand the process thoroughly, an individual employee facing an employer investigatory process may simply choose to not file a grievance.

The *Alexander* decision grants a plaintiff extensive rights under Title VII, even where a union grievance procedure exists. Since the discussion above suggests that an employer grievance procedure may provide even less safeguards to the employee than a union grievance process, the conclusion is inescapable that the rationale of *Alexander* should be the basic precedent for an employee dealing with a *Miller*-type employer grievance procedure.

IMPACT OF *ALEXANDER*

The essence of the *Alexander* holding entitles the plaintiff to a new trial on his or her Title VII claim, *regardless* of whether there exists a collective bargaining grievance procedure or whether or not the grievance procedure has been used. The plaintiff cannot be penalized by a court for her decision to utilize the statutory remedy of Title VII even where there is available a grievance procedure.

> We think, therefore, that the federal policy favoring arbitration of labor disputes and the federal policy against discriminatory employment practices can best be accommodated by permitting an employee to pursue fully both his remedy under the grievance arbitration clause of a collective bargaining agreement and his cause of action under Title VII. The federal court should consider the employee's claim de novo,

the Supreme Court ruled in *Alexander*.

The Supreme Court's holding focused upon the differences between a court of law and an arbitration process. An arbitrator or a set of arbitrators have as their objective the achievement of harmony in the business community. Their perspective is therefore in terms of fairness and common practices in the industry. Arbitrators may also possess an amount of self-interest, because arbitrators chosen by the corporation and by the union are selected in part due to their leanings toward a particular side of the dispute, the Court reasoned.

The court system, on the other hand, has as its perspective in considering Title VII questions a far more expansive standard. There is inherent in Title VII a sense of equity, and the solutions reached under the Act are designed not only to remedy injustices done to a particular person but also attempt to correct the larger problem of industry practices which limit *any* employee's employment opportunities. The courts derive their authority from the Constitution rather than from a collective bargaining agreement and therefore can draw upon a much wider historically accepted body of law for guidance than can the arbitrator. Finally, the Court has no personal or pecuniary interest in either of the two parties and is therefore an impartial tribunal before which disputes are brought, the Court observed.

A de novo trial is necessary when a plaintiff brings a Title VII action. Further, there can be no prejudice against the plaintiff because of the plaintiff's decision to bypass or dispute the results of a collective bargaining grievance process. What, then, of the *Miller* plaintiff? Surely an employee who is faced with the option of an employer personnel department procedure or Title VII lawsuit should also be entitled to a de novo consideration of her Title VII claims without prejudice. The *Miller* decision, to the extent that it imposes any prejudice or raises any questions about the plaintiff's decision to ignore the employer relations department, is inconsistent with the *Alexander* holding and should be reconsidered.

The *Miller* court is willing to give the employer virtual immunity from a Title VII action simply because of the existence of a grievance process and the employer's past history of disciplining amorous supervisors. However, this misses the point of *Alexander* in a second way since under *Alexander* any resolution of a Title VII claim by an organization other than a court should not have *any* evidential bearing on the case unless the court is satisfied that the non-judicial procedure is sufficiently rigorous and imparital to appropriately be considered by the court. The *Alexander* decision permits the district courts to consider an arbitration award which reaches Title VII issues as evidence, but the *weight* or reliance placed on the award must be considered in light of a number of factors.

The arbitration process must accord both parties full procedural fairness (such as opportunity to be notified of charges, time to prepare arguments, ability to call witnesses and to ask questions of parties testifying on behalf of the other side). The arbitration process should also be examined to determine whether the arbitrator had any special competence in deciding Title VII type issues. Further, the transcript or record of the arbitration process should be examined for its completeness. The implication in *Alexander* is that a court should be reluctant to place heavy reliance upon an award which does not adequately explain the underlying facts, the arbitrator's reasoning, information about testimony of the parties, and other information supporting the decision.

The *Miller* opinion makes no mention of the nature of the employer relations department's procedures. Do both parties receive notice? Can they both present their argument? Is there an opportunity to cross examine individuals who are advocating the other party's interest? Is there a written record of all the communications that take place during the examination by the department? Do the members of the department have any special competence in Title VII-type matters to give their decisions additional reliability? Can the *Miller* court assume that the department is as impersonal as a court would be, considering that the department members are themselves employees of the corporation? To reiterate, *Miller* should not be followed as a precedent because of its inconsistency with the *Alexander* opinion.

THE *TOMKINS II* DECISION

The second major decision which finds the corporate employer liable for acts of supervisory harassment is *Tomkins II*, the appellate decision reversing *Tomkins I*. The plaintiff's argument, which the court of appeals accepted as proved during trial, stated that the employer corporation *had* knowledge of the harassment incident and that, instead of investigating or correcting the situation, the corporation permitted further harassment of the plaintiff by other employees of the corporation.

The Third Circuit held:

> we conclude that Title VII is violated when a supervisor with the actual or constructive knowledge of the employer makes sexual advances or demands toward a subordinate employee and conditions that employee's job status—evaluation, continued employment, promotion, or other aspects of career development—on a favorable response to those advances or demands, and the employer does not take prompt and appropriate remedial action after acquiring such knowledge.

Tomkins II presents a three part test. First, harassment by a supervisor must be linked to the victim's job status. Harassment must be coupled with a threat of demotion, or with actual punitive conduct that relates to the individual's position with the corporation.

Secondly, the employer must be shown either to have had knowledge of the supervisor's acts or to have been negligently ignorant of the acts. This second approach is a version of the "reasonable man" standard used in negligence cases. The employer will be held to have knowledge of supervisor misconduct where a reasonable employer in a similar situation *should* have been aware of the misconduct.

Cases dealing with Title VII have made use of this form of liability. For example, a district court in Pennsylvania, in finding a corporation liable for racial harassment by employees and supervisors, stated:

> [The plaintiff] has testified to harassment by several different supervisors over several years. An inference that "management" was aware of his mistreatment, or should have been aware, is unavoidable.[41]

The third component of the *Tomkins II* test focuses on the employer's subsequent efforts to remedy the problem of the harassing supervisor. This test has found support in other courts by way of permitting the employer a defense of "prompt remedial action."

In a 1970 EEOC decision, the problem of discriminatory firing of a female employee by a supervisor was brought to the attention of higher management. The hearing officer concluded that the management's prompt efforts to remedy the supervisor's conduct served to prevent liability from being imputed to the corporation.[42] Similarly, a 1973 Pennsylvania district court decision held that United States Steel was not liable for discriminatory remarks made by workers against an employee of Hungarian descent where there was evidence that the corporation made efforts to protect the plaintiff from harassment where possible and investigated the problem as soon as the corporation was informed.[43]

The most difficult component of the test in *Tomkins II* is the "reasonable person" standard adopted by the court, under which the corporation must reasonably keep itself informed of acts of supervisory personnel. One defense which corporations have raised in other Title VII lawsuits is the argument that the corporation should not be held responsible for a single, isolated misconduct by a supervisor. This approach was adopted by a federal district court in 1977, where the court concluded:

> The court finds that a single insult by an employee, reprehensible as it may be, cannot form the basis of liability against management. If an employee was allowed to continually harass fellow workers without being disciplined, that might be held against the employer.[44]

The same basic approach evidently underlies the *Miller* court's conclusion that the defendant corporation should not be held liable. The court was satisfied that the bank had a record of promptly following up on employee complaints of supervisory misconduct. Thus, under the "single act defense," the bank should not be held liable for a single act of the supervisor, where the bank could not reasonably have made itself aware of the improper act. And since the plaintiff did not inform the higher management about the incident, there was apparently no other way in which the corporation could have informed itself of the problem.

CONCLUDING REMARKS

From the foregoing discussion, it seems apparent that the position of the *Corne* court against finding a federal remedy for sexual harassment with accompanying economic or psychological harm to the employee should yield to one of the principal theories finding a Title VII cause of action for sexually harassed employees. Definitive decisions at the appellate level in the Third Circuit and District of Columbia Circuit indicate that the Arizona court's position should be reconsidered.

Of the possible theories under which an aggrieved employee may bring a Title VII action, the respondeat superior/master-servant liability approach seems to be the most desirable from the employee's standpoint. This approach is desirable provided that the federal courts take the developing approach which the EEOC and some courts place on the employer to maintain a working place free from verbal abuse and other harassment.

The standard requiring employer knowledge (actual or inferred) before liability is imposed, on the other hand, favors the corporation by giving the organization an opportunity to clean its own house before being subjected to Title VII liability. It would seem, however, that an employer cannot merely promise to root out discrimination, and then close its eyes to incidents occurring in the organization.

What factors should a corporation bear in mind when seeking to avoid liability for supervisory acts of sexual harassment? The following points, which serve to summarize some of the issues raised in this presentation, suggest some guidelines for future corporate action aimed at avoiding liability.

(1) Has the employer made an un-equivocal statement, which has reached every employee, that it is *not* company policy to condone sexual harassment or pressure which utilizes the employee's job status as a factor in the "persuasion" of employees? If the employer has not made such a statement, then the employer is leaving itself open to judicial application of the apparent authority doctrine in situations similar to *Southwestern Savings*. Without a formal employer statement denying support of such pressure, an employee cannot be certain that her supervisor's actions are outside of his actual scope of authority. By making this statement, however, the corporation has *not* automatically shielded itself from liability under Title VII. The employer may still be held accountable on a respondeat superior or actual knowledge basis.

(2) Does the employer conduct adequate reviews of supervisory decisions to hire, fire, and promote employees, so that the employer can be expected to become aware of incidents of supervisory misconduct? This is an admittedly vague condition, due to the inability of decisively determining what constitutes an "adequate" review.

However, it can safely be assumed that in a corporation where there is *no* review of supervisory authority, it is quite possible that the employer may be liable for violations of supervisory personnel under a range of theories. A strong argument could be made that the employer has acted unreasonably in that it *should have* made itself aware of activities of its supervisors (the "reasonable man" standard implicit in *Tomkins II*). There will also be liability under the theory of master-servant on the grounds that the employer has, by his inaction, ratified or assented to supervisory decision-making or that, in the alternative, the employer has failed to maintain a working place free from harassment.

(3) Has the injured employee notified someone in higher management of the harassment incident? If the corporation does maintain a comprehensive system

of review as suggested above, then the failure of the corporation to make itself aware of supervisory misconduct might possibly be excusable (this would be a question of fact for the judge or jury). However, even if the employer has such a program, its effectiveness as a "shield" would be seriously undermined by an employee complaint lodged with a member of the organization in a position to act on the complaint.

(4) Once made aware of the existence of a problem, has the employer made a prompt and adequate effort to investigate and resolve the issue? This standard is drawn from the *Tomkins II* decision. "Awareness" or "knowledge" is a state of mind which may be arrived at via many roads: possession of actual knowledge by the employer; failure to make itself aware of the situation; or knowledge after the incident based upon an employee complaint. What constitutes prompt and adequate action is again a question which would necessarily be determined on a case-by-case basis, depending upon the individual circumstances of the case.

The failure of an employer to take prompt and immediate action should provide the plaintiff with an argument that the employer *has*, in fact, acquiesced to the harassment. It must be reiterated, however, that even if there exists an employer resolution process, whether or not the plaintiff uses the process should not be a prejudicial factor in a subsequent federal court Title VII claim. The court should hear the employee's case de novo, pursuant to the *Alexander* decision.

Continuing the *Alexander* analogy, the employer might be permitted to make use of findings from the corporation's resolution process, but only to the extent that these findings have provided the parties with procedural fairness, are supported by a record, and have been decided by a group of individuals with expertise in dealing with the particular dispute. Under no circumstances should

the mere existence of a grievance or employer relations process be the basis for denying a Title VII claim.

It is important to note that the corporate defendant should be particularly concerned about which theory of employer-imputed liability will be used by a reviewing court: the respondeat superior perspective as discussed in cases similar to *Tidewell*; or cases using the concept of "reasonable corporation knowledge", typified by *Tomkins II*, and to a lesser extent by *Miller*.

While the outcome will be the same if the corporation actually has knowledge of the supervisor's misconduct and does nothing, the results may differ in the circumstance where the supervisor has engaged in a single act of harassment. Under the *Tomkins II* approach, it may be possible for the corporation to successfully defend its lack of action on the basis of reasonably being unaware of the supervisor's misconduct. On the other hand, under the respondeat superior approach, the act of supervisor abuse of a delegated power creates liability against the master regardless of whether there was knowledge at all.

NOTES

1. Mim Kelber, "The UN's Dirty Little Secret," *MS*, Vol. VI, No. 5 (November, 1975), 51.

2. Caryl Rivers, "Sexual Harassment—The Executive's Alternative to Rape," *Mother Jones*, Vol. III, No. 5 (June, 1978), 22.

3. See generally the discussion in M. R. Skrocki, "Sexual Pressure On the Job," *McCalls*, Vol. 105, (March, 1978), 43.

4. William Prosser, *Handbook on the Law of Torts*, 3d ed. (St. Paul: West Publishing Co., 1964) p. 476.

5. *Id.*, at 51-52.

6. *Rogers* v. *EEOC*, 454 F2d 234 (CA-5, 1971), 4 EPD ¶ 7597.

7. 42 USC 2000(e)-3(a).

8. 42 USC 2000(e)-5(f) (4,5).

9. 42 USC 2000(e)-5(f) (1).

10. 42 USC 2000(e)-5(k).

11. *EEOC* v. *Detroit Edison Co.*, 515 F2d

301 (CA-6, 1975), 9 EPD ¶ 9997, cert. denied, 97 SCt 2669 (US SCt, 1977), 14 EPD ¶ 7580.

12. Prosser, cited at note 4, pp. 9-12.

13. 42 USC 2000(e)-5(e).

14. As an example, the Texas statute of limitations for injury to persons is two years from the date of the incident. Vernon's Ann. Civ. St. Art. 5526(6).

15. *Tomkins* v. *Public Service Electric and Gas Co.*, 422 FSupp 553 (DC NJ, 1976), 12 EPD ¶ 11,267, rev'd and rem'd 568 F2d 1044 (CA-3, 1977), 15 EPD ¶ 7954. Hereinafter, references to the district court opinion of this case will be referred to as *Tomkins I*. References to the Third Circuit Court of Appeals will be noted *Tomkins II*.

16. *Tomkins I*, cited at note 15. See also *Barnes* v. *Train*, 561 F2d 984.

17. Blumrosen. "Arbitration and Title VII Backlog", 98 *Labor Relations Reporter* 192 (July 3, 1978).

18. *Barnes* v. *Costle*, 561 F2d 983 (CA DofC, 1977), 14 EPD ¶ 7755.

19. 42 USC 2000(e)-2(a).

20. *Williams* v. *Saxbe*, 413 F2d 654 (DC DofC, 1976), 12 EPD ¶ 11,130.

21. *McDonnell Douglas* v. *Green*, 411 US 792, 93 SCt 1817 (1973), 5 EPD ¶ 8607. Although a race discrimination case, *Green* has been used to establish a prima facie case of sex discrimination. A class action case of sex discrimination would be governed by *Griggs* v. *Duke Power Co.*, 401 US 424, 91 SCt 849 (1971), 3 EPD ¶ 8137, the seminal case is the law of employment discrimination.

22. *Corne* v. *Bausch and Lomb*, 490 FSupp 161 (DC Az, 1975), 9 EPD ¶ 10,093.

23. 42 USC 2000(e)-(b).

24. Restatement (Second) of Agency, Sec. 2(1).

25. *Id.*, Sec. 2(2).

26. Prosser, cited at note 4, p. 472.

27. *Slack* v. *Havens*, 8 EPD ¶ 9491 (DC Ca, 1973).

28. *Tomkins II*, cited at note 15, at case note 1.

29. EEOC Decision 72-0957, CCH EEOC DEC ¶ 6346.

30. EEOC Decision 72-0779, CCH EEOC DEC ¶ 6331.

31. EEOC Decision 72-1114, CCH EEOC DEC ¶ 6347.

32. EEOC Decision 72-05, 6 FEP 834.

33. 464 F2d 723 (CA-6, 1972), 4 EPD ¶ 7901.

34. *Tidewell* v. *American Oil Co.*, 332 FSupp 424 (DC Ut, 1971), 4 EPD ¶ 7544.

35. Restatement (Second) of Agency, Sec. 27.

36. Case note 7, 509 F2d 140 (CA-5, 1975), 9 EPD ¶ 9995.

37. 418 FSupp 233 (DC Cal, 1976), 13 EPD ¶ 11,357.

38. *Alexander* v. *Gardner-Denver Co.*, 415 US 36, 94 SCt 1011 (1974), 7 EPD ¶ 9148.

39. 29 USC 158(b)(1)(A). See also *Local 12, United Rubber Workers* v. *NLRB*, 368 F2d 12 (CA-5, 1966), 54 LC ¶ 11,554, cert. denied 389 US 837 (US SCt, 1967), 56 LC ¶ 12,214. *Local 12* is a good example of a union that has, through its inactivity in processing a member grievance, violated the duty of fair representation.

40. Note that this problem is largely avoided under Title VII by section 704(a), which protects against employer retaliation. The National Labor Relations Act also protects an employee petition to the NLRB in section 8(a)(4) of the act (29 USC 158(a)(4)).

41. *Croker* v. *Boeing Co. (Veritol Div.)* 437 FSupp 1138 (DC Pa, 1977), 16 EPD ¶ 8185.

42. EEOC Decision 70-432, CCH EEOC DEC ¶ 6130.

43. *Feteke* v. *U.S. Steel Corp.*, 353 FSupp 1177 (DC Pa, 1973), 5 EPD ¶ 8569.

44. *Dickerson* v. *U.S. Steel Corp.*, 439 FSupp 55 (DC Pa, 1977), 14 EPD ¶ 7570.

17. Interim Amendment to Guidelines on Discrimination Because of Sex under Title VII of the Civil Rights Act of 1964, as Amended*

EQUAL EMPLOYMENT OPPORTUNITY COMMISSION

SUMMARY

The Equal Employment Opportunity Commission (EEOC) is amending its Guidelines on Discrimination Because of Sex on an interim basis, in order to clarify its position on the issue of sexual harassment and to invite the public to comment on the issue. This amendment will re-affirm that sexual harassment is an unlawful employment practice. These Interim Guidelines are in full effect from the date of their publication; however, EEOC will receive comments for 60 days subsequent to the date of publication. After the comment period EEOC will evaluate the comments, make whatever changes to the Interim Guidelines may seem appropriate in light of the comments, and publish the final Guidelines.

SUPPLEMENTARY INFORMATION

Sexual harassment like harassment on the basis of color, race, religion, or national origin, has long been recognized by EEOC as a violation of Section 703 of Title VII of the Civil Rights Act of 1964, as amended. However, despite the position taken by the Commission, sexual harassment continues to be especially widespread. Because of the continued prevalence of this unlawful practice, the Commission has determined that there is a need for guidelines in this area of Title VII law. Therefore, EEOC proposes to amend its Guidelines on Discrimination because of Sex (37 FR 6836, April 5, 1972, as amended) to add Section 1604.11, Sexual harassment.

Proposed Subsection 1604.11 (a) provides that harassment on the basis of sex is a violation of Title VII and states that such unwelcomed behavior may be either physical or verbal in nature. The proposed section also sets out three criteria for determining whether an action constitutes unlawful behavior. These criteria are (1) submission to the conduct is either an explicit or implicit term or condition of employment; (2) submission to or rejection of the conduct is used as the basis for employment decisions affecting the person who did the submitting or rejecting; or (3) the conduct has the purpose or effect of substantially interfering with an individual's work performance or creating an intimidating, hostile, or offensive work environment. It is the Commission's position that sexual harassment, like racial harassment, generates a harmful atmosphere. Under Title VII, employees should be afforded a working environment free of discriminatory intimidation whether based on sex, race, religion, or national origin. There-

---

Source: 29 CFR Chapter XIV, Part 1604.11 (March 11, 1980).

fore, the employer has an affirmative duty to maintain a workplace free of sexual harassment and intimidation.

Proposed Subsection 1604.11 (b) recognizes that the question of whether a particular action or incident establishes a purely personal, social relationship without a discriminatory employment effect requires a factual determination. In making such a determination, the Commission will look at the record as a whole and at the totality of the circumstances, emphasizing the nature of the sexual advances and the context in which the alleged incidents occurred. The determination of the legality of a particular action will be made from the facts, on a case by case basis.

Proposed Subsection 1604.11 (c) applies general Title VII principles to the issue of sexual harassment and states that an employer is responsible for the acts of its supervisory employees or agents, regardless of whether the acts were authorized or forbidden by the employer and regardless of whether the employer knew or should have known of the acts. This subsection further states that the Commission will determine whether an individual acts in either an agency or a supervisory capacity on a case by case basis, examining the circumstances of the particular employment relationship and the job functions performed by the individual, rather than accepting an individual's title as being controlling.

Proposed Subsection 1604.11 (d) distinguishes the employer's responsibility for the acts of its agents or supervisors from the responsibility it has for the acts of other persons. This subsection states that liability for the acts of those persons not mentioned in subsection (c) exists only when the employer, or its agents or supervisory employees, knows or should have known of the conduct. The subsection further provides that the employer may rebut this apparent liability for the conduct by showing that it took immediate and appropriate corrective action.

Consistent with the policy of voluntary compliance under Title VII, subsection 1604.11 (e) recognizes that the best way to achieve an environment free of sexual harassment is to prevent the occurrence of sexual harassment by utilizing appropriate methods to alert the employees to the problem and to stress that sexual harassment, in any form, will not be tolerated. This subsection requires an employer to take all steps necessary for the prevention of sexual harassment and gives the following as examples of steps which might be deemed necessary: affirmatively raising the subject, expressing strong disapproval, developing appropriate sanctions, informing employees of their right to raise the issue of sexual harassment under Title VII, and developing methods to sensitize all concerned.

This amendment to the Guidelines on Discrimination Because of Sex is a significant regulation under Executive Order 12044, "Improving Government Regulations" (43 FR 12661, March 24, 1978). There are no regulatory burdens or recordkeeping requirements necessary for compliance with the amendment. The Commission has determined that these proposed guidelines will not have major impact on the economy and that a regulatory analysis is not necessary.

In compliance with Executive Order 12067 (43 FR 28967, July 5, 1978), the Commission has consulted with representatives of the Office of Personnel Management, Department of Justice, Department of Labor, and Department of Health, Education and Welfare. At the end of the 60 day comment period, the Commission will again consult with these agencies on the issues raised through the public comment process.

INTERIM AMENDMENT

Accordingly, 29 CFR Chapter XIV, Part 1604 is amended by adding Section 1604.11 to read as [shown in accompanying box]:

PART 1604 — GUIDELINES ON DISCRIMINATION BECAUSE OF SEX

Section 1604.11 Sexual harassment.

a) Harassment on the basis of sex is a violation of Sec. 703 of Title VII.[1] Unwelcome sexual advances, requests for sexual favors, and other verbal or physical conduct of a sexual nature constitute sexual harassment when (1) submission to such conduct is made either explicitly or implicitly a term or condition of an individual's employment, (2) submission to or rejection of such conduct by an individual is used as the basis for employment decisions affecting such individual, or (3) such conduct has the purpose or effect of substantially interfering with an individual's work performance or creating an intimidating, hostile, or offensive working environment.

b) In determining whether alleged conduct constitutes sexual harassment, the Commission will look at the record as a whole and at the totality of the circumstances, such as the nature of the sexual advances and the context in which the alleged incidents occurred. The determination of the legality of a particular action will be made from the facts, on a case by case basis.

c) Applying general Title VII principles, an employer, employment agency, joint apprenticeship committee or labor organization (hereinafter collectively referred to as "employer") is responsible for its acts and those of its agents and supervisory employees with respect to sexual harassment regardless of whether the specific acts complained of were authorized or even forbidden by the employer and regardless of whether the employer knew or should have known of their occurrence. The Commission will examine the circumstances of the particular employment relationship and the job functions performed by the individual in determining whether an individual acts in either a supervisory or agency capacity.

d) With respect to persons other than those mentioned in subsection (c) above, an employer is responsible for acts of sexual harassment in the workplace where the employer, or its agents or supervisory employees, knows or should have known of the conduct. An employer may rebut apparent liability for such acts by showing that it took immediate and appropriate corrective action.

e) Prevention is the best tool for the elimination of sexual harassment. An employer should take all steps necessary to prevent sexual harassment from occurring, such as affirmatively raising the subject, expressing strong disapproval, developing appropriate sanctions, informing employees of their right to raise and how to raise the issue of harassment under Title VII, and developing methods to sensitize all concerned.

EEOC MANAGEMENT DIRECTIVE ON SEXUAL HARASSMENT

Harassment on the basis of sex is a violation of Title VII of the Civil Rights Act of 1964, as amended. The Office of Personnel Management (OPM) has issued a policy statement that sexual harassment is also a prohibited personnel practice.

Agencies are instructed to include as supplement to their Phase II Affirmative Action Planning Process a plan indicating the steps the agency will take to prevent sexual harassment. Such supplements are to be submitted by May 1, 1980.

Agency plans will be evaluated on the extent to which they utilize training and/or other methods to prevent sexual harassment. This evaluation will be part of the EEOC analysis of agency affirmative action plan submission.

EEOC has published Interim Guidelines on Sexual Harassment. Agencies should refer to these

Guidelines for further information and for guidance in developing or modifying their affirmative action plans.

EEOC invites comments on the Interim Guidelines during the comment period. As interim guidelines these are effective upon publication. However, comments submitted will be evaluated, changes will be made as appropriate and formal interagency consultation will be conducted prior to publication as final Guidelines.

NOTE

1. The principles involved here continue to apply to race, color, religion or national origin.

Bibliography

Abramson, Joan. *Old Boys New Women: The Politics of Sex Discrimination* (New York: Praeger Publishers, 1979).

Atkinson, Joseph D., Jr., and Dianne R. Layden. "A Federal Response to Sexual Harassment: Policymaking at Johnson Space Center, NASA" (May 1980).

Backhouse, Constance and Leah Cohen. *The Secret Oppression: Sexual Harassment of Working Women* (Toronto: Macmillan of Canada, 1978).

Backhouse, Constance, et al. *Fighting Sexual Harassment: An Advocacy Handbook* (Cambridge, Mass.: Alliance Against Sexual Coercion, 1979).

Bradford, David L., Alice G. Sargent & Melinda S. Sprague. "The Executive Man and Woman: The Issue of Sexuality," in Francine E. Gordon & Myra H. Strober, (eds), *Bringing Women Into Management* (New York: McGraw Hill, 1975), pp. 39-58.

Brown, Helen Gurley. *Sex and the Office* (New York: Pocket Books, Inc., 1965).

Bularzik, Mary. "Sexual Harassment at the Workplace: Historical Notes," *Radical America*, Vol. 12, No. 4, (July/August 1978), pp. 25-41.

Carey, Sandra Harley. "Sexual Politics in Business," unpublished, (University of Texas at San Antonio, 1976).

Crull, Peggy. "The Impact of Sexual Harassment on the Job: A Profile of the Experiences of 92 Women," Research Series, Report No. 3 (New York: Working Women's Institute, Fall 1979).

"Employment Discrimination—Sexual Harassment and Title VII . . ." *New York University Law Review*, Vol. 51, No. 1, (April 1976), pp. 148-166.

Equal Employment Opportunity Commission. "Title 29—Labor, Chapter XIV—Part 1604—Guidelines on Discrimination Because of Sex Under Title VII of the Civil Rights Act of 1964, as Amended Adoption of Interim Interpretive Guidelines," Washington, D.C., April 1980.

Evans, Laura J. "Sexual Harassment: Women's Hidden Occupational Hazard," in Jane Roberts Chapman and Margaret Gates, (eds), *The Victimization of Women* (Beverly Hills, Calif.: Sage Yearbooks in Women's Policy Studies, Vol. 3, Sage Publications, 1978).

Farley, Jennie. *Affirmative Action and the Woman Worker: Guidelines for Personnel Management* (New York: AMACOM, 1979).

Farley, Lin. *Sexual Shakedown: Sexual Harassment of Women at Work* (New York: McGraw Hill, 1979).

Faucher, Mary D. and Kenneth J. McCulloch. "Sexual Harassment in the Workplace—What Should the Employer Do?" *EEO Today*, Vol. 5, No. 1, (Spring 1978), pp. 38-46.

Ginsberg, Gilbert J. and Jean Galloway Koreski. "Sexual Advances by an Employee's Supervisor: A Sex Discrimination Violation of Title VII?" *Employee Relations Law Journal*, Vol. 3:1 (Summer 1977), pp. 83-92.

Goldberg, Alan. "Sexual Harassment and Title VII: The Foundation for the Elimination of Sexual Cooperation as an Employment Condition," *Michigan Law Review*, Vol. 76, No. 6, (May 1978), pp. 1007-1035.

Goodman, Jill Laurie. "Sexual Demands on the Job," *The Civil Liberties Review*, Vol. 4, No. 6, (March/April 1978), pp. 55-58.

Government of the District of Columbia, Mayor's Order 79-89, Subject: Sexual Harassment" (May 24, 1979).

Harragan, Betty Lehan. *Games Mother Never Taught You*. New York: Warner Books, Inc., 1977.

Hooven, Martha and Nancy McDonald. "The Role of Capitalism: Understanding Sexual Harassment," *Aegis*, (November/December 1978), pp. 31-33.

Korda, Michael. *Male Chauvinism! How It Works*. New York: Random House, 1972.

Kreps, Juanita. *Sex and the Marketplace: American Women at Work*. Baltimore: The Johns Hopkins Press, 1971.

Lindsey, Karen. "Sexual Harassment on the Job," *Ms.*, (November 1977), pp. 47-52.

MacKinnon, Catharine A. *Sexual Harassment of Working Women*. New Haven, Conn.: Yale University Press, 1979.

McGee, Jack I., Jr. "Civil Rights: Sexual Advances by Male Supervisory Personnel as Actionable Under Title VII of the Civil Rights Act of 1964. *South Texas Law Journal*, Vol. 17, No. 3, (1976), pp. 409-415.

Mead, Margaret. "A Proposal: We Need Taboos on Sex at Work," *Redbook*, (April 1978), pp. 31-33.

Memo from J. C. Crouch to J. P. Dooley, Office of the Regional Director, Rocky Mountain Region, Office of Personnel Management (November 13, 1979).

"Memorandum of Understanding between the Investigations Subcommittee of the Post Office and Civil Service Committee and the Equal Opportunity Employment Commission, concerning the Problem of Sexual Harassment of Federal Employees" (unpublished, undated).

Miller, Jon, Sanford Labovitz and Lincoln Fry. "Inequities in the Organizational Experiences of Women and Men: Resources, Vested Interests and Discrimination," *Social Forces*, Vol. 54, No. 2, (December 1975), pp. 365-381.

Nardino, Marie. "Discrimination: Sex—Title VII—Cause of Action," *Seton Hall Law Review*, Vol. 9, No. 1. (1978), pp. 108-129.

Pogrebin, Letty Cottin. "Sex Harassment," *Ladies Home Journal*, Vol. XCIV, No. 6, (June 1977), pp. 24-28.

Quinn, Robert E. "Coping with Cupid: The Formation, Impact and Management of Romantic Relationships in Organizations," *Administrative Science Quarterly*, Vol. 22, No. 1, (March 1977), pp. 30-45.

Quinn, Robert E. and Noreen A. Judge. "The Office Romance: No Bliss for the Boss," *Management Review*, Vol. 67, No. 7, (July 1978), pp. 43-49.

"Responses of Fair Employment Practices Agencies to Sexual Harassment Complaints: A Report and Recommendations," Research Series, Report No. 2 (New York: Working Women's Institute, Fall 1978).

"Results of Preliminary Survey on Sexual Harassment on the Job," Research Series, Report No. 1 (New York: Working Women's Institute, 1975).

Ripskis, Al Louis, (ed). "Sexual Harassment Rampant at HUD," *Impact Journal*, Vol. VII, No. 11 and 12, (July/August 1979).

Safran, Claire, "What Men Do to Women on the Job: A Shocking Look at Sexual Harassment," *Redbook*, (November 1976), pp. 149, 217-224.

"Sex in the Office," *Fortune*, Vol. 101, No. 7 (April 7, 1980) p. 42.

"Sexual Harassment in the Federal Government," Hearings Before the Subcommittee on Investigations of the Committee on Post Office and Civil Service, U.S. House of Representatives, Ninety-Sixth Congress, First Session, October 23, November 1, 13, 1979, Serial No. 96-57 (Washington, D.C.: U.S. Government Printing Office, 1980).

"Sexual Harassment: A Hidden Issue," Project on the Status and Education of Women, Washington, D.C.: Association of American Colleges. Adopted from a pamphlet "Sexual Harassment at the Workplace" (Cambridge, Mass.: Alliance Against Sexual Coercion, undated).

"Sexual Harassment Lands Companies in Court," *Business Week*, (October 1, 1979), pp. 120-122.

"Sexual Harassment on the Job: Results of Preliminary Survey" (New York: Working Women's Institute, 1975).

Seymour, William C. "Sexual Harassment: Finding a Cause of Action Under Title VII," *Labor Law Journal*, Vol. 30, No. 3, (March 1979), pp. 139-156.

Silverman, Dierdra. "Sexual Harassment: Working Women's Dilemma," *QUEST: A Feminist Quarterly*, Vol. III, No. 3, (1976-77), pp. 15-24.

Somers, Patricia A. and Judith Clementson-Mohr. "Sexual Extortion in the Workplace," *The Personnel Administrator*, Vol. 24, No. 4, (April 1979), pp. 23-28.

Sullivan, Elizabeth. "Survey Shows Few States Have Systems to Resolve Sexual Harassment Complaints," *Intergovernmental Personnel Notes* (Washington, D.C.: United States Office of Personnel Management, November–December 1979), p. 3.

The Women's Advisory Council to the Salt Lake County Merit Council.

"Report on Barriers for Upward Mobility for Women" (Salt Lake City, Utah: Salt Lake County Merit Systems Council, July, 1979).

United States Commission on Civil Rights. *A Guide to Federal Laws and Regulations Prohibiting Sex Discrimination* (Washington, D.C.: U.S. Government Printing Office, Clearinghouse Publications 46, July 1976).

U.S. Department of Health, Education and Welfare. "Memorandum to Heads of Principle Operating Components, Principle Regional Officials, Subject: Sexual Harassment" Washington, D.C., October 5, 1979.

U.S. Department of Housing and Urban Development. *HUDDLE*, Vol. X, No. 3, (March 1980).

U.S. Office of Personnel Management. "Memorandum to Heads of Departments and Independent Agencies. Subject: Policy Statement and Definition of Sexual Harassment," Washington, D.C., December 12, 1979.

Uris, Auren. *The Blue Book of Broadminded Business Behavior* (New York: Thomas Y. Crowell Co., 1977).

Weisel, Kerri. "Title VII: Legal Protection Against Sexual Harassment," *Washington Law Review*, Vol. 53, No. 1, (December 1977), pp. 123-144.

Workshop on Sexual Harassment, Participant's Manual and Trainer's Manual (Washington, D.C.: Supervisory and Communications Training Center, U.S. Office of Personnel Management, undated).

List of Legal Cases Involving Sexual Harassment

Barnes v. *Train*, 13 FEP Cases 123, 124 (D.D.C. 1974): *Barnes* v. *Costle* 561 F. 2d.983 (D.C. Cir 1977).

Continental Can Co., et al. v. *State by William Wilson, Commissioner, et al.* June 6, 1980. Minnesota Supreme Court.

Corne v. *Bausch & Lomb, Inc.,* 390 F. SUPP 161 (D. Ariz. 1975). Reversed 562 R. 2d. 55 (9th Cir 1977).

Elliott v. *Emery Air Freight,* No. C-C-75-76 (W.D.N.C. June 21, 1977).

In re. Nancy J. Fillhouer, Case No. SJ-5963, William J. Costello, Referee (San Jose Referee Office, April 28, 1975).

Garber v. *Saxon Business Products, Inc.,* 552 F. 2d. 1032 (4th Cir 1977).

Gates v. *Brockway Glass Co., Inc.,* 93 L.R.R.M. 2367 (C.D. Cal. 1976).

Hamilton v. *Appleton Electric Co.,* E.R.D. Case #7301025, State of Wisconsin, Department of Industry, Labor and Human Relations, October 1, 1976.

Heelan v. *Johns Mansville Corp.,* 451 F. SUPP. 1382 (D. Colo. 1978).

Miller v. *Bank of America,* 418 F. SUPP. 233 (N.D. Cal. 1976).

Monge v. *Beebe Rubber,* 316 A. 2d. 549 (N.H. 1974).

Munford v. *James T. Barnes & Co.,* 441 F. SUPP. 459 (E.D. Mich. 1977).

Tomkins v. *Public Service Electric and Gas Co.,* 422 F. SUPP. 533 (D.N.J. 1977), Reversed on Appeal, 568 F. 2d. (3rd Cir. 1977).

William v. *Saxbe,* 413 F. SUPP. 654 (D.D.C. 1976).

In re. Carmita Wood, Case No. 75-92437. New York State Department of Labor Unemployment Insurance Appeals Board, Decision and Notice of Decision, March 7, 1975 (unreported), Appeal No. 207,958, New York State Department of Labor, Unemployment Insurance Division Appeal Board (October 6, 1975).

Index of Persons and Proper Names